Nation on Board

NEW AFRICAN HISTORIES

SERIES EDITORS: JEAN ALLMAN, ALLEN ISAACMAN,
AND DEREK R. PETERSON

*Books in this series are published with support
from the Ohio University Center for International Studies.*

David William Cohen and E. S. Atieno Odhiambo, *The Risks of Knowledge: Investigations into the Death of the Hon. Minister John Robert Ouko in Kenya, 1990*

Belinda Bozzoli, *Theatres of Struggle and the End of Apartheid*

Gary Kynoch, *We Are Fighting the World: A History of the Marashea Gangs in South Africa, 1947–1999*

Stephanie Newell, *The Forger's Tale: The Search for Odeziaku*

Jacob A. Tropp, *Natures of Colonial Change: Environmental Relations in the Making of the Transkei*

Jan Bender Shetler, *Imagining Serengeti: A History of Landscape Memory in Tanzania from Earliest Times to the Present*

Cheikh Anta Babou, *Fighting the Greater Jihad: Amadu Bamba and the Founding of the Muridiyya in Senegal, 1853–1913*

Marc Epprecht, *Heterosexual Africa? The History of an Idea from the Age of Exploration to the Age of AIDS*

Marissa J. Moorman, *Intonations: A Social History of Music and Nation in Luanda, Angola, from 1945 to Recent Times*

Karen E. Flint, *Healing Traditions: African Medicine, Cultural Exchange, and Competition in South Africa, 1820–1948*

Derek R. Peterson and Giacomo Macola, editors, *Recasting the Past: History Writing and Political Work in Modern Africa*

Moses E. Ochonu, *Colonial Meltdown: Northern Nigeria in the Great Depression*

Emily S. Burrill, Richard L. Roberts, and Elizabeth Thornberry, editors, *Domestic Violence and the Law in Colonial and Postcolonial Africa*

Daniel R. Magaziner, *The Law and the Prophets: Black Consciousness in South Africa, 1968–1977*

Emily Lynn Osborn, *Our New Husbands Are Here: Households, Gender, and Politics in a West African State from the Slave Trade to Colonial Rule*

Robert Trent Vinson, *The Americans Are Coming! Dreams of African American Liberation in Segregationist South Africa*

James R. Brennan, *Taifa: Making Nation and Race in Urban Tanzania*

Benjamin N. Lawrance and Richard L. Roberts, editors, *Trafficking in Slavery's Wake: Law and the Experience of Women and Children*

David M. Gordon, *Invisible Agents: Spirits in a Central African History*

Allen F. Isaacman and Barbara S. Isaacman, *Dams, Displacement, and the Delusion of Development: Cahora Bassa and Its Legacies in Mozambique, 1965–2007*

Stephanie Newell, *The Power to Name: A History of Anonymity in Colonial West Africa*

Gibril R. Cole, *The Krio of West Africa: Islam, Culture, Creolization, and Colonialism in the Nineteenth Century*

Matthew M. Heaton, *Black Skin, White Coats: Nigerian Psychiatrists, Decolonization, and the Globalization of Psychiatry*

Meredith Terretta, *Nation of Outlaws, State of Violence: Nationalism, Grassfields Tradition, and State Building in Cameroon*

Paolo Israel, *In Step with the Times: Mapiko Masquerades of Mozambique*

Michelle R. Moyd, *Violent Intermediaries: African Soldiers, Conquest, and Everyday Colonialism in German East Africa*

Abosede A. George, *Making Modern Girls: A History of Girlhood, Labor, and Social Development in Colonial Lagos*

Alicia C. Decker, *In Idi Amin's Shadow: Women, Gender, and Militarism in Uganda*

Rachel Jean-Baptiste, *Conjugal Rights: Marriage, Sexuality, and Urban Life in Colonial Libreville, Gabon*

Shobana Shankar, *Who Shall Enter Paradise? Christian Origins in Muslim Northern Nigeria, ca. 1890–1975*

Emily S. Burrill, *States of Marriage: Gender, Justice, and Rights in Colonial Mali*

Todd Cleveland, *Diamonds in the Rough: Corporate Paternalism and African Professionalism on the Mines of Colonial Angola, 1917–1975*

Carina E. Ray, *Crossing the Color Line: Race, Sex, and the Contested Politics of Colonialism in Ghana*

Sarah Van Beurden, *Authentically African: Arts and the Transnational Politics of Congolese Culture*

Lynn Schler, *Nation on Board: Becoming Nigerian at Sea*

Nation on Board

Becoming Nigerian at Sea

Lynn Schler

OHIO UNIVERSITY PRESS ✍ ATHENS

Ohio University Press, Athens, Ohio 45701
ohioswallow.com
© 2016 by Ohio University Press

To obtain permission to quote, reprint, or otherwise reproduce or distribute material
from Ohio University Press publications, please contact our rights and permissions
department at (740) 593-1154 or (740) 593-4536 (fax).

Printed in the United States of America
Ohio University Press books are printed on acid-free paper ∞™

26 25 24 23 22 21 20 19 18 17 16   5 4 3 2 1

Library of Congress Cataloging-in-Publication Data

Names: Schler, Lynn, author.
Title: Nation on board : becoming Nigerian at sea / Lynn Schler.
Other titles: New African histories series.
Description: Athens : Ohio University Press, 2016. | Series: New African
  histories | Includes bibliographical references and index.
Identifiers: LCCN 2015044414| ISBN 9780821422175 (hc : alk. paper) | ISBN
  9780821422182 (pb : alk. paper) | ISBN 9780821445594 (pdf)
Subjects: LCSH: Merchant marine—Nigeria—History. | Merchant
  mariners—Nigeria—Social conditions. | Merchant mariners—Legal status,
  laws, etc.—Nigeria. | Nigerian National Shipping Line—History.
Classification: LCC HD8039.S42 N557 2016 | DDC 387.509669—dc23
LC record available at http://lccn.loc.gov/2015044414

With love,
to George, Amos, Ellie, and Mika

Contents

Illustrations

Acknowledgments

Many research projects spring from personal experiences and connections to a certain topic, while others are born out of fascination with something extremely foreign or misunderstood. This project unquestionably falls into the second category. My curiosity about the lives and experiences of Nigerian seamen is undeniably linked to my own fear of the sea, and my sheer fascination with those whose livelihoods required them to spend days, months, and years crossing the oceans. As Nigerian seamen were recruited as an underpaid and undervalued labor force on both colonial and postcolonial ships, the hardships and challenges they faced were particularly pronounced. This research was thus driven by reverence for the struggles and adventures these seamen experienced in the face of endless difficulties both onboard ships and ashore. Because the project began with my lack of familiarity with this world, it required a full education into the many facets of African seafaring in the colonial and postcolonial eras. I slowly entered into a world of knowledge concerning life on board ships, including ship hierarchies, work regimens, and tasks, as well as deck-based social relations and cultural life. I also learned about the political economy of international shipping in general, and the politics of shipping in postcolonial nations in particular. To close the gaps of knowledge, I had to rely on countless sources of information and support. The final product is based on material gathered from a wide range of archives, interviews, and the published research of others. Thus, I am deeply indebted to a long list of people and institutions that made this book a possibility.

First and foremost, I am indebted to the former Nigerian seamen, officers, seamen's wives, and former NNSL managers who generously gave me their time, opened up their homes and their offices to me, responded to a wide array of questions, and tolerated my lack of knowledge regarding the material lives of seafarers in the international shipping industry. More than seventy men and women shared their stories, some of which were uplifting, others that were testimonies of abuses suffered and disillusionment. Every interview opened up a world onto itself, and I never could have undertaken this project without the detailed and insightful testimonies that emerged in each meeting. In particular, I am grateful to Adeola Lawal, Capt. Alao Tajudeen, Ari Festus, Ben Achilefu, Evelyn Miekumo, Lawrence Miekumo, Muritala Olayinka alli-Balogun, Pa Agbaosi, Rita Anomorisa, and Jackson Anomorisa. Sadly, some of the most notable informants have passed away since we last met: Joseph Kehinde Adigun, Anthony Davies Eros, Capt. Cosmos Niagwan, and Reuben Lazarus. Although the final product will appear long after the last of the interviews was conducted, it is my hope that all those interviewed will find their stories accurately portrayed in the pages that follow.

There were several institutions and individuals in Nigeria who contributed in significant ways to this study. The officers of the Nigerian Union of Seamen in Apapa, Lagos, helped me to locate former seamen, and also enabled me to conduct interviews in their offices. Adeola Lawal, the late Joseph Kehinde Adigun, and Jackson Anomorisa all referred me to key informants. I also had the honor of working with outstanding research assistants in Lagos. Lanre Davis located the first set of retired seamen. He also conducted a preliminary set of interviews that were extremely rich in content and served as an important basis for the rest of the research. Adeola Thomas Ayannubi and Alex Tayo located and interviewed some of the seamen's wives and assisted with transcriptions. I have the most sincere gratitude for the assistance I received from Friday Aworawo. With great perseverance and personal dedication, Friday sought out informants, set up interviews, and helped to locate important archival sources. Throughout very long days and weeks of interviews, he guided me through dozens of chaotic neighborhoods and suburbs of Lagos. Friday's engagement with the project and the insights he shared throughout helped to shape many of the ideas that emerged during the fieldwork, and his contribution was fundamental to this research. I also thank his wife, Biola, for her support.

The staff at the Nigerian National Archives in Ibadan helped me to locate many key documents. The Nigerian Institute of International Relations holds a very well-organized collection of newspaper articles related to shipping. I am indebted to Capt. Alao Tajudeen, who suggested I search a forgotten closet in the Apapa headquarters of the Nigerian Shipping Federation. There I discovered a large collection of uncataloged ship logbooks from the entire era of the Nigerian National Shipping Line. These logbooks were an invaluable source of information regarding the daily lives of crews on NNSL ships. I would also like to acknowledge the late Capt. Cosmos Niagwan, who gave several lengthy interviews regarding the liquidation of the NNSL and allowed me to review his personal archive of the proceedings. Lawal Bello Dogarawa, of the Nigerian Maritime Administration and Safety Agency, shared his research on Nigerian shipping. Ayodeji Olukoju has been an extremely warm and helpful colleague every time that I have been in Lagos. Paul Osifodunrin graciously helped me to locate research assistants.

Several archives outside of Nigeria provided essential documentary evidence of Nigerian seamen employed by British shipping lines. The Elder Dempster archive at the Merseyside Maritime Museum in Liverpool was a vital source of information for this study, and the staff there provided tremendous assistance on several research trips. The Modern Records Centre of the University of Warwick houses the archive of the International Transport Workers Federation, and the staff there was extremely helpful in providing material on the Nigerian seamen's union. I was also aided by records on British shipping at the British National Archives in Kew Gardens, and the Peter Waterman Papers at the International Institute of Social History in Amsterdam. I would also like to express my sincere gratitude to several people in the United Kingdom who provided interviews and answered endless queries about the historic relationship between Elder Dempster and the Nigerian National Shipping Line. The historian Peter Davies has published extensive and detailed research of the Elder Dempster Lines that provided essential background for my work, and Peter also gave a very informative interview early in the project. I would also like to express my sincere gratitude to Kenneth Birch, former Elder Dempster executive. Following an initial interview in Liverpool in 2009, Ken has generously provided thoughtful responses and clarifications to several queries over the years. I also thank former seaman Derek Bailey, who worked on NNSL ships in the very early years. Derek provided a wealth of information regarding the inaugural journeys of Nigerian ships, and his experiences and insights have greatly enriched this book. Photos were generously provided by Chris Clarke, Claes Moburg, Malcom Cranfield, Paul Strathdee, and Pete Bass.

I prepared the final manuscript while on sabbatical leave at the HUMA Institute at the University of Cape Town. As a visiting scholar at HUMA, I was provided with the space and resources that enabled me to complete the manuscript. I would like to thank Deborah Posel, Shamil Jeppie, Ilana van Wyk, Zethu Matebeni, Heather Maytham, and Rifqah Kahn for the opportunity to be a part of their vibrant intellectual community. A particular thanks goes to Deborah Posel for helping me to jump-start the concluding arguments of the book. I would also like to thank the Department of History at UCT for the opportunity to present my work, and for the encouraging feedback. While in Cape Town, we were assisted in numerous ways by Ronit and Stephen Segerman and Janine and Werner Thetard, all of whom have become lifelong friends.

There are several institutions and people in Israel that provided support for this project. Funding for the research was provided by an individual research grant from the Israel Science Foundation. Nurit Klein helped with the administration of these funds. Additional sources came from the dean's office in the Faculty of Humanities and Social Sciences. I was assisted by several graduate students with the bibliography and references, and I would like to thank Hilah Segal, Itamar Dubinsky, Noa Ginosar, Roy Knafo, and Tally Eyal for their hard work.

I divide my time at Ben Gurion University between two homes. I am honored and extremely fortunate to be a member of the Department of Politics and Government. This community of scholars embodies the best mixture of intellectual rigor, professional support, and deep dedication to human rights and political and social justice. Despite the ongoing challenges presented by the encroachment of antidemocratic forces, the Department of Politics and Government promotes a multiplicity of opinions and vantage points, evidenced by the crucial role the department played in the revival of African studies in Israel. For providing me with this exceptional and valued institutional home, I am extremely grateful to Gal Ariely, Dani Filc, Michal Givoni, Neve Gordon, Becky Kook, David Newman, Jennifer Oser, Sharon Pardo, Rene Poznanski, Ahmad Sa'di, Haim Yacobi, and Dina Zisserman-Brodsky.

My second home is the community of Africanist scholars, including colleagues in the Inter-University Program in African Studies and the Tamar Golan Africa Centre at Ben Gurion University. I would like to thank Ruth Ginio, Louise Bethlehem, Galia Sabar, and Ella Keren for years of camaraderie in the effort to promote African studies in Israel. A special thank you is due to Ruth Ginio, who has been the ideal colleague for many years. It has been my great fortune to work so beneficially with someone whose research interests overlap so closely with my own, and who has consistently provided a critical eye, enthusiastic encouragement, and friendship. I am also extremely privileged to work with the talented and dedicated staff of the Africa Centre. It is impossible to enumerate the countless ways in which Ayala Kuriel, Noga Miller, Moran Mekamel, Noa Levy, Itamar Dubinksy, and Tamar Ben Moshe work tirelessly to promote knowledge of Africa in Israel, and the human rights of Africans in and beyond Israel. Individually and as a staff, they constitute an example to follow.

This project was born in the course of field research for my PhD that focused on the history of Douala in the colonial era. Richard Roberts was my adviser then, but many years later, he continues to be a source of intellectual and professional guidance. And as a teacher and mentor, Richard is a rare role model that all his former students aspire to emulate. From those days in graduate school until the present, Kathryn Barrett-Gaines, Walter Hawthorne, Benjamin Lawrance, Thom McClendon, and Emily Osborn continue to provide support and friendship. Becky Kook, Walter Hawthorne, Tijani Hakeem, Ayodeji Olukoju, Louise Bethlehem, Ruth Ginio, Emily Osborn, and Gai Rofeh have read all or parts of the manuscript and gave important feedback. A special thanks to Haggai Ram, who has heard and commented on each of the arguments in endless car rides to Beer Sheva. I owe an intellectual debt to the scholars whose work has fundamentally shaped the theoretical and empirical grounding of this research. This list includes, but is not limited to, the work of Toyin Falola, Ayodeji Olukoju, Peter Davies, Diane Frost, Frederick Cooper, Carolyn Brown, and Tijani Hakeem. I have learned from each one of these scholars, but the shortcomings of this work are, of course, mine alone. To the editors of the New African Histories series at Ohio University Press: Jean Allman, Gillian Berchowitz, Allen Isaacman, and Derek Peterson, and I would like to express my sincere appreciation for their hard work and support of this book. The final product has been much improved by their close reading, insightful criticisms, and their strong commitment to high-quality scholarship. The entire field of African studies has been greatly enriched by the many important works that this editorial team has put their support behind over the years.

Several friends have been enthusiastic supporters, despite having little connection to or knowledge of African history. Danny Rosen, Lisa Russ, Debbie Hill, and Gayle Kirschenbaum have pushed me for detailed updates at every stage of the project, thus helping me more than they each realize to clarify the arguments to myself, and to make sure that I always had some progress to report. My sister, Miriam, remains my most enthusiastic reader even without reading, and I cherish her for being my link to every part of my past and present.

The final thanks go to those who deserve them the most. At some point in the course of writing, I realized that the storage shed in our yard would make an ideal office space. I thought George would talk me out of my sudden need for "a room of one's own," but instead he immediately took part in the planning and implementation. Ellie and Mika helped with the painting. Amos provided some sharp critique of the decor. In these symbolic gestures, and in countless acts of similar significance, my family has provided me with the physical, intellectual, and emotional spaces that I have needed for both work and home. To George, Amos, Ellie, and Mika—all of my love and deepest gratitude.

Introduction

MY FIRST ENCOUNTER with Nigerian seamen was in the stories I heard and collected in Douala, Cameroon, in the late 1990s. I was in this West African port city to research and interview residents about the social and cultural history of the colonial era, and several of the testimonies and reminiscences that I gathered made reference to the African seamen who passed through Douala while employed on colonial ships. Women in particular described the spectacle of the eye-catching seamen in their bright white uniforms as they crossed the city from the port to the bars and brothels of the popular quarters. These seamen inspired admiration among the local residents, but the former beer brewers and prostitutes of Douala also remembered the seamen as a raucous bunch of troublemakers. The larger-than-life portrayals and stories of these African seafarers stuck with me, and ultimately inspired the research that led to the writing of this book.

My initial imaginary of these African seamen was a romantic one, as I envisioned adventurous men traversing seas and cultures and social landscapes, leaving their indelible mark along the way as evidenced in the popular memory of Doualans. Opportunities such as these for transnational mobility were extremely rare among working-class Africans in the colonial era, and I was deeply curious about the worlds that opened up to seamen in the course of their travels. At the same time, as a historian of colonialism in West Africa, I was also keenly aware of the ways in which seamen's status as colonial subjects must have shaped and limited the freedoms and opportunities they enjoyed in the course of their travels. While seamen were extraordinarily unique among colonial subjects in Africa for their experiences of transnational mobility, I believed that research into the history of their lives on and off colonial vessels could shed new light onto the ways in which colonialism shaped and limited the opportunities of African subjects.

The early stages of research into Nigerian seafaring in the colonial era confirmed this anticipated trajectory. Beginning in World War II, British shipping companies began the mass recruitment of African seamen in Lagos. From the very start, Nigerian seamen's entrance into the colonial shipping industry was characterized by contradictory experiences. On the one hand, these seamen were cast as cheap and unskilled labor performing menial tasks on vessels where hierarchies of class intersected with hierarchies of race. Both on board with European crews and offshore among local populations, seamen experienced discrimination and hardships that characterized the experiences of black working classes across the Atlantic World in the post–World War II era. At the same time, transnational travel opened up a world of opportunities that seamen were quick to seize. To supplement meager wages, many developed a lucrative business as traders of secondhand goods. Offshore hours also provided seamen with opportunities to encounter cultural and social landscapes far removed from Nigeria, and many nurtured relationships that traversed racial and ethnic boundaries. Thus, as unskilled labor in the workforce of the colonial shipping industry, Nigerian seamen confronted discrimination and poor working conditions on the one hand, but they also exploited numerous opportunities for both adventure and personal gain on the other.

Although my focus was the colonial era, numerous interviews with former Nigerian seamen quickly revealed that seamen's life stories and experiences were not molded by colonialism alone. Moreover, I was surprised to hear many of those interviewed describing colonialism as an idealized era that had been lost. While seamen acknowledged the discrimination they suffered on board British ships, most remembered their employment on colonial vessels as years of golden opportunities, justice, and propriety. In fact, seamen described their most poignant experiences with injustice and disempowerment as taking place following the transition from colonialism to independence. In the postindependence era, seamen in Lagos were no longer recruited directly by British shipping companies, and many took up employment with the Nigerian National Shipping Line (NNSL). Inspired by nationalist fervor, seamen were initially optimistic about the creation of the national line, and many hoped that conditions would be more favorable aboard Nigerian ships. But a lack of sufficient resources and mismanagement doomed the venture, and seamen ultimately experienced deep disappointment with the move to the NNSL. The bitter disillusionment these seamen experienced in the context of their work in the postcolonial era impacted the ways in which seamen remembered and described colonialism. It became clear to me that the history of Nigerian seafaring in the colonial era could not be studied in isolation from postcolonial experiences.

Seamen's testimonies thus led me to reshape the focus and scope of the project. Rather than a history of colonialism, this book evolved into a working-class perspective on decolonization, nationalization, and the meaning of the "postcolonial" for labor in Nigeria. By looking at the history of Nigerian seafaring from the colonial period through independence, I could gain a better perspective on how seamen experienced and interpreted the broader strokes of Nigerian history over the last sixty years. The history and life stories of Nigerian seamen provide poignant testimony into the complex and contested process experienced by working classes while "becoming Nigerian."

What follows is a history of Nigerian seafaring from the late colonial period of the 1950s through the processes of decolonization and the first decades of independence in Nigeria. The aim is to provide a working-class perspective on the critical developments and transitions of this volatile period in the modern history of Africa. While histories of the end of colonialism abound, they often privilege a familiar trajectory. They outline the anticolonial struggles of Westernized African politicians, European concessions, and a negotiated transition to the establishment of independent nation-states. Much has been written about the ways in which elite interests, both African and European, were protected in this process. Largely missing from this narrative are the working classes and their perspectives and experiences on the end of colonialism, the promise of nationalism, and the significance of independence.

AN OVERVIEW ON NIGERIAN SEAFARING
IN THE TWENTIETH CENTURY

From the very beginning of international shipping between Africa, Europe, and the New World, Africans were employed on merchant vessels as crewmen. Particularly from the eighteenth century onward, the increase in commercial traffic on these routes led to the large-scale recruitment of Africans on European ships, serving as a cheaper and more efficient alternative to white sailors, who suffered from the tropical climate and its associated diseases.[1] "Coloured" seamen[2] engaged in ports throughout the British Empire were paid considerably lower rates than white seamen, and shipping companies increasingly exploited this cheap source of labor. From the era of the slave trade until the outbreak of World War II, the vast majority of Africans who worked on European vessels were Kru sailors recruited in Freetown, Sierra Leone. As the forerunners in the evolution of a pool of seafaring labor in West Africa, the Kru exploited colonial dependency upon them to establish relatively favorable conditions of employment for African seamen.

The Second World War changed the hiring practices of shipping giants such as Elder Dempster, which controlled the lion's share of cargo, mail, and passenger shipping between the United Kingdom and the West African coast. The war greatly increased demands on the company, and the need for seamen was acute. Hiring was moved to Nigeria, where Elder Dempster could sign on inexperienced fresh recruits for salaries lower than those of the Kru. Nigerian recruits came from a wide range of ethnic groups spanning southern Nigeria, and they lacked the social and cultural cohesion that had facilitated Kru labor organizing over the years. Colonial shipping companies exploited the Nigerians' lack of experience and organization, and paid Lagos recruits considerably lower wages than the Kru. Elder Dempster established a four-tiered pay scale during the war: At the bottom of the scale were the Nigerians signed on in Lagos, followed by the Kru recruited in Freetown. The third level of pay was given to Africans employed from Liverpool, while the highest salaries were reserved for European seamen, who were paid the National Maritime Board rates.

Thus, seamen recruited in Nigeria were embraced by colonial shipping companies as the cheap alternative to the Kru, with the additional benefit of being inexperienced in labor contract negotiating. But Nigerian seamen did not accept this inferior status passively, and they immediately sought ways to improve the conditions and benefits of their work. They soon formed the Nigerian Union of Seamen and began agitating for better working conditions. Seamen also exploited unofficial channels and opportunities to improve their lot. The primary source of additional income was the independent trade conducted by seamen, and most men leveraged whatever resources they had to engage in this trade. In Europe, seamen bought a wide variety of secondhand goods for resale in Africa, such as electronics, kitchen appliances, furniture, mattresses, ceramic goods, clothing, tires, and even used cars. Seamen nurtured and negotiated their relations with captains, immigration officers, customs officials, dockers, European retailers, African customers, and fellow crewmates in order to ensure their ability to buy, transport, and sell goods from one continent to another, and seamen had to continually adapt their activities to changing circumstances. Trading was a vital aspect of seamen's activities, and proof of seamen's ability to creatively and autonomously improve their financial standing.

While independent trade sustained seamen financially, it was the allure and intrigue of meeting new people and seeing new places that seamen associated most centrally with the core of the seamen's existence. The exploration of foreign lands and the bonding across geographic and cultural spaces provided seamen with a sort of spiritual compensation for their hard work and meager salaries. Seamen sought to re-create home wherever they were, and many spoke with great pride of their foreign wives and children in ports scattered across the world. The social bonds formed during their travels became the self-fashioned cornerstone of each individual's identification with a seaman's lifestyle.

Nigerian seamen's encounters with the work and lifestyle of seafaring thus nurtured a unique cosmopolitanism. But this exposure to cosmopolitanism also taught them the power of national identities and the hierarchies of the passports that accompanied them. Seamen were thus poised to engage with the nationalist fervor that grew in Nigeria during the post–World War II era, but they did so from their position as seamen. The demand for indigenization was a central focus of the nationalist elite, and included calls for the indigenization of shipping through the establishment of the Nigerian National Shipping Line. Seamen measured and appropriated nationalist ideology through the prism of the national shipping venture, and they equated the end of colonialism with the "Nigerianization" of shipping. Seamen could finally imagine a sense of home and belonging on board Nigerian ships, and they were enticed by the NNSL promise of higher wages and an end to discriminatory practices toward African seamen. Thus, the "freedom dreams" of working-class seamen in the era of nationalist organizing were starkly different from those of the political elite.[3]

For these seamen who had invested much hope in the outcome of decolonization, optimism quickly gave way to discontent and disappointment with the Nigerian national line. The Nigerian government was never fully committed to the success of the NNSL, and from the outset, politicians refrained from taking the necessary financial and legislative steps that would protect and bolster the enterprise. While the establishment of the national line was extolled as a vital step in freeing the Nigerian economy from colonial exploitation, this ideological support was not enough to ensure its success. Mismanagement and a lack of technical expertise perpetually plagued the enterprise, and company resources were slowly pillaged by management and government officials. Ships were used by captains and management for personal gain, and seamen were forbidden to conduct their own trade. In the context of their employment in the NNSL, seamen encountered a new set of prejudices based on ethnic rivalries and injustices around new forms of corruption and exploitation. The seamen, who had once seen themselves as "workers of the world," ultimately found themselves without employment or prospects as the Nigerian National Shipping Line underwent liquidation in the early 1990s. Just as seamen had embraced nationalism from the prism of seafaring, so, too, did they evaluate the outcome of decolonization through their experiences as seamen, and disillusionment with the NNSL was translated into a broader critique of corruption and inequality in postcolonial Nigeria.

REVISITING AFRICAN LABOR HISTORY

Nation on Board: Becoming Nigerian at Sea signifies a return to labor history, a field that has been largely neglected in the historiography of Africa over the last two decades. While historians attributed a crucial role to working-class organizations and struggles in the years leading up to independence, labor has slowly disappeared from histories of the postcolonial era. The move away from labor and working classes as categories of analysis is apparent not only in the field of African history, but can be seen as part of a general departure from a strict materialist agenda across the social sciences in the last two decades. This was not always the case in the field of African studies. To measure the sea of change that has taken place, one needs only to recall the 1984 proclamation of Bill Freund: "No subject has in recent years so intruded into the scholarly literature on Africa as the African worker. Labor has become a fundamental issue to those who seek to develop African economies or to revolutionize African polities. The elucidation and debate about the relationship of labor to historical and social issues is currently under way over an impressive range of places and a number of languages."[4]

Beginning in the colonial era, labor became a focus of Western research in Africa, but early studies produced on African workers and productivity were permeated with the colonial agenda. Particularly from the 1930s, European regimes advanced increasingly complex development schemes, and the need to extract labor from Africans became more pressing.[5] Colonial officials commissioned sociologists and demographers to study the cultures, migration patterns, living quarters, and birth rates of African workers in an effort to maximize their productivity.[6] In the postwar era, African working classes came under more scrutiny as labor movements played an increasingly prominent role in anticolonial agitation. European officials sanctioned the formation of trade unions in an effort to contain the discontent.[7] These concessions were not enough to quell the unrest, and, by 1960, organized labor and working classes had joined broad-based nationalist movements to successfully negotiate a transfer of power. Historians of nationalist movements throughout the continent have highlighted the pivotal role played by African labor unions in the transition from colonialism to independence.

In the first decades of independence, labor continued to draw the attention of historians and sociologists in Africa, with research deeply shaped by both Marxist ideology and an idenitification with the nationalist agendas of postcolonial states in Africa. Trade unions were seen as the uncontested representatives of working classes, while their role in nation-building was scrutinized and debated.[8] The conceptualization of these histories remained faithful to a universalist narrative of proletarianization, and evidence of solidarities among laboring constituencies that were not class-based were deemed to require analysis and explanation. By the 1970s and 1980s, "labor" became one of the most researched fields within African history.

Within this broader field, Nigeria played a prominent role as the site of some of the most influential studies produced on African labor in this era. Research in the 1960s and 1970s focused on the evolution of wage labor from the colonial era through independence, and was generally preoccupied with evaluating the effectiveness of the proletariat in organizing against economic and political exploitation. Tijani Yesufu's pioneering work was one of the first broad studies of the evolution of industrial relations from the late colonial era into independence in Africa. Yesufu evaluated the extent to which joint consultation and collective bargaining had taken root in employee-employer relations in Nigeria. Using Great Britain as his model, he explained Nigeria's failure to evolve according to the principles of industrial democracy as "problems of adolescence."[9] Most of the subsequent work focused on Nigerian labor unions themselves, and scholars engaged in heated exchanges concerning the role unions played in advancing pro-labor legislation. This debate was set off by a 1964 article by Elliot Berg and Jeffrey Butler, who claimed that Western scholars had highly exaggerated the role that trade unions played in advancing the political agendas of African working classes.[10] A dispute around the significance of trade union organizing ensued, and the General Strike of 1964 in Nigeria provided fodder for scholars on both sides of the issue. W. M. Warren and Peter Kilby each argued that unions had indeed played an effective role in the achievement of wage increases, while John Weeks countered that unions were fairly limited in their ability to pressure the government on the issue of wage legislation.[11] Other studies looked at specific sectors of the working class in an effort to understand the nature and significance of working-class activism. In an in-depth examination of shop-floor organizing among factory workers in Lagos, Adrian Peace concluded that urban working classes were most effective when they mobilized against their specific employers for better working conditions.[12] Peter Waterman's study of worker organization at the Port Authority of Lagos attempted to understand how conservatism among dockworkers prevented the emergence of broad alliances among working classes.[13] Robin Cohen's seminal work, *Labor and Politics in Nigeria, 1945–71*, provided a broad view of the relationship between wage earners and working classes in transition from colonialism to independence, and concluded that unions could claim "occasional" successes in the struggle for higher wages.[14] Theoretical and empirical differences notwithstanding, all these studies adopted a strict Marxist perspective from which to examine and evaluate the role of organized labor in Nigeria. As Adrian Peace wrote, "The Nigerian working classes are those wage-earners who stand in a consistently subordinate relationship in the industrial mode of production, whose surplus product is appropriated by those who own the means of production . . . and who on the basis of this relationship can identify a common opposition to their own economic interests and act accordingly."[15]

The commitment to the classic narrative of proletarianization in African labor history began to unravel in the wake of widespread disillusionment with socialist regimes both inside and outside Africa at the end of the 1970s. The corrolary weakening of labor movements at the end of the twentieth century led to a general crisis in labor studies, as William Sewell has noted, "because the organized working class seems less and less likely to perform the liberating role assigned to it . . . the study of working class history has lost some of its urgency."[16] It was increasingly evident that Africans had not been transformed into a revolutionary proletariat even when engaged in wage labor within capitalist enterprises. In addition, universalist conceptions were challenged by the growing body of literature focusing on local meanings for productivity and materiality. As Robin Cohen conceded in 1980, the major weakness of research into African working classes was the uncritical adoption of "traditional formula dichotomies," and a narrow focus on strikes and unionization, with no attention to the ways in which local cultural and social influences shaped labor consciousness.[17]

Post-structural criticisms cast doubt on the applicability of Marxist analysis to African contexts, and the growing discomfort with universalist categories led many historians to avoid class all together as a category of analysis. But rather than joining the retreat from the study of labor, some scholars have mobilized post-structural and postcolonial critiques to revisit materialist perspectives in African histories, and thus reinstate class as a valuable means of historical analysis. Recent studies are grounded in specific cultural and social contexts, and describe the ways in which African laborers have negotiated class interests in dialogue with ethnic, religious, regional, and gender-based alliances.[18] There is a more complex understanding of the interactions and contestations that exist between capitalist and noncapitalist sectors, and the multiplicity of strategies and ideologies leveraged by laborers. These are timely efforts, especially in the face of the gradual slide of working classes toward economic, political, and social marginalization in recent decades. African labor has experienced persistent poverty, failed schemes of development, and disempowerment, and there is a pressing need for more research on the ways in which African workers have lived, interpreted, and responded to their changing material and political circumstances. We need to better understand the diverse histories and cultures of work in Africa, and the impact that broader processes have had on African working lives over time.

In the Nigerian context, recent scholarship demonstrates that there is much to be gained from a reinvigorated focus on the working class. Several studies focused on the experiences and perspectives of labor have informed us of how work and productivity take on meaning and operate in specific social and cultural contexts. This can be seen in Paul Lubeck's work, which examined the coexistence of precapitalist and capitalist social and economic institutions in postcolonial Kano. Lubeck found that Koranic students and malams constituted a vocal and influential subgroup within the industrial proletariat. Rather than occupying a separate sphere, Lubeck claimed, the ideologies and social practices of Islamic institutions articulated with capitalism and shaped class consciousness.[19] Carolyn Brown's study of coal miners in the Enugu Colliery during the colonial era also emphasized the role played by local culture in the construction of work regimes, class consciousness, and organizing among Igbo miners. According to Brown, Igbo miners drew upon local ideologies, cultural practices, and economic spheres to negotiate "what they would and would not do" in the face of exploitative structures in the mines.[20] Finally, Lisa Lindsay examined the impact of wage earning on the construction of gendered identities and roles among Yoruba railway workers and their wives in southern Nigeria. Similarly to Brown, Lindsay argued that local notions of gender were resilient in the face of colonial modernizing projects, and shaped the ways in which working classes and their families navigated the colonial workforce.[21]

Taken together, these contributions affirm that the ideologies, experiences, and identities of African working classes cannot be understood outside of the local contexts from which they emerged. Each of these groups of laborers resisted or modified the process of proletarianization within the context of the Islamic, Igbo, or Yoruba cultural and social institutions in which they operated. At the same time, the focus on a specific regional and cultural context has made it difficult to problematize the role of ethnicity in the construction of consciousness among the Nigerian working class, or to offer an alternative to the trope of ethnicity that has dominated the study of Nigeria in the past and present. As seamen were drawn from a broad range of ethnic groups and did not share a common cultural or social foundation, their experiences provide an alternative case study that can further complicate our understanding of the experiences of postcolonial labor in Nigeria. Among the socially diverse group of seamen, it will be seen that the lack of ethnic cohesion gave birth to new types of solidarities and conflicts within this one sector of the working class in the postcolonial era.

The focus on seamen can further deepen and broaden our understanding of labor in the national context of Nigeria by including a transnational perspective in the examination of working-class lives. Leading scholars in the field of labor history have argued that a major limitation of classical labor history in Africa was that most studies were confined to the boundaries of national histories. As Philip Bonner, Jonathan Hyslop, and Lucien Van Der Walt argued, when national borders define the unit of analysis in the history of labor, we lose sight of the regional or transnational solidarities that often shape and define working-class identities and organizing.[22] Bonner and his coauthors advocate for a transnational approach to labor history, which "does not accept that its field of enquiry should stop at the 'national' border, or that a 'national' unit is self-evident, or necessarily a particularly useful unit of analysis."[23] This investigation into the experiences of Nigerian seamen confirms that a transnational perspective can be imperative for understanding African working-class histories. Beginning with an analysis of the transcontinental migrations and cosmopolitan lifestyles that characterized seamen's working lives, the narrative that unfolds problematizes and destabilizes the nation-state as a fixed context of analysis in the study of African labor. As will be seen, seamen's working lives were deeply shaped by the broader histories of British imperialism and the black diaspora. Their organized struggles and working lives were inherently connected to the ideological currents and social ties linking communities across what Paul Gilroy has called the "Black Atlantic." Seamen's ties to the black diaspora provide rare insights into working-class expressions of Pan-Africanism. But as will be seen, seamen also forged bonds that cut across boundaries of race. Seamen's organized and individual struggles exposed the broad array of cultural, religious, and ideological discourses that attracted them, inspired them, and shaped their worldviews.

This was not an unbridled process, and as discussed later in this book, nationalism and nationalization became hegemonic forces that slowly ruled out these transnational alliances. The broader context of decolonization was characterized by the triumph of European capitalist interests and their

African elite collaborators in constructing a postcolonial future favoring and protecting elite economic and political interests at the expense of rank-and-file labor. As several scholars have shown, African working classes have continually confronted limitations on their ability to assemble and exploit solidarities when these have come into direct conflict with the political and ideological agendas of power elites.[24] Thus, in the era of decolonization, African labor was corralled into allegiances reflecting the political programs of the African power elite in collusion with colonial capitalist interests. Both local and transnational imaginaries lost ground to the nationalist perspectives, and it was ultimately the nation-state that became the preeminent framework within which class struggles were negotiated and fought in the postcolonial era.[25] Thus, only by maintaining an awareness of seamen's transnational experiences and perspectives can we more fully appreciate the ways in which Nigerian seamen experienced the rise of nationalism and the bordering processes that accompanied it.[26]

VISIONS OF DECOLONIZATION, NATIONALISM, AND THE POSTCOLONIAL FROM BELOW

This history of Nigerian seamen aims to broaden our understanding of how nationalism and the nation-state were imagined by everyday Africans. To date, the history of nationalism in Africa is largely concerned with expressions of anticolonial agitation that brought about European decolonization and the establishment of independent, modern nation-states within the borders of former colonial territories. Across most of the continent, nationalist movements were led by Westernized elites who adopted political discourses, tactics, and platforms deeply influenced by Western-style political activity and political entities. In most contexts, members of this small male-elite were educated in Europe and the United States, and returned to lead the struggle that resulted in the transfer of power from colonialism to independence. Thus, in the words of Susan Geiger, the historiography and master narrative of nationalism have focused "almost exclusively on the lives, actions and contributions of 'a few good men.'"[27]

Recent decades have seen significant efforts to broaden this body of literature to include alternative (and sometimes subversive) voices to the history of nationalism in Africa. Jean Allman's work on Asante nationalism argues that ethnic movements such as the Asante National Labor Movement that gave voice to anticolonial aspirations were not merely reenactments of primordial, tribal politics, but in fact constituted an alternative voice of African nationalism.[28] Susan Geiger's work also expanded the narrow boundaries defining nationalist organizing by documenting the central role women played in constructing and organizing the nationalist movement in Tanganyika, thus debunking previous claims that women had filled only an auxiliary or reactive function in the Nyerere-led movement.[29] Tefetso Mothibe makes a similar case with regard to working-class nationalism in Zimbabwe, claiming that organized labor was not subordinated to petit bourgeois nationalism, but instead played a proactive and creative role in determining the direction the nationalist movement took.[30]

But while important works such as these have made significant contributions to broadening and deepening our understanding of how nationalism emerged and took shape in Africa, they still remained confined to an overly narrow vision of what the "postcolonial" signified for African masses both on the eve of decolonization and into the period of independence. The historiography of nationalism in Africa, with all its modifications and expansions, largely adopts the political vision of the Western-educated male elite for the postcolonial nation-state. Fred Cooper argued, "Nationalist leaders often began to channel the variety of struggles against colonial authority on which they had drawn—embracing peasants, workers, and intellectuals—into a focus on the apparatus of the state itself and into an ideological framework with a singular focus on the 'nation.' In the process, many of the possible readings of what an anticolonial movement might be were lost."[31]

The agenda of the nationalist elite did not reflect the aspirations of all Africans. As colonialism drew to a close, individuals and communities from across the continent conjured up visions and interpretations of what decolonization could and should mean, but many of these have been subordinated, lost, or silenced by narratives of nation-building. Even within the context of nationalist ideologies, formulations that diverged from the political agenda seeking to establish modern nation-states existed, but they have been largely lost in the historical record. Although many of the paths taken in the era of decolonization became irrelevant, outdated, or even oppositional with independence, their significance should not be measured by their ultimate fate in the postcolonial landscape. As Fred Cooper has argued, the difficulty in writing a contoured history of decolonization and accurately assessing the significance of the new possibilities born in this era is that "we know the end of the story."[32] Looking back from the present, historians tend to privilege narratives describing processes of nation-building as the main theme of decolonization. Left behind are the other possible routes and outcomes—cultural, political, and economic alliances not corresponding to the physical or conceptual borders of postcolonial African nation-states.

Histories of decolonization in African contexts have insufficiently examined how everyday Africans embraced and promoted alternative visions
of postcoloniality rather than those ultimately enforced by political elites.
And, little attention has been paid to the individual and communal journeys taken by nonelites toward the assumption of national identities and
ideologies, and the consequences of their entwinement in this historical
trajectory. One notable exception is Gregory Mann's work on the fluid and
changing notions of political belonging invoked by Senegalese veterans in
the colonial and postcolonial eras. Mann argued that national identity was
part of a broad and changing set of statuses inhabited by veterans in an effort
to claim political and material benefits. For Senegalese veterans, national
identity was a "claims-making" instrument that diverged from more formal,
legal notions of citizenship signified by decolonization and the establishment of nation-states in Africa.[33] Similarly, it will be seen that Nigerian
seamen's formations of nationalist consciousness bore little resemblance to
elite visions, which were aimed at constitutional reform, political emancipa-
tion from foreign domination, and nation-building. For seamen, becoming
"Nigerian" was a strategy for achieving better pay, more just relations with
management, and an end to racial discrimination. Thus, this investigation
into the Nigerianization of seamen unpacks the meaning and significance
of a Nigerian identity and highlights its fluidity and evolution over time.
It will be seen that decolonization was a process that everyday Africans responded to, interpreted, and experienced, rather than one merely dictated
from above.

While this book illustrates how ordinary people exploited opportunities
to create a political agenda and postcolonial vision tied to their particular
circumstances, it ultimately draws attention to the processes and institutions
that finally prevented seamen from representing themselves and protecting their interests. For masses of Africans, decolonization was a process that
ultimately ended in unfulfilled promises. The transition to independence
was characterized by the collaboration between European capitalists and
African political and economic elites to construct a postcolonial future favoring and protecting their specific interests. Once independence arrived,
these elites had to confront the tremendous challenge of meeting the needs
of the masses. Fred Cooper has claimed that while most African states took
up projects of development, few had the necessary resources or dedication to
serve the interests of the people. Instead, postcolonial ruling elites ensured
their own survival and prosperity by becoming "gatekeepers" over the limited
resources that moved into and around the newly born nation-states.[34]

This book provides a clear illustration of the processes described by Cooper. Seamen's expectations of the postcolonial reality went unfulfilled because the management of the Nigerian National Shipping Line had insufficient resources and managerial experience to develop the national line into a viable enterprise. Instead, Nigerian officers tightened their control over the resources moving in and out of Nigeria through the ships of the NNSL. Against this backdrop, seamen experienced a worsening of employment conditions on board ships, and a narrowing of possibilities for those engaged in independent trade. This case study thus illustrates how political and economic developments associated with the transition from colonialism to independence ultimately limited the autonomy of African labor in crafting postcolonial identities, and provides background for understanding the disillusionment working classes expressed toward the postcolonial reality. In chronicling the defeats and failures experienced by Nigerian seamen, the study exposes precisely how power was consolidated in the processes of nationalization at the expense of labor, and how deals struck between European and African elites on the eve of independence continue to limit the choices and opportunities available to African working classes today.

CORRUPTION AND DECLINE
OF A POSTCOLONIAL BUSINESS VENTURE

The history of the establishment, functioning, and ultimate demise of the Nigerian National Shipping Line can be seen as a microcosm of the broader fate of countless political and economic schemes in postcolonial Nigeria. This focused investigation into one enterprise provides insights into how the promise of economic nationalism slowly evaporated as it confronted the political and economic realities of postcolonial Nigeria. The story of the NNSL can be woven seamlessly into a larger narrative of mishaps and failures of government planning and economic development in the postcolonial era. These narratives of unrealized opportunities, failed government, underdevelopment, and corruption abound in the history of postindependence Nigeria, and scholars across disciplines have attempted to provide an appropriate theoretical framework for understanding their causes and long-term effects. Academics have debated the roots of the political and economic instability that has plagued Nigeria since independence, as well as the stark inequalities and misappropriations that only seem to deepen over time. Indeed, these debates are not limited to Nigeria, and many scholars inside and outside the continent struggle to understand the persistent economic and political difficulties faced by postcolonial African states.

Several distinct approaches have taken shape in these debates. There are those who find explanations in institutional weaknesses, many of which are attributed to the legacy of colonialism. Thus, Mahmood Mamdani has argued that the roots of inequality in postcolonial Africa are found in the colonial legacy that institutionalized unequal structures of power that served the needs of only a small elite at the expense of the masses.[35] Scholars from the schools of underdevelopment theory and dependency theory also argue that the colonial legacy is largely responsible for instituting a world system that leaves postcolonial states at a perpetual disadvantage in international markets. But while acknowledging the immense obstacles colonialism placed on Africa's road to development, many are beginning to feel ill at ease with these explanations that do not confront the postcolonial factors shaping Africa's present. As Timothy Burke summarized the situation, "The *problem* of postcolonial Africa is treated by the majority of scholars, especially anthropologists and historians, as an extension of or continuation of the *problem* of the colonial, that the moral and political challenge of postcolonial society is subordinated to or situated within a modernity whose character is largely causally attributed to colonial intervention."[36]

As we move further away from the colonial era, there is a growing need for understanding postcolonial realities beyond the impact of the colonial legacy. In recent years, several significant works have argued that the postcolonial instability and weakening of African polities and economies must be understood against the backdrop of the cultural contexts of local societies. Thus, argue Patrick Chabal and Jean-Pascal Daloz, African states will never evolve into exact replicas of the Western state because this transplanted model does not serve the interest of local elites. African elites prefer to maintain a deeply rooted traditional system based on "a reciprocal type of interdependence between leaders, courtiers and the populace. And it is a system that *works*, however imperfectly, to maintain social bonds between those at the top and bottom of society."[37] The persistence of patron-clientism and moral obligation has been cited by many scholars as a prominent cause of misappropriation and corruption in African political and economic systems. Jean-François Bayart wrote, "A man who manages 'to make good' without ensuring that his network shares in his prosperity brings shame upon himself and acquires the reputation of 'eating' others in the invisible world."[38] J. P. Olivier de Sardan also cites local cultures as the source of poor governance and corruption in Africa. Included in his survey of widespread social practices that ultimately lead to corruption are practices of negotiation, gift-giving, and the logics of predatory authority and solidarity networks. But unlike Chabal and Daloz, de Sardan rejects the notion that these are precolonial carryovers: "All these logics are syncretic, none is 'traditional,' none comes directly from any so-called pre-colonial culture."[39] While hardly an exhaustive survey, these few examples illustrate the types of polarities that exist in the ongoing debates about the "failures" of postcolonial Africa.

This history of the Nigerian National Shipping Line reveals that there are no simple formulas for explaining the unsuccessful economic and political ventures of the postcolonial era. As we will see, the NNSL began as an ideological project. For Nigerian politicians and businessmen, the indigenization of shipping was a powerful symbol of decolonization, representing a reversal of centuries of economic exploitation at the hands of European colonizers. But the success of an international shipping venture required far more investment than just ideological zeal. From its creation, the national line suffered because of inadequate financial support from the very politicians who had reaped political rewards by grandstanding its establishment. Political motives, rather than economic ones, hindered decision-making processes, evident in the hasty buyout of the technical partners, Elder Dempster and the Palm Line, after only two years of operations. This move greatly weakened the already scarce managerial resources of the company, and the NNSL suffered from a lack of expert knowledge essential to running an international shipping line. Political instability further exacerbated this situation, as the revolving door of ministers led to constant hirings and firings of staff, and no one stayed around long enough to ensure solid business practices. The lack of leadership and authority at the NNSL ultimately led to the unchecked pillaging of the company by politicians and their networks of clients who had no interest in the success of the shipping venture. With time, there was a trickle-down effect seen in practices of misappropriation and corruption. All parties involved in the shipping line, from the management to officers and captains, down to the rank-and-file crew, looked for ways to maximize opportunities. By the 1980s, illegality flourished at all levels: seamen engaged in theft and drug trafficking, captains and officers used the ships for their own private enterprises, and management embezzled millions in company resources.

The history of the NNSL demonstrates that a complex array of factors, spanning the colonial and postcolonial eras, led to the demise of the Nigerian National Shipping Line. From the start, material inequalities became a breeding ground for abuses of power, illegality, and misappropriation. Local responses to the instability and scarcity of resources were indeed culturally rooted, but they cannot be understood in isolation from inequality and injustice. In his work on corruption in postcolonial Nigeria, Daniel Smith has argued that the roots of corruption are neither purely institutional nor purely cultural, but rather can be found at "the intersection of local culture and larger systems of inequality."[40] Against the backdrop of political and economic insecurity and inequality, Smith argues, people exploit all available resources, whether they be economic, political, or cultural, in order to survive and thrive.

This history of the Nigerian National Shipping Line provides a unique view into the evolution of a postcolonial enterprise from multiple perspectives. By focusing on the evolution of the NNSL from the perspective of seamen, but also engineers, captains, and management, it aims to reveal how each class fared against the backdrop of broader political, economic, and ideological developments. In maintaining a view of all the actors involved, the study provides insights into the divergent ways in which working classes and elites experienced the opportunities and limitations that characterized the history of postcolonial Nigeria.

ON SOURCES

Histories of enterprises and the workers employed by them are profoundly lacking in the history of Africa, largely because archival evidence either has not been preserved out of disinterest or has been deliberately destroyed. This study overcomes the absence of a well-organized and preserved archive, and demonstrates that it is nonetheless possible to write postcolonial histories of African enterprises and the labor employed by them. While no complete archive of the NNSL has survived, I have located a broad base of primary documents in government, corporate, and personal archives in Nigeria, Liverpool, London, and Amsterdam.

The archives of the Merseyside Maritime Museum in Liverpool and at the British National Archives in Kew Gardens provided vital documentation on British shipping interests in the colonial era. The archives of Elder Dempster in particular, located at the Merseyside Maritime Museum, provided rich information about the shipping company's involvement in Nigeria, as well as information about recruitment and employment of seamen, and relations between the company and the Nigerian Union of Seamen. Colonial policies toward "coloured" seamen in general, and Nigerians in particular, could be found at the National Archives. The archives in Liverpool and London also included vital information on the process of decolonization, and on the negotiations behind the founding of the Nigerian National Shipping Line in partnership with Elder Dempster and the Palm Line. For the 1960s–1980s, the British National Archives contain records of the Port Authority regarding illicit trade and drug smuggling involving seamen in general and Nigerians in particular. The Peter Waterman Papers at the International Institute of Social History in Amsterdam contain primary and secondary material concerning labor organizing in Nigeria in the postcolonial era. Finally, archives in Liverpool and London included correspondence concerning the various shipping conferences operating between Africa and Europe in the colonial and postcolonial eras.

In Nigeria, few records of the former Nigerian National Shipping Line have survived. But several important sources of information were available in various archives in Lagos and beyond. The Nigerian Shipping Federation houses a partial collection of official ship logbooks from the 1960s through the 1980s. These captain's logs contain rich and detailed documentation of specific incidents that took place on board NNSL ships, and provide rare insights into hierarchies of power and relations between officers and rank-and-file seamen, as well as any disciplinary actions, medical emergencies, and personal issues concerning crew members that arose. The Nigerian Institute of International Relations contains a well-organized collection of Nigerian newspaper articles relating to shipping and seamen from the colonial era to the present. In the collections of the National Archives in Ibadan, I was able to find correspondence about seamen in the colonial era, with an important collection of files concerning repatriations. I supplemented the information found in these archives with official documents, photos, personal letters, and various keepsakes found in the personal archives and photo albums of former seamen, labor union officers, captains, officers, and NNSL management. Many of these records have never been used before by historians.

Without detracting from the significance of all these written sources, this study was largely made possible by the information obtained through oral interviews. Over the course of three research trips to Nigeria from 2007 to 2011, I conducted more than seventy interviews with Nigerians who had varying degrees of involvement with the Nigerian National Shipping Line. As the study began with a focus on seamen themselves, I initially concentrated on interviewing rank-and-file seamen who had worked on colonial and NNSL ships. With the help of research assistants, I located some former seamen and these men directed me to others. The officers at the Nigerian Union of Seamen in Apapa, Lagos, also provided assistance in contacting former seamen, and they generously allowed me to conduct some of the interviews in their offices. While this was an extremely helpful arrangement that enabled me to schedule consecutive interviews over a few days, the interviews that I conducted in seamen's homes were often richer for the insights they provided me. Through dozens of visits to former seamen's homes across greater Lagos,[41] I was able to get an invaluable glimpse into seamen's offshore lives, and to gain a deeper understanding of how their careers as seafarers had shaped their lives and the lives of their family members. Some had a piece of furniture or another keepsake from their time at sea, while others had pictures of their foreign girlfriends and children on the walls of their homes. But mostly, visits to seamen's homes in the low-income neighborhoods of Lagos provided physical evidence of the dire fate of the working class within the history of the NNSL. The interviews I conducted with seamen were open-ended, but they covered a range of topics including seamen's recruitment and training, life on board ships in both the colonial and the postcolonial eras, time spent at international ports of call, their involvement with independent trade, relations with their families abroad and back in Nigeria, the seamen's union and labor protests, and seamen's perspective on the circumstances leading to the demise of the NNSL. Often, seamen's wives were present at the interviews, and I was able to use this opportunity to interview the women as well. Seamen's wives told very different stories than those of their husbands, as they had to struggle with many months and years of maintaining the household and caring for their children in their husbands' absence. Women provided an essential perspective on the financial significance of men's independent trading enterprises, and they also provided fascinating insights into the romantic relationships their husbands maintained abroad.

As the interview process progressed, and more and more seamen voiced criticisms of Nigerian officers and management, I soon realized that in order to gain a fuller perspective of life on board NNSL ships, it was imperative to interview former captains, engineers, and managers. Interviews with captains and engineers offered a very different perspective from those of seamen. These NNSL officers received far more extensive training than rank-and-file seamen, which included several years of academic study in Britain, and thousands of hours of practical training logged on foreign vessels. They therefore possessed a wealth of knowledge, and the ability to draw comparisons, about the technical and economic aspects of running ships and cargo in the international shipping industry, and the functioning of the NNSL within it. Captains and officers had their own criticisms of both rank-and-file seamen and management, and their perspectives were an important complement to seamen's testimonies. As opposed to the officers, it was fairly difficult to locate former managers of the NNSL who were willing to provide an interview. Many who had occupied positions of influence and power in the former company were not willing to meet with me, probably in light of the rampant misappropriation and corruption that led to the NNSL's failure. But a few key informants from both middle and upper management of the NNSL did provide important information on the general running of the company, financial issues, and the links between the volatile political history of postcolonial Nigeria and its impact on the National Shipping Line. Finally, one former government official who oversaw the process of liquidation also provided a key interview regarding the final years of the NNSL.

This research would not have been possible without these interviews, as no official or complete archive of the NNSL exists. Even in the presence of the available sources, interviews provided me with invaluable insights that brought to life, enriched, and contradicted the written material found in archives. But as historians of Africa are well aware, the use of oral histories can raise its own set of concerns, including issues of remembering and forgetting, and questions of accuracy, authenticity, and bias. I attempted to overcome many of these problems by conducting over seventy interviews with a range of informants, thus enabling me to find common threads and themes that emerged again and again from the interviews. Yet, throughout the research, and particularly in this effort to overcome biases and partialities in oral testimonies, I remained keenly aware that many of my informants did not necessarily share my agenda. While my primary concern was to produce a book that *accurately* portrayed their experiences, I realized that those who provided interviews did so with the earnest hope that telling their stories *would make a difference*. For rank-and-file seamen, officers, and managers, the intersections between their lives and the history of the NNSL were not simply a matter of historic interest, but an unfinished business that still evoked varying claims. This issue was all the more complicated by the fact that there were stark contrasts between the agendas of each class of informants. Officers and managers offered systematic analyses of the political economy of shipping in Nigeria, and how the wrongdoings of the past could be overcome and corrected by reestablishing the national line. Working-class seamen, on the other hand, gave testimonies full of pride, anger, disillusionment, and a sense of betrayal around their experiences with the NNSL, and interviews often ended with a bitter lament of their extreme poverty and lack of prospects. Despite stark differences in the material and political agendas that characterized each class of informants, none told their stories to merely enrich the historical record. For all those interviewed, the story of the NNSL strongly resonated in the present, and there had to be utility and impact in its retelling. While conducting interviews, and later analyzing and interpreting the testimonies, I was confronted with the dissonance that existed between my primary concern for constructing an accurate account and my informants' efforts to convey a story that addressed the injustices and disappointments they experienced. I hope that the narrative that has taken shape, and the lessons it can provide, resolves this issue by signifying something of use to those who shared their insights with me.

AN OVERVIEW OF THE CHAPTERS

The first two chapters of the book trace the origins of Nigerian seafaring in the late colonial period and describe the work and lifestyles of seamen employed on colonial vessels. Chapter 1 provides background on African seafaring in the modern age, and the processes that led to the recruitment of Nigerians en masse. This chapter describes work on board the ships, and the types of jobs seamen were engaged in, training provided, relations with European crews, incidents of racism and discrimination, and the background of union organizing among Nigerian seamen and labor relations between seamen and management of the colonial shipping lines. Chapter 2 examines the cosmopolitanism that characterized the economic, social, and cultural lives of seamen offshore. This chapter describes the trade conducted by seamen in secondhand goods such as electronics, small and large appliances, foodstuffs, clothing, and even in scrap metals and used cars. The chapter also looks at the social lives of seamen abroad, and examines particularly the romantic relationships seamen established with European, Asian, and Latin American women in the course of their travels. This review of the centrality of cosmopolitanism in seamen's consciousness and experiences provides essential context for understanding the eventual impact of nationalism and nationalization on seamen's working lives.

Chapters 3 and 4 evaluate the seamen's organizing efforts and relationship with the Nigerian Union of Seamen, and the impact the rise of nationalism had on this organizing. Chapter 3 focuses on the history of labor organizing and the Nigerian seamen's union in the shadow of decolonization. The chapter examines cooperative efforts between Nigerian seamen and diaspora communities, and highlights the ideological and political support the seamen obtained from these transnational alliances in organizing protests and strikes. This chapter describes how the process of decolonization ultimately limited the potential for cooperative efforts between Nigerian seamen and diaspora working classes. The role played by union leadership in Lagos in bringing about this shift is scrutinized. Chapter 4 examines the establishment of the Nigerian National Shipping Line, reviewing the economic and political motives for its establishment, the terms by which the enterprise was launched, and the relationship between the NNSL, British shipping lines, and international shipping conferences. A close investigation into the negotiations that took place between Nigerian and British officials reveals the ways in which elite interests prevailed in the history of decolonization. The chapter reviews the intense critique this business relationship between the NNSL and Elder Dempster received from the broader public, who questioned the autonomy of the Nigerian shipping line under the arrangement.

Chapters 5 and 6 trace the history of the Nigerian National Shipping Line and the fate of the seamen employed by it. Chapter 5 examines the process of "Nigerianization" of shipping and the impact this process had on the working lives of seamen on board ships. Based largely on a review of official logbooks, the chapter documents how shipboard hierarchies, labor relations, and working cultures evolved over time and became "Nigerian." It will be seen that what seamen once anticipated as an act of homecoming ultimately ended in deep disappointment. The scarcity of resources doomed the venture from the start and resulted in corruption and pillaging by those with access to resources. Class conflicts and ethnic tensions from the broader Nigerian political landscape found their way on board. Chapter 6 studies the multiple and complex set of factors leading to the decline and eventual demise of the Nigerian National Shipping Line. This chapter attempts to provide insights into the economic insecurity and inequalities that led to misappropriation and illegality. The examination of the demise of the NNSL demonstrates that material inequalities became a breeding ground for corruption, and corruption can therefore not be understood in isolation from inequality and injustice. It will be seen that the turn to illegality, in the forms of theft and drug trafficking on the part of seamen, or misappropriation of company resources on the part of officers and management, cannot be divorced from broader political and economic contexts.

The concluding argument of the book is that the uneven impact of nationalization on each of the classes involved in the shipping industry can be linked to the broader history of postcolonial Nigeria. The history of the Nigerian National Shipping Line can be taken as a metaphor for the postcolonial economy and society, and the disempowerment of seamen can be linked to the narrowing of opportunities that characterize the political, economic, and social lives of working-class Nigerians to the present. This study helps us to understand that the mismanagement and cronyism of postcolonial states were not just political failures, but processes with broad and consequential effects on the everyday lives of working people who were, at one point, deeply committed to the project of independence, and who believed in the rights and benefits it promised.

1 ⌇ The Working Lives of Nigerian Seamen in the Colonial Era

THE ORIGINS OF NIGERIAN SEAFARING can be linked to a deeper history of African seafaring in the Atlantic World. The history of economic and political relations between Africa and the Western world was constructed largely by the traffic of ships, passengers, crews, and cargoes crossing the ocean. From the very beginning of international shipping between Africa, Europe, and the New World, Africans were employed to supplement crews on vessels arriving from Europe. This was usually necessary due to the high mortality rate among European seamen, who contracted malaria and yellow fever in large numbers. African recruits, readily available in ports throughout West Africa, provided labor as deckhands, cargo handlers, or translators at a much lower cost than seamen signed on in Europe. Thus, from the very start of seagoing trade between Africa and the West, European shipping companies became dependent upon African labor. African crews were a cheap alternative to European ratings, and shipping companies made continual efforts to maintain this source of labor at the lowest possible cost. For their part, African seamen employed in the transatlantic trade attempted to exploit the economic, social, and cultural opportunities that opened up to them through work on European vessels. This dynamic of mutual dependency, coupled with an attempt of all those involved to maximize opportunities, characterized the history of African seafaring in the Atlantic World from the slave trade throughout the colonial era and the era of decolonization. The entry of Nigerians into the history of African seafaring came only in World War II, but largely followed dynamics and patterns established centuries before.

Historians of the eighteenth and nineteenth centuries have argued that seafaring was empowering for black men and enabled them to overcome prejudices and social hierarchies structuring relations between Europeans and Africans in the era of the slave trade. Out on the open sea, ships brought multiracial crews together in tight quarters, and the collective work on board ships fostered a rare solidarity among black and white sailors that was not possible back in port. According to Jeffrey Bolster, race never fully disappeared on ships, but black seamen enjoyed membership in a deck-based camaraderie and egalitarianism that temporarily mitigated against racial divisions.[1] Seafaring was thus empowering for Africans, fostering a potent masculine identity. Walter Hawthorne has argued that this empowerment was evidenced on slave ships, where African seamen "were free to commit depraved acts on shackled women and men."[2] The mobility and displacement that characterized the working lives of African seamen engendered the emergence of creolized and hybrid identities. In this world of the multiethnic "Atlantic proletariat" described by Peter Linebaugh and Marcus Rediker,[3] black seamen exploited new solidarities and ultimately challenged relations of power throughout the Atlantic World.

Whether or not this positive assessment of black seamen's early history is overly optimistic, there was a clear deterioration of their status on board colonial merchant vessels with the conversion to steamships from the 1870s onward. The technological innovations behind the transition from sailing to steam engines were accompanied by the replacement of traditional seamen's work with the work of unskilled labor. Colonial subjects were now hired to fill lower-status positions on board, and a new industrial division of labor emerged. Following the conversion to steam engines, up to 50 percent of African crewmen were engaged in jobs not traditionally found on sailing ships: stoking the engine, housekeeping, and catering. Many seamen deprecated these new shipboard tasks as less than proper seafaring.[4]

The segregation of African crews into jobs that did not require seafaring skills or training largely erased the "rough equality"[5] described on sailing ships. From the beginning of the twentieth century, labor hierarchies on board steamships were entrenched in colonial racial ideologies. It was argued that "coloured" men from the tropics were better suited for jobs such as firemen in the engine room, as they were naturally more capable than whites to handle the heat. "Coloured" seamen engaged in ports throughout the British Empire were paid considerably lower rates than white seamen, receiving one-third to one-fifth of a British seaman's wage, and took on jobs perceived as menial, unskilled, and feminine.[6] From the beginning of the twentieth century, the unraveling of British maritime dominance as a result of growing international competition only intensified the desire to cut costs by underpaying colonial seamen.[7]

Nigerian seamen, whose recruitment began during World War II, thus entered a world of shipping that had largely erased any kind of benefits enjoyed by black seamen in the Age of Sail. The working lives of Nigerian seamen in the late colonial era bore the political and ideological imprints of colonialism. Nigerian crews were employed on ships where race largely determined the division of labor and shipboard hierarchies. Difficult working conditions and discrimination ultimately led them to organize their own union, but this body had little success as an effective advocate for improving working conditions. Thus, Nigerian seamen shared a solidarity with colonial seamen recruited throughout the British Empire, united by a political and historical relationship of colonial subordination.[8] This chapter will outline the beginnings of Nigerian seafaring on British vessels from the end of World War II. We will review the historical circumstances that led to widespread hiring in Lagos, the jobs that seamen performed and the working conditions on board colonial ships, problems of prejudice and discrimination that characterized the working lives of these seamen in the late colonial era, and the early efforts at organizing a Nigerian seamen's union.

RECRUITING NIGERIANS: HISTORICAL AND POLITICAL BACKGROUND

European vessels arriving in West Africa in the era of the slave trade were met by fleets of canoes manned by African mariners occupying the coastal regions. Historical records recount the respect and surprise of European seamen at the skillful handling of canoes that enabled Africans to navigate waterways that were impassable by European deep-sea ships.[9] Certain groups stood out for their competence as mariners and began supplying European crews additional deckhands, navigators, and interpreters. In particular, the Kru, inhabitants of the Liberian coast, impressed the Europeans as expert boatmen, and by the eighteenth century became the main source of local recruits on European ships. Although originating from a heterogeneous collection of fisherman clans on the coast of Liberia, the seamen recruited from this region for work on foreign vessels were commonly identified by European merchants as "Kru." This labeling took on official status by the Liberian government's recognition of the Kru ethnic group in the nineteenth century.[10] The emergence of the Kru social construct thus represents the earliest coalescing of African identities and social groupings around maritime employment. The Kru were employed on steamships as deckhands and stevedores moving cargo from ship to shore, and later as firemen and stokers on deep-sea steamships.[11] European shipping companies eventually became reliant on these African seamen, and most ships from Europe would stop in Freetown to pick up Kru coal handlers, deckhands, and firemen before continuing down the coast.[12]

The Kru in turn exploited this dependence. They controlled the supply of seamen through a system of labor recruitment based on a headman and his apprentices. Headmen acted as middlemen between seamen and their employers, recruiting laborers from the interior and negotiating terms of employment. Headmen decided who went to sea and for how long, took care of lodging and food, and represented their apprentices in any grievances. The system opened the door to many abuses, and the colonial administration received complaints that crewmen were forced to pay large bribes to headmen in order to get employment on ships. In some cases, in the initial period of employment, the headmen earned the wages of the young men in training and thus amassed considerable wealth and influence for themselves. Headmen took pains to develop personal relations with European captains, who would in turn give them preferential treatment in the process of recruitment. Shipping companies also paid headmen large sums for providing labor. The system was well entrenched by the beginning of the twentieth century, enabling the Kru to establish a near monopoly on the supply of seafaring labor until the Second World War. It was not only the headmen who benefited, and years of specialization and efficient organizing enabled the headmen to continually negotiate for improved terms of employment for all the African crew engaged in Freetown. This earned the Kru a position of relative prosperity, symbolized by the fact that Kru women were never allowed to work outside the home in petty trading or market work, as most other Freetown women did.[13]

Until the period following World War II, European shipping companies overwhelmingly favored this system of labor recruitment based in Freetown because it passed the responsibility for monitoring the labor supply, crew behavior, and work supervision onto the Kru headmen and away from them as employers. The preference for this arrangement substantiates Fred Cooper's claim that European economic interests prior to World War II preferred to cast African labor in a tribal mold, and argued that even workers migrating to the city should remain subordinated to Native authorities. In proposing that labor remain linked to "a traditional African way of life," employers and the colonial administration could avoid taking responsibility for masses of "detribalized" Africans.[14] Likewise, rather than acknowledging the proletarianization of the Kru as laborers in a modern, industrialized economy, and thereby clearing the way for potential demands for workers' rights and benefits, the system of headmen and apprentices enabled shipping companies to abdicate their responsibility for the newly born African working class. Within this model of preserving a premodern workforce, there was no room for trade unions, and British shipping companies, led by the Liverpool-based giant Elder Dempster, refused employment to union members up until World War II.[15]

From the end of the nineteenth century, the Elder Dempster company controlled the lion's share of cargo, mail, and passenger shipping between the United Kingdom and the West African coast.[16] Elder Dempster was founded by Alfred Jones, a one-time clerk who slowly rose to managerial positions in the African Steamship Company in Liverpool. Over the course of the years 1884–1891, Jones gradually orchestrated the merger of six smaller shipping companies to form what would ultimately be known as the Elder Dempster Lines.[17] The shipping company was one of the largest in UK history and, in addition to operating hundreds of deep-sea vessels, also provided small-vessel services to transport cargo and passengers from inland, riverside bases to and between coastal ports. By the time of his death in 1909, Alfred Jones had led Elder Dempster in the establishment of an extensive and integrated transport and storage infrastructure throughout West Africa.[18] The company held a monopoly for carrying mail and coal between the UK and West Africa, and, in addition to shipping, held large interests in banking, agriculture, and the trade in oil, coal, and cement.[19] By 1925, Elder Dempster had a share of 85 percent of the West African Shipping Conference, which controlled all trade to and from West Africa.

Until the outbreak of World War II, Elder Dempster routinely recruited the Kru of Freetown as supplemental labor for their ships. But the war increased demands on the company, as their headquarters in the port cities of West Africa oversaw ship repairs, in addition to handling the increase in cargo activity associated with the war.[20] Janet Ewald has argued that in times of hardship, European shipping companies historically sought out fresh sources of "coloured" seamen to recruit throughout the maritime world, and tapped them to offset rising costs of labor.[21] The acute need for seamen pushed Elder Dempster to begin hiring in Nigeria, where the company could enjoy several advantages. In Lagos, European shipping companies readily found ratings at much cheaper rates than in Freetown. The Nigerians were initially hired directly by representatives of the shipping companies, and came from a wide range of ethnic groups including Yoruba, Igbo, Ijaw, and Urhobo. The multiethnic Nigerians lacked the deep-rooted headman system for organizing seamen that the Kru had developed over decades. During the war, the shipping companies came to see this as an advantage. There were growing concerns that the Kru recruitment system had become increasingly corrupt with the additional demand for seamen. According to Diane Frost, the Trades Union Congress Colonial Advisory Committee received a complaint from Sierra Leone during the war concerning the increasing abuses and improprieties in the system of Kru recruitment. It was claimed that the practice of bribery intensified as a result of increasing demands for labor. Thus, Frost wrote, "the Wages Board was so disturbed by the amount of bribery and corruption characteristic of headmen recruitment that it was suggested the Labour Department should take over responsibility for it."[22] Following the war, it was decided that recruitment in the ports of West Africa would be under the control of the Port Labour Board rather than headmen. Bribes were no longer allowed, and shipping companies filled vacancies on board ships through official employment exchanges.

Elder Dempster's move to hire in Lagos was thus designed to circumvent the highly organized and increasingly corrupt Kru establishment in Freetown. Shipping companies seized upon the opportunity to cut costs by hiring in Lagos, and Elder Dempster established a four-tiered pay scale during World War II: at the bottom were Nigerians recruited in Nigeria, then Africans recruited in Freetown, then Africans employed from Liverpool, and finally European seamen who were paid the National Maritime Board rates.[23] The discrimination Nigerians faced did not go unnoticed by seamen, as one recalled, "In the shipping world, we were the most poorly paid seamen."[24] Sierra Leone officials complained to the Colonial Office that Elder Dempster's new methods of recruiting "cheap labour" in Lagos were "deplorable," and left many skilled seamen in Freetown without jobs.[25] Officials in Lagos, on the other hand, were highly supportive of the move. The 1942 governor of Nigeria, Sir Alan Burns, did not see any reason to protest the cheap wages, and instead expressed great enthusiasm for Elder Dempster's new hiring policy. He wrote, "The development which has taken place is natural and inevitable and provides opportunities of employment for the more adventurous spirits in Nigerian which cannot well be denied them."[26]

But while the Nigerians were a cheap alternative, hired to undercut Kru wages and terms of employment, the shipping companies initially paid a price for the lack of experience that characterized Nigerian crews in the early years. Many Nigerians recruited during the war lacked the knowledge and training required to successfully fulfill their responsibilities on board.

In some cases, recruits claimed that they were completely uninformed or even misled by shipping companies about the work for which they were being recruited. In one archival account, two Nigerian boys at the age of secondary school jumped ship in Liverpool and were eventually intercepted by an immigration officer, who reported, "They told me they were recruited by Elder Dempster. A Mr. Dyson, a European employed by the Company, came to their homes and told them that the Government needed men to go on ships and suggested to them that they might like to take the journey to England."[27] Fresh recruits such as these were completely lacking in skills needed on board, and some captains began to complain about the new hiring policy.[28] Ships were slowed down or nearly stalled at sea when inexperienced Nigerian firemen did not feed the boilers properly. As one Kru seaman recounted, a British captain who went to recruit in Lagos during a wartime strike in Freetown paid dearly for taking on the inexperienced Nigerian crew: "Was a captain called J. J. Smith of Elder Dempster, he said, okay if Sierra Leoneans don't want the job, I'm taking my ships to Nigeria — took all the ships to Nigeria to start taking Nigerians. This Elder Dempster got three sister ships with 21 fires. So these Nigerian they can't stand it, they can't fire the ships! From Lagos to Takoradi, they don't fit. They have to send to Freetown back."[29]

ROUTINE AND RISKS
IN THE AFRICAN SEAMAN'S WORK

As employees of British shipping companies in the colonial era, Nigerian seamen performed a range of duties on board cargo vessels and passenger ships known as mail boats. The workforce of the steamship was divided into three distinct crews: sailors on deck, firemen and trimmers in the engine room, and stewards in the catering and housekeeping departments.[30] The three departments were strictly demarcated, and seamen were trained for specific positions.

According to Diane Frost, most of the Africans recruited for work on European vessels worked as deckhands, which included both maintenance chores and cargo handling. Deckhands did stevedoring work, which involved loading and discharging cargo at ports of call. Before the container shipping industry emerged in the 1960s, boxes and bundles of goods of various types and sizes were used to transport cargo, and despite some technical innovations involving derricks and winches, the system was slow and inefficient. The labor-intensive process could take several days, and ships could spend more time at port than at sea while dockers and seamen unloaded and loaded cargo. Upon arriving in port, deckhands removed the hatches, rigged the booms and falls, and began the work of swinging the ship's cargo out upon the pier. Prior to the mechanization of the loading and unloading processes, seamen also carried cargo on and off vessels. As soon as compartments were emptied and cleaned, crews began loading the outbound freight that was waiting on the pier. The coal gang took on the laborious task of filling the ship bunkers with the fuel.[31] Although considered unskilled labor, the work of cargo handlers was at times very dangerous and required caution in dealing with the machinery moving heavy loads. Seamen could be seriously injured, crushed to death, or knocked overboard by loads that were poorly secured or mishandled. Some seamen interviewed described the difficulty of handling cargo on deck in the bitter cold of winter in Europe.[32] In West Africa, African deckhands were hired "to save white seamen from exposure to the sun and mosquito-infested swamps."[33] While at sea, deckhands worked on upkeep and repair of the ship, with chores including painting, overhauling gear, rust removal, and cleaning. Scrubbing the deck was also a task performed each morning. Diane Frost described a job that was known as holystoning "because the men cleaning the deck did it on their knees. The decks were sprinkled with water and then sand. Krooboys would kneel four abreast (if the ship was wide enough), each kneeling on a small pad, and push up and down a piece of sandstone the size of a house brick."[34]

The work of the stewards and catering crews varied with the size and type of ship. Cargo ships needed only a small catering department that was responsible for feeding the crew. On passenger ships, the responsibilities of the stewards were far more extensive, but most of the work centered around housekeeping and personal service. Stewards cleaned cabins, did laundry, and attended to the personal needs of passengers when necessary. They also prepared and served food, and cleaned up afterward. While these jobs were less dangerous and demanding than those of deckhands, stewards were exposed to demeaning attitudes of passengers and European crews. This could be seen in the following description of an African steward by a British ocean-liner passenger: "The first-cabin passenger is apt to look upon the steward as not exactly human. To him the steward is an automaton who serves deftly and silently, appears at the right moment, anticipates wants, and when not wanted keeps out of sight, but within call."[35]

The seamen who worked "down below" were responsible for the boiler rooms and coal bunkers. Work in the engine rooms was the most physically challenging on the ship. The firemen were responsible for firing the boilers and keeping up steam by shoveling coal into the furnaces. Firemen worked in two four-hour shifts, four hours on and eight hours off. Stoking a steam engine with coal was dirty work, and firemen and trimmers were known as the "Black Gang" because of their work with the coal.[36] As Laura Tabili described it, the engine room was "hotter than hell," and had up to twenty boilers with three to four fires each. At each boiler worked a fireman, who threw coals on the fire and sliced them with a hundred-pound iron bar to keep them burning.[37] A 1900 account of the firemen's work describes the perils of the engine room:

> A stoker works four hours at a stretch, and during that time the temperature of his surroundings varies from 120 degrees to 160 degrees Fahrenheit. One stoker usually has four furnaces to attend to, and while feeding one furnace a man has to be extremely careful or his arm may be burned by the furnace behind him. As a rule a man is occupied about three minutes at each furnace, and directly he has finished he rushes to the air pipe and waits until his turn comes again. The intense heat of the furnaces has sometimes rendered stokers temporarily insane, and there are many cases on record where they have jumped overboard after having made their way to the deck.[38]

For every three firemen, the stokehold watch carried two coal trimmers, who provided coal to the firemen and had to work quickly to make sure that there was always a pile of coal within reach of the fireman's shovel. Trimmers had the most difficult job of all, working quickly to supply firemen with a constant supply of coal while struggling with the heat and coal dust. A British seaman, David Simpson, gave a vivid description of their work: "Trimmers have always had the dirtiest and the most physically demanding jobs on the ship—the absolute bottom of the engineering hierarchy. Needless to say—they received the lowest pay."[39] Trimmers would wheelbarrow the coal from the bunkers and drop it on plates at the fireman's feet. They were in constant motion, moving coal and "trimming" each pile into evenly arranged groupings, ready for the fireman's shovel. They also took away ash and raked out the ashpits and fires, cleaned and degreased machinery, and painted the engine room when necessary. In short, trimmers did "any unpleasant and filthy job you can think of that didn't require the touch of a skilled or semi-skilled rating."[40] The trimmers' responsibilities kept them working even when the ship docked, as Simpson explained: "While in port, most of the crew could count on 'going ashore' at one time or another—and blow off a little steam. Unfortunately for the trimmers, when the ship is 'bunkering,' they had to stow the coal being loaded and trim as the coal was loaded and moved about—with nothing more than a wet rag tied over their face to keep the choking dust out of their lungs. All, of course, under the watchful eye of the chief engineer."[41]

The division of labor on board ships on Europe-Africa routes was largely determined by race. Until the final years of colonialism, and the establishment of the Nigerian National Shipping Line (NNSL), the officers in each of the departments were Europeans. In the engine room, the chief engineer and the second, third, and fourth engineers were all Europeans. On deck, the chief mate, as well as the first, second, and third mates and the boatswain and carpenters, was also European. Finally, in the catering department, there was a European chief steward, second steward, and cook.[42] In the colonial era, the vast majority of Africans worked as ordinary seamen, stewards, firemen, and trimmers, and virtually no Africans rose to the rank of officer before the final years of colonial rule.[43] As will be seen in chapter 5, the lack of officer training among Africans in the colonial era meant that initially Europeans had to fill the top-ranking positions on the ships of the Nigerian National Shipping Line. The establishment of the national line finally opened the way for large numbers of Nigerian seamen to become officers, but it took several years before any ships were fully under the command of Nigerians, leaving some ratings to wonder what had actually changed.

Throughout the colonial era, African seamen worked on the average ten hours a day, with the workday beginning at 5:00 a.m. and finishing normally at 5:00 p.m. Hours varied with the types of vessels, and fluctuated over a journey according to the work at hand. On mail boats, African crews worked a 60-hour week, or 120 hours over 14 days. On cargo ships, the workweek was 45 hours long, with an average of 135 hours worked over a period of 22 days.[44] But routinely, seamen were forced to work overtime. This was particularly the case when there was cargo to load and unload. Some seamen recalled working for twenty-four hours at a time as British captains pushed the crew to finish the work in order to get on with the voyage. Diane Frost quoted one Kru seaman as saying: "Sometime the captain in a rush to go to England so we start at 530 am and finish at 1200 am."[45] Shipping companies did not pay for overtime, and as will be seen, this became the single greatest complaint among Nigerian seamen in their protest against British management.

For African seamen signed on in West Africa, wages were considerably lower than for those signed on in England. According to Diane Frost, a fireman engaged in 1940 in West Africa earned £6 a month, while West African firemen engaged in Liverpool earned £12, and white firemen earned £16. Shipping companies rationalized these differences by claiming that the cost of living was lower in Africa. But the disparities angered seamen; as one explained, "There was a big difference between the salaries of the European crew and the African crew. What often bothered us is that we are all working on a ship, and if an accident should happen, it does not know whether you are a black man or white man."[46] Wages also varied between the crew departments, with firemen earning the highest wages, followed by able-bodied seamen, and then trimmers and ordinary seamen.[47]

The length of voyages varied according to the types of ships, with cargo ships taking longer than passenger ships to make the journey to Europe. Making frequent stops to load and unload cargo, these ships were slower than passenger ships that kept to a fixed schedule. Some seamen preferred to work for cargo vessels, as the voyages were longer and more wages could be earned. During the colonial era, African seamen signed articles as "running agreements," for up to six months; or "voyage" articles, lasting for up to two years.[48] For many seamen, the waiting time in between signing articles was very difficult, as they were not paid for the months ashore. Seamen could be dropped in England at the end of the voyage, and many stayed on, usually in Liverpool, for months or years in between articles. It was commonplace for seamen to take up shore work, and some stayed on permanently in the UK. In most cases, seamen were away from home for months, or even years, at a time. Some welcomed this as an opportunity to spend time in England and other destinations around the world. But there was also much difficulty and uncertainty associated with this type of employment. Voyages could be suspended in ports around the world due to repairs or delayed because of cargo. Thus, one seaman reported waiting in Bremen, Germany, for six months while his ship was being repaired.[49]

For families back home, seamen's terms of employment posed many difficulties. Seamen were regularly away from home for three to six months at a time, but some reported staying abroad for years in between journeys.[50] Seamen's wives had to manage all the affairs of the household, and they faced many difficulties, often without their husbands' knowledge. As one woman said, "It was not easy at all. I was doing the work that was meant for two people in the family."[51] Another claimed, "I tried to cope as a wife and mother of my children, but it was not easy for me. I had to be determined in such a situation."[52] Women interviewed reported giving birth to their children while husbands were away, and having to deal with sickness and economic hardships all alone. One woman recalled, "I had babies born while he was away. I even had a stillbirth because he was away for eight months and there is no money to take care of myself, even to buy medicine. Nobody came to help me."[53] Many wives complained that they had to rely on help from their extended families and neighbors in times of need. One woman sought help from local churches: "Particularly when he traveled to Congo and there was a lot of fighting over there and no letter from him, I was very worried. I just had a baby during this period and also lost one child and he was away for about nine months. It was very tough. I was just moving from one church to another seeking solutions to different sickness the kids were having."[54] Women also had to deal with loneliness and isolation; as one woman said, "I always tell my husband because of my lonely staying, I don't feel any happiness. I feel very, very bad, extremely bad. One year plus and your husband will not get to his house."[55] The long absences were particularly difficult for children, one seaman's wife explained: "It was very difficult for them because it was like having a parent that you do not know much about his identity. Because, the father came in for about one or two months, then go back again for a very long time. It was not for them at all."[56] When they finally returned home, seamen's families had to readjust to a new reality. Some even reported that children did not recognize their fathers. As one woman recounted:

> At the initial stage it was very difficult. I couldn't explain so many things to the children. When the last two children, though they are a bit big now, two years after he left, he came back and I was at the market at that time. They did not allow him to enter the house. He explained to them that he is their father but they told him they had no father. Even my sister who was living with me tried to explain but they refused. It was when their elder sister came back from school and welcomed him, saying, "Daddy welcome," that they calmed down and allowed him to enter the house. After settling down, they asked him why he left for so long and he told them he went to look for *garri* [cassava flour] for them to eat. They objected and led him to the kitchen to show him buckets of garri, rice, beans and other foodstuffs and told him that mummy has provided them. When he went back to work after the holiday, he decided to send his pictures home so that the children can know him very well.[57]

For seamen's wives and families, there was the additional hardship of worrying about their husbands in this risky line of work, and going long periods without hearing any news of their well-being or whereabouts. Ship work could be dangerous, and many accidents took place, particularly around loading and unloading cargo. Seamen also fell overboard and drowned, and many suffered chronic diseases such as kidney disease, heart failure, and tuberculosis.[58] As F. J. Lindop explained, "Exposure to all weathers, over-crowding, inadequately ventilated accommodation, poor food and negligible medical provision aboard ship and a dissipated life ashore took a toll in health."[59] When accidents on ships were reported, wives and families were very worried, and they often had great difficulty in verifying which ships their husbands were on and if they were safe. Some of the women felt that a seaman's line of work was not worth all the hardship. One said: "The work is a life-threatening job and there is very little money with all the risk involved. Is this a good job?"[60] When asked if she would allow her son to become a seaman, another woman said, "Never. God will never allow a bad thing to happen to my children and family. Working as a seaman in this Nigeria is a bad thing."[61]

RACIAL DISCRIMINATION AND VIOLENCE ON COLONIAL SHIPS

Nigerian seamen working on colonial ships often faced miserable working conditions, replete with racial discrimination and dehumanizing treatment. The archives abound with incidents of discrimination against black seamen on the part of both European crews and officers. Many black seamen suffered physical abuse, name-calling, and random punishments by the officers they served under, and group beatings or other violent attacks by white seamen. Often, these incidents would land black seamen in the hospital, but the majority suffered these abuses and remained on board, lacking any record or verifiable proof against those who perpetrated these crimes. African seamen who did seek justice usually came up against an uninterested or unconvinced captain, and when it was a case of a black seaman's word against that of a white seaman, there was little hope that any justice would be served. In one letter of protest, seamen complained to the shipping company that the provocations led Africans to respond with violence for which they, and not the white crews, were ultimately punished:

> The habit of several white seamen, as we said, is to collectively beat up on African crew. We protest against this, because it can lead to a situation where African Seamen can join forces to retaliate white seamen, leading to developments of unpleasant proportions. Captains do not call into evidence African crews to refute or say what leads to reports against them by white crews. . . . The mode of addressing them employed by white seamen borders on provocation. It is

sometimes so appalling that they are confused or annoyed to point of disobedience and as soon as this happens, the report reaches the Captain divorced of the circumstances under which the disobedience occurred.[62]

In the colonial era, crews were generally segregated, with blacks and whites occupying separate quarters. They often ate in separate areas, and African seamen complained that they were served poor-quality food compared to Europeans. This segregation was the result of a ship hierarchy based on the intersections of race and class biases. Thus, ship hierarchies drew clear distinctions between officers and the rank and file, and in most vessels, these distinctions also coincided with racial difference. Opportunity for advancement in the hierarchy was reserved for Europeans only, as representatives of seamen complained in 1959, "No African seamen . . . irrespective of their number of years are in responsible posts. We always serve in a subordinate role. The African seamen who do the same type of work as white crews cannot share equal advantages with them in the sphere of working conditions, after many years of contribution to the progress of the Companies."[63] White officers ate better food, lived in superior accommodations, and enjoyed unlimited rations of cigarettes and beer. The officers socialized in their own bar, which was better furnished than that of regular seamen. While hierarchies such as these were not explicitly racist, African seamen were keenly aware of the connections between race, class, and status on colonial ships. Seamen's perceptions of discrimination touch upon these intersections; as one explained: "If you talk about maltreatment from the European officers, it was general. They prevented us from their quarters."[64]

In ports of call, the situation was not better, and seamen's missions were segregated by race. In times of illness and hospitalization, African seamen complained that shipping companies did not give the same treatment to blacks as to whites, as can be seen in the following complaint filed by seamen in 1958: "When an African seaman is stranded, due to no fault of their own, proper care is not taken of them. When Mr. J. Woin, deckboy in a cargo boat, was sick on December 3, 1958, he was discharged after seven days in Victoria hospital. The shipping master at Victoria gave him 3 newspapers to sleep on in the streets. This is a sample of the sort of action which makes cooperation sometimes absurd. We are not sure that the shipping master would serve 3 newspapers to any white crew for supper or sleeping pillows."[65]

Nigerian seamen suffered racist attacks by white crews, but the racialized hierarchies on board ships meant that captains and officers would often side with European crews in times of conflict. The officers themselves were also accused of making racist remarks toward African crews. As seamen's representatives complained in 1958, "We know of instances where officers have told African crews quite openly that they hate not only them but Africans on the whole."[66] European officers were known to abuse their power in requiring Africans to work overtime for them personally. For these types of jobs, the payment was usually in kind, but sometimes Africans were not paid at all. This could be left to the officer's discretion, as one captain explained: "The chief steward may wish to have a storeroom cleared out, or have the inside of the storeroom alleyway painted. He would be paid in goods—in rice and biscuit. Likewise, the chief or second steward would have their laundry done for free or rather would pay the head washman in rice or biscuit."[67] The practice of asking African crews to do personal work for white officers was a source of great contention, as one seaman recalled: "It was a long story. That is why I said there was maltreatment by the white officers. The chief steward used to bring his car to the dock and he asked one of the black stewards to wash his car. We all resisted and refused to obey because the car in question was not the company's car, but a personal one. If you want to wash your car, take it to the car wash and pay them. The steward wanted to wash his during the working hours and at free of charge too. We said, we weren't doing that again."[68]

African seamen were not always so empowered to resist the discriminatory practices of officers. This was painfully evident on the MV *Egori*, when, in 1958, the Nigerian crew complained bitterly of the racist attitudes of Captain Everall. After many reports of abuse, seamen in Lagos refused to sign articles with him, and a representative of the seamen went on board to investigate the matter. In a report to Elder Dempster, it was claimed that the entire crew complained of Everall's "hatred and wickedness towards members of the African crew." The crew was particularly angered by the captain's demand that they work long hours of overtime, with no breaks, on the weekends. According to the report, the captain met with the seamen's representative, and assured him that the seamen would cease to work from Saturdays at 1300 until Monday morning. The seamen were told of the promise and signed articles on the ship. But once at sea, the captain ordered them to work for the whole weekend. The seamen asked the captain about his promise, and, according to the report, "he turned round to ask them whether they have known of any Englishman who has kept his promise to a black man? They informed him that the man he was talking about happened to be their President. The captain then asked, he is a black man. Is he not?" They offered the captain to work all day Saturday to finish the tasks at hand so that they might have Sunday off. The captain agreed and they worked as hard as they could, finishing all the work by 1700. Yet, on Sunday, the captain called them up to start work again. The African seamen reported, "This man then said that Africans have been serving Englishmen for centuries and that he wants to inform them that the cities of Liverpool, Manchester and London were not only built by African slaves but by the profit made by selling them to the American planters. He continued to say that he would use them as he pleased and they were already committed by signing the Article." The seamen refused to work, and the captain called in the police from Takoradi, Ghana, when they were in port. The men were arrested in Ghana, fined, and banned for over six months. At their trial, the local magistrate asked the captain whether or not the African crews were being paid for their overtime, and whether or not European crews were paid for overtime. The captain replied that only the Europeans were paid for overtime, and that this was the policy of ED Lines and he could not change it.[69]

The incident demonstrates the vulnerability of rank-and-file seamen to the abuses of power by European officers. Regular crew were also victims of abuses committed by the very few African seamen who rose to positions of power on board such as head stewards. Owning their positions of privilege to their proximity to the European officers, these headmen could not always be counted on to represent the needs of the rank-and-file seamen. Thus, on the MV *Accra* in 1959, seamen complained to their head steward, Joseph Akintayo, that there was not enough food being fed to the African crew. Akintayo did not pass this information on to the chief steward, and following a lack of action, the crew went directly to complain to the chief steward themselves. This breaking of rank infuriated Akintayo, and they reported, "He jumped from the cabin and abused all of us and came back after five minutes with porthole keys and broke the door of the cabin for we locked the door because he made a lot of noise after he had gone out. He used porthole keys, axes, and knives to chase us." The problem was resolved only when the captain intervened. He reported to the shipping company that there was indeed not enough food for the African crews, and he arranged for more supplies.[70]

UNION ORGANIZING

Nigerian seamen did not remain passive in the face of what they perceived as unjust treatment. Colonial shipping companies had imagined that the Nigerians would be more easily exploited than the Kru because they were less organized than their Sierra Leonean counterparts, and they lacked the same experience in labor contract negotiating. What the colonial employers did not anticipate was the quick turnaround among the Lagos-based recruits from easily exploited and inexperienced manpower to agents of industrial discord and protest. Sir Alan Burns reported that two unions for seamen and shipping workers were already registered in Nigeria in 1942.[71] In the early years, the seamen's union was hardly a broad-based organization, with membership dropping to an all-time low of six in 1946. But the Nigerian Union of Seamen underwent reorganization in 1947. Following this spirit of revival was a swift climb in dues-paying membership, reaching 2,250 by 1953. The union's declared objectives remained the same from the earliest years: to protect the interests of its members, regulate work hours and wages, ensure adequate accommodation for all seamen on vessels and ashore, to promote the general welfare of seamen, and to regulate relations between employers and employees.[72]

At first Elder Dempster attempted to avoid any recognition or contact with the organization. But suddenly, in 1948, in what appeared to be a stark turnaround, Elder Dempster conceded recognition of the Nigerian Union of Seamen as the sole representative of seamen engaged in Lagos. This conciliation was followed by several years of limited contact. But in 1952, the two sides formed a local board with representation from the union, the shipping companies, and local government to monitor the recruitment and supply of seamen working out of Lagos.[73] The board was to establish and maintain a register of seamen, and West African ratings were to be recruited only from those whose names were on the register. Both parties agreed that all matters pertaining to Nigerian seamen should be decided in Lagos. Cooperation began in earnest in 1954, when representatives of the Nigerian Union of Seamen met with Tom Yates of the National Seamen's Union in Britain, and the British union helped to negotiate an effective working relationship between the Nigerian seamen and the British shipping lines.[74]

The change in the shipping companies' position toward the Nigerian seamen's union was in line with an overall shift in colonial policy toward African labor unions in the post–World War II period. A wave of strikes across the continent forced colonial governments and business interests to make some concessions in their stance toward organized labor. But while recognizing the need for reform, Fred Cooper has argued that governments and employers "wanted to confine the labor question to a set of institutions and practices familiar to them from the industrial relations experience of the metropole: to treat labor as [separate] from politics. The threat of a labor crisis becoming unbound—linked to people other than waged workers . . . made governments especially willing to pay the costs of resolving labor issues [through recognized unions]."[75]

In the case of the Nigerian Union of Seamen, the shipping company fully engaged with the union following a formal request from the colonial Labour Department in Lagos in 1952. While reluctant to comply at first, officials in the shipping company ultimately came to the conclusion that cooperation with the union would be the most efficient means for dealing with labor disputes. The local agent wrote, "Whilst we are still far from satisfied that the present officers of the Union are responsible and trustworthy persons, there has of late admittedly been a marked improvement in their demeanor and attitude, and the resumptions of Meetings of the Board would provide a means of negotiation preferable to attempts by the Union to send deputations on the slightest pretext."[76] To ensure that the union would not be any source of real agitation, the shipping company nurtured good relations with union officers and provided them with special benefits that would ultimately prevent these officers from agitating for the union. This could be seen in 1956, when the general secretary of the union, Franco Olugbake, wrote to the managing director of Elder Dempster to inquire about a new job with better pay at the United Africa Company. He wrote:

> I have no alternative but to continue to hang on to my present employment—the seamen. What was more, I can not help but to keep the job, even though the salary is anything but compatible with my status in life. My Executive, knowing full well that my efforts to land another job seem gloomy, they tied me to all sort of conditions. For instance, my Executive pressed on me to agitate for the question of overtime, etc. I had to do this reluctantly. I had to write a memo covering overtime, Sundays as sea and holidays—you will probably see it.[77]

In developing a close relationship with the union leadership, Elder Dempster hoped to ensure that unrest among seamen remained at a minimum.

Thus, the decision to engage with the Nigerian Union of Seamen was a calculated attempt at making limited yet controlled concessions to Nigerian seamen, but did not represent any fundamental shift in the shipping companies' views on seamen's rights, and the whole endeavor was undertaken with a frustrated yearning for the good old prewar days when African seamen had not yet awoken to claim their rights. As one Elder Dempster official wrote in 1959, "We have looked through the rules of the Nigerian Union of Seamen. . . . It is a shocking document and much of what the Union appears to be aiming to do could not possibly be accepted by the [shipping] lines. I am referring to ship committees and so forth. I suppose in the old days there would have been someone in Nigeria who would have told the Unions not to be silly in framing rules of this kind, but I do not know whether there is anyone bold enough or authoritative enough to do so at the present time."[78]

The document this official was referring to was the Rules of the Union, formulated and submitted to the shipping companies in 1959. These rules were aimed at regulating the internal workings of the union, and formalized procedures such as elections, dues collection, and the running of general assemblies. The union's rules also made it a priority to maintain harmony among seamen and reduce incidents of tribalism, corruption, and conflict. But the detailed document was largely focused on a long set of demands and ideological positions taken by the union toward the shipping companies. The Rules of the Union called for improved working conditions, salary increases, the payment of overtime, and the upgrade of accommodations on board ships. The issue of hiring and recruitment was also raised, with the union calling for the institution of a closed shop. This demand was totally unacceptable to officials at Elder Dempster, who insisted that shipping companies reserved the right to select seamen according to personal ability and availability, regardless of their union membership.[79] The shipping companies were also strongly opposed to crews organizing representative bodies on ships. The union had proposed electing a "ship's committee" on board each vessel that would "settle all minor matters or disputes between European crews and African crews on board ships; settle all minor matters or disputes between the representatives of the shipping companies and the African crews on board ships; and try to settle all minor matters or disputes between one African and another or one group of African crews and another group."[80] This proposition was preposterous to the officials at Elder Dempster, who argued that the hierarchy of the ship was based on an established chain of command, with the captain the ultimate commander, and this would not be compromised by the establishment of elected seamen's committees.

The most fundamental point of contention between the shipping companies and the seamen's union emerged around allegations of racism. The existence of racism on ships was clearly acknowledged in the union's rules, which demanded that "the committee should see to it that the African crews are not misused or unduly insulted because of the colour of their skin, which is a common practice on board ships."[81] This was an issue of immense sensitivity among officials at Elder Dempster, and they categorically rejected any allegations of racism on board their ships. They refused to even engage in any dialogue around the subject, and consequently would take no steps to stop it. Thus, while the shipping company had begrudgingly recognized the union, the ways in which they dealt with the explosive issue of racism on board demonstrates that the shipping company still hoped to limit and frame the terms of debate between shipping company officials and union representatives. For Elder Dempster, the issue of racial discrimination or prejudice was completely off-limits, and officials went to great efforts to strike the allegations from the lists of complaints and demands made by the union.

For seamen and their representatives, racism was a pervasive and inescapable feature of life on board colonial vessels. One seaman interviewed said, "On the British ships, you may be lucky to meet a nonracist. Your right is recognized and is given to you, but they don't mingle easily."[82] Time and again, the issue was raised by union leadership in meetings and correspondence with Elder Dempster officials. Thus, in a letter written by union officer Akpan Monday in 1958, it was reported that "Africans are ill-treated by the English seamen with whom they work and 'their so-called superior officers.'" He described several incidents when African crewmen were beaten by gangs of English seamen, and claimed that these incidents were reported but nothing was done about them. "In each case, the culprits went free without even receiving a warning." Akpan provided vivid descriptions of racial violence against black seamen on several voyages and the lack of response from officers on board:

> On the *Aureol's* last trip, an English sailor threw hot water on the back of Mr. S. Ikpi, an African greaser. When Ikpi turned around and asked why, he was attacked by five other English sailors. When he ran to the Engine room for help, the officer said he was busy and could not come. Another African seaman was called a "bastard nigger" by the chief store keeper. When he reported this to the chief steward, the chief steward defended the store keeper. . . . This goes to show that whatever the black man says, right or wrong, he is always wrong in the eyes of the white man who is always prepared to defend his white brothers.[83]

The shipping companies' refusal to acknowledge racial discrimination on board ships infuriated the seamen's union. They claimed that management's denial of the problem allowed it to continue unabated, and this inaction was in fact at the root of the problem. This could be seen in an impassioned letter from General Secretary Sidi Khayam, submitted to Elder Dempster in 1959. Khayam claimed that white crews had made a hobby out of provoking African crews, but because of their close relations with the European captains, they were never punished for it. On the contrary, Khayam claimed, those black seamen who filed complaints against white seamen were black-listed from further employment. He claimed that the situation was unbearable for African crews, "when they realize they have no possibility of defense before the shipping master." Under these circumstances, Khayam charged that the shipping company must stop denying that racism existed on board ships, and take measures to put a stop to it. He wrote:

> Our Union first of all, wants to express its concern for the continued denial that there is no discrimination whereas actual fact everyone realizes that it is there. If the shipping companies refuse to recognize that discrimination exists, then they cannot see the need to ask white crews to stop the habit. It will be very difficult for you to enjoy the confidence of African crews when you dismiss the reality of discrimination, which occurs almost in every ship, when many white crews are well known for their attitudes towards Africans. You must admit that we are not in a position to gain anything by manufacturing imaginary stories which have not happened, you will also agree that the situation must be so desperately disappointing that special emphasis is always placed by the Union about it whenever we approach you. This problem is daily becoming more complex. The treatment is so miserable that it is now psychologically resulting in conflict, quarrels, near-tension which finally are put in other forms as delinquency on part of African crews.[84]

These impassioned pleas made little impact on Elder Dempster officials. General Manager Glasier came to Lagos in late 1959 to demand that "all talk about racial hatred must cease." According to notes from a meeting between the union and management, Glasier complained that over the last two months, difficulties had culminated with "certain letters." The shipping company official rejected their contents, as the meeting notes read: "Mr. Glasier said that never in all the years of his experience with Trade Unions had he ever received or read such letters from a Union and he was very gravely disturbed as they created an atmosphere in which the Lines would find it very difficult to maintain their usual harmonious relations with the Union; he was quite sure that the letters did not express the feelings of the seamen."[85] Glasier claimed that disputes on board ships were routine affairs, both between crews and officers and among crews themselves, and these occurrences were not the result of racism, even if they erupted between whites and blacks. He threatened that continued allegations of racism would result in a change of Elder Dempster hiring practices, and he warned the union: "Seven years ago there were 400 Nigerian seamen, now the three lines employed 1700. We will continue to employ Nigerian seamen for preference at Lagos as a convenient port of changing crews, but if there was not an immediate cessation of the demonstration and other commotions which had been current in recent months, the Lines would be compelled to consider engagement of further Freetown crews."[86] The intimidation apparently worked, because at another meeting two days later, the union leadership backed down from their previous allegations. The notes from this meeting demonstrate the success of Glasier's strong-arm tactics: "As Mr. Glasier had nothing further to add, Mr. Ekore went on to say that his Union wished to cooperate peacefully." Mr. Glasier asked if what Mr. Ekore wanted to say was that the question of race hatred had been dropped for good. Mr. Ekore agreed and mentioned that at the first meeting he had said that race discrimination was not a company policy.[87]

POWER AND POLITICS IN THE NIGERIAN UNION
OF SEAMEN IN THE COLONIAL ERA

The ineffective efforts of union officials to reshape the terms of the debate between seamen and shipping companies reveal the limits of power of the seamen's union. Despite the rhetoric of demands, throughout the 1950s the Nigerian Union of Seamen did not pose a serious threat to the shipping companies' designs of maintaining the status quo. This was partially because union leaders in Lagos were preoccupied primarily with internal political struggles for control over the organization rather than agitating for seamen's rights. The infighting that characterized the union in the 1950s engrossed both the leadership and dissenting factions, and left little time to effectively challenge the shipping companies. According to Hakeem Tijani, leadership of the seamen's union continually changed hands, as "existing officials were thrown out of office through the same methods of intrigue which they themselves had employed to get into power."[88] The shipping companies and the colonial government followed the conflicts almost with amusement. One government review from the period stated, "The record of the Union's activities over the years makes a most pathetic reading. Almost from its inception, there have always been instances of endless strife, distrust, intrigues, tribal discrimination, police arrests, litigation, rifts of members into factions, one faction trying at one time or the other, and often quite successfully, to overthrow the other from office, and to install itself into power. No set of officials of the union would appear to have held office happily together for any reasonable length of time."[89]

The self-serving practices of the union leadership created additional obstacles standing in the way of effective organizing among seamen. Union officers routinely attempted to leverage their proximity to the shipping company in order to advance their own interests. This could be seen in a report from an Elder Dempster official in 1958 following his meeting with President Ekore. According to the report, President Ekore complained of his low salary from the union, and claimed that he would be far better off back at sea. Ekore asked the shipping company if he could be allowed to supply chickens to Elder Dempster vessels as a ship chandler, thereby earning more income. The conflict of interest was noted by the local official: "We think this was the most important point of the meeting so far as Ekore was concerned. We pointed out that, under the present circumstances, this would not be desirable and that we already had an efficient Ships' Chandler."[90]

The focus of the leadership constituted a colossal divide between the concerns of union officials and the everyday experiences of seamen on ships. This divide was partly unavoidable, as the unique nature of seamen's work took them away from Lagos and union headquarters for most of the time they were under contract. On the other hand, officers based in Lagos were either Westernized elites posing as professional trade unionists and never actually employed as seamen, or seamen who had been denied work due to disciplinary actions taken against them on board or criminal activity such as smuggling or drug trafficking. Thus, the gap separating the rank-and-file seamen from the leadership and decision-making organs of the union was exceptionally wide. In a May 1959 address to the union, President Ekore described the problematic situation: "The Seamen's Union is not like any other and why trouble always finds a way easy, is because when a resolution has passed and [been] adopted by a handful of members ashore without the knowledge of members at sea, on arrival they will declare their stand of ignorance and thereby seek to oppose the adopted resolution which actually is right."[91]

The internal conflicts in the union were attributed time and again to tribalism, as competition for leadership positions and resources often fueled ethnic tensions between members. As Ekore said in his address, "From its origin, there had been no time of peace and understanding among [the union's] members. . . . [A] fact that lay low the glory and reputation of the Union is a Tribal Hatred and discrimination among its members. The daily struggle is, I want me Tribe's man in the office."[92] According to the chief steward of the MV *Aureol*, the conflict was mainly between coastal groups originating in eastern and western Nigeria, as he reported to Elder Dempster officials: "The bone of contention in the Union is Tribal rivalry of who are to hold Office, at present it is dominated by Eboe and Ejaw tribes who come from the Eastern region, and it would appear that the Warri and Calabar people are objecting to all the officers being from these two tribes. . . . I do not anticipate any upset with the men, it is just that being mostly illiterate, they can be so easy led up the Garden Path, and that would seem what is happening."[93]

While union officials busied themselves with power struggles and political intrigue, everyday seamen continued to confront the tough realities of onboard discrimination and poor working conditions. It has been seen that seamen endured grueling, and at times perilous, working lives on board colonial ships. They worked long hours in jobs that were demeaning, physically difficult, and dangerous. They suffered from wage discrimination in the colonial shipping industry, and lacked the organizational means for effectively improving their conditions of work. Journeys took them away from their families for months or years, and their wives back home had to endure the challenges of maintaining a household in their husbands' long absences. In addition, Nigerian seamen suffered from racism on board ships and in ports of call, but their protests against this mistreatment fell on deaf ears. The union leadership, preoccupied with Lagos-based politics, remained largely useless and irrelevant in organizing and initiating seamen's protests, and did little to address the sources of their discontent.

But as will be seen, seamen did not wait around for the union to address their needs. Rather, they employed a full range of options and leveraged the skills that were available to them in their unique position as seamen in order to improve the conditions of their lives. Instead of accepting their disempowerment, seamen continually exploited the various opportunities that presented themselves on each voyage across the sea. The next chapter will examine entrepreneurial efforts, cultural alliances, and social ideologies of resistance that seamen mobilized to meet basic needs and better their lives.

2 ⤳ Seamen and the Cosmopolitan Imaginary

The social imaginary is not a set of ideas; rather it is what en-
ables, through making sense of, the practices of a society.

—Charles Taylor

WHEN COSMOS NIAGWAN was a youth in the village of Shendam in
northern Nigeria during the colonial era, he dreamed of becoming a truck
driver. As he recalled, "My idea was to do something manly," and he envisioned himself behind the wheel of a larger trailer truck. This plan for his future quickly changed one night while he was still in secondary school. The
colonial Information Service arrived in Shendam with a mobile cinema,
and he went along with the rest of the village to watch a film projected onto
a makeshift screen set up in front of the local chief's house. During the
newsreels, he saw images of new trailer trucks arriving in Nigeria and being
unloaded from a large cargo ship. As he recalled, he was suddenly struck
with the realization that a ship is much larger than a truck. Impressed with
the immense size of these seagoing vessels, he told himself, "Now THAT
is what I am going to drive!"[1] As soon as he finished secondary school, he
set out on a journey that indeed culminated in his commanding of ships.
Niagwan began his career as a seaman with the Nigerian Port Authority
(NPA) in 1963 as a marine officer cadet. That year, he was sent by the NPA
for study and training at the King Edward VII Nautical College in London,
and he worked with Elder Dempster until he earned his second mate cer-
tificate of competency in 1967. Following his formal studies, he worked
for seven years with the Black Star Line of Ghana and then moved to the

47

Bangladesh Shipping Corporation for two more years before returning to work for the Nigerian National Shipping Line (NNSL) in 1987.

Captain Niagwan's journey to becoming a seaman began with a set of social imaginaries that organized his view of the world and grounded his course of action. His recounting of the process that brought him to seafaring began with a clear vision of his own potent masculinity and an unhindered sense of possibility. When considering the obstacles that might have stood in the way of the son of a farmer born eight hundred kilometers from the sea in northern Nigeria under the shadow of British colonial rule, his recounting of how he came to command ships appears all the more extraordinary. The sense of empowerment and opportunity revealed in his story is a crucial starting point for any investigation into Captain Niagwan's life trajectory. Indeed, for most of the Nigerian seamen whose stories are presented here, the journey to seafaring began with an anticipation of opportunity and an openness to adventure. Although many had never left Nigeria before becoming seamen, they were keenly attuned to the prospects that transnational migrations might bring, and they were quick to exploit the economic, social, and cultural opportunities that presented themselves along the way.

This is not to suggest that these men were not confronted with obstacles and injustices that barred them from carving out their lives in the image of their idealized imaginaries. Without doubt, the Nigerian seamen recruited by the British shipping industry in the 1950s entered a world of colonial hierarchies and biases, a hostile landscape of intersecting geographies of race, class, gender, and nation that converged on and limited the opportunities seamen had for navigating transnational spaces at their own will. Decolonization did not improve Nigerian seamen's standing abroad. On the contrary, the 1960s and 1970s were marked by increasing hostility toward the presence of former colonial subjects in England in particular, and Africans faced increasing restrictions on their movement and settlement in the United Kingdom. Nonetheless, in their testimonies, Nigerian seamen celebrated transnational migrations as potential opportunities for unrestricted agency and freedom. Journeys beyond Nigerian borders were sometimes harsh confrontations with multiple methods of exclusion in both the colonial and the postcolonial eras, but they also held the potential for reaching new social and economic horizons. Seamen's ability to circumvent or overcome exclusionary or racist practices and policies began with their capacity for imagining and then implementing countering strategies. Here, Charles Taylor's notion of "social imaginaries" is very useful. Taylor's theory refers to "the ways in which people imagine their social existence, how they fit together with others, how things go on between them and their fellows, the expectations that are normally met, and the deeper normative notions and images that underlie these expectations."[2] Social imaginaries are the background and foundation of social practice; indeed, they enable certain actions and collective "self-understandings" that are constitutive of a society.[3] Nigerian seamen's experiences and the stories they tell about themselves overcome cultures and politics of exclusion by embracing a brand of cosmopolitanism as an organizing principle of their lives.

We must be careful not to overstate seamen's power to fully resist all or even some of the hegemonic forces they confronted in their social and cultural encounters. As will be seen in subsequent chapters, the turn to nationalist ideologies and policies in the era of decolonization was a calculated response to confrontations with racism and exclusionary practices of colonialism. But while keeping this final outcome in mind, we have much to gain from a close examination of how African seamen described their ability to rearrange and redefine social and political forms in specific times and specific locations. Our understanding of seamen's experiences would not be complete without a consideration of the role cosmopolitanism played in their self-imaginings. Seamen's cosmopolitan imaginaries enabled them to first envisage, and later construct, alternative forms of association and alliance that challenged hegemonic notions of identity and community, even if only temporarily.

The idea of cosmopolitanism has been increasingly invoked to describe worldviews and identities emerging in globalized spaces. As we seek out ways to describe the fluidity and hybridity resulting from transnational migrations, the notion of cosmopolitanism can help capture the kinds of aspirations and transitions that characterize experiences in these transnational spaces. But we must identify just what is intended by the term, "as many competing and contested claims are being made under the banner of cosmopolitanism."[4] In the case of seamen, Stuart Hall's definition is applicable: "It means the ability to stand outside of having one's life written and scripted by any one community, whether that is a faith or tradition or religion or culture—whatever it might be—and to draw selectively on a variety of discursive meanings."[5] In crossing nation-state boundaries, seamen were able to "articulate complex affiliations, meaningful attachments, and multiple allegiances to issues, people, places, and traditions that lie beyond the boundaries of their resident nation-state."[6]

This chapter will focus on the cosmopolitan imaginaries and practices of Nigerian seamen as they made their way across the globe in the context of their work. As many scholars have argued, cosmopolitanism is an outlook that is often born in enduring circumstances of prejudice, discrimination, and exclusion. Thus, the discussion will begin with a brief review of popular antagonism toward the presence of colonial seamen in British port cities throughout the twentieth century, and the gradual process by which widespread racism was translated into reforms of British immigration policies toward colonial subjects. This will provide the necessary background for evaluating the ways in which seamen in fact defied or circumvented exclusionary practices. We will review the ideological and cultural attitudes of seamen and highlight the ways in which Nigerian seamen who began working on British vessels in the late colonial era saw themselves as "workers of the world." Special attention will be paid to the social lives of seamen abroad, and particularly the romantic relationships seamen established with European, Asian, and Latin American women in the course of their travels. We will then turn to an investigation of the independent trade conducted by seamen in secondhand goods. In establishing these individual trading enterprises, seamen rejected their proletarianization by colonial shipping companies, and used their position as seamen on board colonial ships to develop their own autonomous transnational trade networks. Taken together, this review of the social, cultural, and economic networks that seamen created in the context of their transnational travel offers us a view of the cosmopolitanism that defined and shaped seamen's experiences beginning in the late colonial era.

Cosmopolitan imaginaries and connections continued to play a role in seamen's self-understandings following independence, and seamen working for the NNSL continually endeavored to leverage the social and economic opportunities of transnational mobility to their benefit. But it will be seen that the process of nationalization slowly limited seamen's freedom to craft and exploit these transnational and migratory solidarities and networks. Thus, this focus on the role of cosmopolitanism in seamen's working lives provides essential context for measuring the outcome and significance of nationalization in seamen's lives. Only against the background of these cosmopolitan imaginaries can we fully grasp the price that seamen paid when nationalization eliminated the opportunities that seamen had fundamentally come to rely upon.

RACISM AND THE EXCLUSION OF "COLOURED" SEAMEN IN BRITAIN

The massive recruitment of "coloured" seamen for British shipping enterprises during the colonial period ultimately had far-reaching repercussions for British society, as many of these colonial seamen chose to abandon their ships and settle in the United Kingdom. Some were seeking higher wages as seamen contracted out of British rather than colonial ports, while others took up residence and sought out new opportunities beyond seafaring. While these seamen enjoyed the right of free entry into British ports as British colonial subjects, tensions with local populations grew along with the numbers of these new immigrants in port cities such as Cardiff, Liverpool, and London. The presence of colonial subjects on British soil fueled antagonism among local populations, who opposed their growing numbers as potential competition for employment and for the perceived social and cultural threat they posed to local societies. From the outset, white seamen were leading agitators against black seamen, as they feared the competition for seafaring jobs. But the periodic riots that broke out against "coloured" seamen in ports throughout Britain, such as those in 1919, were fueled by angry mobs sometimes numbering in the thousands.[7] Particularly in the post–World War II era, the issue of colonial immigration to Britain became increasingly contentious within the political sphere, as emigration from the colonies began to rise at what were seen as alarming rates.[8]

Following the riots of 1919, the British government began making moves to limit the rights of seamen to settle permanently in the UK. The first proposed solution was legislated in the form of the Coloured Alien Seamen Order of 1925, a law mandating all "coloured" seamen to register with local police, and requiring them to carry documentation proving their status as British subjects. All those unable to produce documentary evidence could be declared aliens and deported. As seamen generally lacked this kind of official documentation, most found themselves in a compromised position following the passing of the Order of 1925. The law also required that colonial seamen be hired for round-trip voyages and receive their salaries back in their colonies of origin, thus helping to ensure that most would not stay in the UK. While many seamen were able to avoid or work around the law, the order has been identified as a crucial turning point in the British government's efforts to redraw the lines of nationality along the lines of race. Laura Tabili noted, "In the space of a few years, Black seamen went from welcome additions to the empire and particularly to the seafaring workforce, with or without 'proper passports,' to undesirables barred from entry to British ports or deported when destitute, whether British subjects or aliens, to presumptive aliens illegitimately in Britain."[9]

Within British port cities, the deepest anxieties around the presence of colonial seamen were linked to the social and sexual liaisons between white women and black seamen. These relations were thought to compromise the morality of white women, and spawn half-caste children who threatened the colonial racialized order. Mixed-race couples thus became a lightning rod for moral and social policing efforts both in Britain and back in the colonies. According to Carina Ray, anxieties over interracial sexual relations were at the root of a massive repatriation campaign for black seamen in the inter-war era.[10] The dilemma posed by mixed-race couples became evident in this campaign, as officials were highly reluctant to repatriate those who requested to be returned home with their white wives. The reasoning was that the ar-rival of these couples in the colonies would threaten the stability of colonial race relations, and thus authorities attempted to limit the number of these couples allowed to repatriate.[11] Ray found that the repatriation of interracial couples was tolerated only in cases of wealthy African businessmen married to European women, as they could guarantee that their wives would be main-tained at a standard of living fitting for a white woman. Mixed-race couples of lower classes, on the other hand, aroused "deep-seated anxieties" of colo-nial officials, who feared that European women would be forced to live the destitute lifestyle of the native populations. The panic of British officials led to "bureaucratic strong-arming" to prevent these couples from "violating the racial geography" of colonial rule by returning to the colonies.[12]

The ferocity of British official opposition to racial mixing is perhaps best exemplified in the writings of Muriel Fletcher, a social scientist who con-ducted research on black seamen in Liverpool in 1928–1930. Fletcher wrote in the report of her findings: "In their own country they are not allowed to mix freely with white people or have relations with white women. Once having formed unions with white women in this country, they are perhaps loathe [sic]to leave England. . . . In this country [the black seaman] is cut adrift from [tribal restrictions] before he has developed the restraint and con-trol of Western Civilization. In Liverpool there is evidence to show that the negro tends to be promiscuous in his relations with white women. [Their] sexual demands impose a continual strain on white women."[13] Fletcher's deepest fears, and indeed those of the British public at large, were linked to the "half-caste" children born out of these unions and raised in an en-vironment characterized by immorality. Far from being a marginal view, Fletcher's findings have been identified as both constructive and represen-tative of "systematic social and political disempowerment of Black people" in Liverpool until the present.[14] According to Jacqueline Brown, "It would be hard to state emphatically enough how thoroughly racial politics in Liverpool/Britain reflect the legacy of the Fletcher Report."[15] Indeed, stud-ies from the 1980s and beyond confirmed the ongoing marginalization and stigmatization of the black and mixed-race community in Liverpool.[16]

Popular opposition to the growing presence of colonial subjects in Britain did not translate into official changes in immigration policies until the period of decolonization. Prior to this time, there was an official commitment to keep borders open to all citizens of the Commonwealth. This open-door policy was intended to enable Australians, Canadians, and New Zealanders to immigrate to Britain freely, but the policy extended these rights to all citizens of the New Commonwealth as well. According to Randall Hansen, British officials wanted to avoid placing overtly racist restrictions on some Commonwealth citizens, and until the late 1950s, no one could imagine the threat of mass immigration of colonial subjects, who remained, in British consciousness, inherently fixed in traditional and premodern natural settings.[17] This was all to change in 1962, when popular fears over the colonial presence in Britain were turned into tightened restrictions on immigration, and several legislative measures were taken to officially close the door on former colonial subjects. Beginning with the Commonwealth Immigrants Act of 1962, those Commonwealth citizens seeking to immigrate had to apply for a work voucher, which were limited in number, before being permitted to settle in the UK. The 1968 amendment to this act denied citizenship to Commonwealth citizens who did not have parents or grandparents born in Britain, and was aimed specifically at stripping East African Asians of their British passports. Finally, the Immigration Act of 1971 ended the distinction between "aliens" and Commonwealth citizens.[18] The act served to restrict the entry of people from the New Commonwealth by decreeing that only those with connections of descent, such as white South Africans or Australians, would be granted unrestricted entry.[19]

Nigerian seamen entered the colonial shipping industry many years before the Commonwealth Immigration Act of 1971. But already in the post–World War II era, popular antagonism toward African immigrants converged with official policies, creating an environment that was increasingly hostile to the presence of colonial subjects in local societies. Thus, Nigerian recruits began arriving at a time when British society was becoming progressively more unaccepting of the presence of African seamen. These grievous realities of colonialism and racism were certainly not unique to England, and seamen were exposed to varying degrees of discrimination and disempowerment beyond Britain in their travels to the United States, South America, and Asia.[20] Yet this broader political and social context is curiously downplayed in many seamen's accounts of their years as colonial seamen. On the contrary, seamen's testimonies of their lives at sea reflect an unexpected sense of empowered agency and opportunity in their transnational travels. In what follows, it will be seen that while seamen's lives resonated with these encounters with exclusion, they also represented a powerful resistance to the subjectivities constructed and imposed upon black working-class men in colonial and postcolonial contexts. Seamen's testimonies reflect an unexpected sense of empowered agency and opportunity in their transnational travels. The border crossings they experienced exposed them to circumstances, resources, and knowledge that enabled them to cross and disrupt bounded identities and embrace a vision of themselves as citizens of the world, thus circumventing both official policies and popular practices of racial exclusion.

A SEAMAN'S WAY OF LIFE

Q: Why did you become a seaman?

R: It was because I like to travel all over the world to see what is happening.[21]

The stories that seamen told about how they became seamen are very revealing for what they can teach us about seamen's sense of autonomy and agency. Seamen gave a variety of responses when asked how and why they became seamen, but nearly all of the answers they provided reflected a strong belief in their own self-fashioning. Over and over, men explained that they became seamen because the job attracted them personally, and this led them to sign up. As one man explained, "I saw the type of job and I liked it, and later I joined them."[22] Another simply explained, "For the purpose of adventure, nothing more."[23] Many claimed that they were drawn to the job after seeing other seamen around Lagos. One seaman replied, "I used to see seamen coming from abroad to Lagos then. When I saw how they dressed and their actions, I was attracted to these things."[24] Another man gave a similar response: "When I was in school, I used to see the seamen from Freetown. Their manner of dress attracted me to become a seaman. Really, their clothes and shoes made me want to join seamen."[25] Some got the job through connections to Europeans with links to the shipping industry. One man explained that he had fought as a soldier in World War II, and when he returned to Lagos and looked unsuccessfully for a job, his British military colonel suggested that he go to the Elder Dempster offices to sign on as a seaman.[26] Another man explained that he was working in a shoe store in Lagos when a British manager from Elder Dempster came in to have his shoes repaired. The two men began talking, and according to the seaman, "He said he was teaching people on how to travel all over the world. From there, I developed an interest in what to know about the whole world. So, I asked how he could help me. He said I am too small. I was fifteen years old at the time."[27] Despite his young age, he soon began working as a greaser on Elder Dempster ships. Some men relied on personal connections to local friends or family who helped them to get the job. But even with these connections, men's responses implied that going to work as seamen was a decision rooted in their own desire for travel and adventure. As one man explained, he secured the job through a connection with an Urhobo friend he knew from back home in the Delta State, but his personal interest in becoming a seaman was peaked when he moved to Lagos and heard a lot of talk of travel abroad: "It was because it's only in Lagos that people talked about England. They say, 'I want to go to England,' and from this urge to travel, I went to England."[28]

Travel to distant corners of the globe opened up a myriad of opportunities for seamen to create social bonds that challenged and transcended cultural, social, and ideological boundaries of both their home communities and those abroad. Seamen were often able to negotiate and redefine the cultural, racial, class, and national landscapes they inhabited within the contexts of their travels. Through the bonds they formed, seamen nurtured a sense of alterity and cosmopolitanism, and imagined a sense of belonging in a myriad of volatile, and sometimes hostile, social and cultural landscapes.

For many seamen, Pan-African connections provided an important basis for community. This was particularly true in Liverpool, which, as the headquarters for Elder Dempster shipping and the point of departure and return for most voyages, was the perceived home base for seamen. It was therefore not unusual that seamen visiting Liverpool found a large community of former seamen from across West Africa as well as Liverpool-born blacks to socialize with.[29] Seamen's testimonies revealed the central importance Pan-Africanism played as the antecedent for forming social, cultural, and economic alliances.[30] Histories of Pan-Africanism from the postwar era are usually concerned with the intellectual movements of the political elite in their anti-imperialist struggles. Barbara Bush wrote, "By the First World War this intellectual black nationalism, which had been concerned with establishing a racial and cultural bond between Africa and its diaspora, had embraced more directly political objectives."[31] By contrast, the Pan-Africanism of seamen was a popular, working-class expression of black solidarity and affiliation. Rather than a political or intellectual movement, seamen's experiences reflected a lived Pan-Africanism.[32] As one seaman recalled the scene in Liverpool: "We were really welcomed and we made new friends. . . . There were a lot of Africans, whether Ghanaians, Togolese, Liberian, or Sierra Leoneans—we were treated as brothers."[33] Descriptions of the social scene in Liverpool in particular revealed the extent to which seamen identified with the Pan-African community. Nightclubs bore the names of ethnic and national groups originating in Africa, but seamen claimed that all the clubs welcomed mixed populations. One reported, "Sometimes I stayed in Liverpool with my European girlfriend for three months whenever I dropped from the ship. I know the Yoruba, Igbo, Ghanaian, and Freetown Clubs in Liverpool. . . . At night, after the day's work, we went round the clubs and that was a seaman's life."[34] Liverpool-born blacks and emigrants from the Caribbean frequented the same social clubs, creating many opportunities for social and cultural mixing among blacks of the diaspora. The Stanley House, a community center in Liverpool, also served as an important meeting point for local blacks and visiting seamen.[35]

The same attraction and affiliation to local black communities could be identified in seamen's recounting of their experiences in South America, Canada, and the United States. Several recounted their satisfaction over seeing Africans in Brazil, and the discovery of close affinities between blacks there and back at home. As one said, "South America is also good. In fact, in South America you will see Africans; it is just like Africa where you will see some of them working barefoot."[36] Particularly for the Yoruba seamen, the meeting with local communities in Brazil was deeply moving, as they found an unexpected familiarity among Yoruba descendants. One recalled, "I had a peculiar experience in Brazil. I was in Santos for the first time, I was in the black community and the people are predominantly Yoruba. These people called me 'a fresh brother from home.' They spoke Yoruba language but they spoke more in Portuguese language. They never wanted me to come back to Nigeria again, but I told them that was not possible."[37]

At the same time that seamen made strategic use of Pan-African and black diaspora relations, their mobility and resourcefulness led them to construct alliances that also cut across boundaries of race. Perhaps the most outstanding tribute to seamen's defiance of racial, class, and national boundaries was the romantic partnerships they formed abroad with European women, and the children born of these unions. According to seamen's testimonies, the taking of a "wife" or "wives" in one or several foreign ports of call was commonplace. While these were not official marriages in the legal sense, seamen referred to these women as wives because they relied on them to provide a sense of home, community, and belonging in foreign countries.[38] Retired seamen spoke with pride of their families abroad, and some claimed to have several "wives" and children spread over a few countries. When asked if he had girlfriends abroad, one seaman claimed, "Definitely, there should be."[39] A seaman interviewed claimed that he had a wife and two children in Holland, as well as a wife and two children in Brazil.[40] Another informant boasted that in addition to his two wives and seven children in

Nigeria, he had a wife and children in Liverpool, and a wife and children in Spain.[41] A former captain told the following story of one of his crew:

> There was a case when we traveled to Freetown. When we got to Freetown, this guy said, my wife is coming to greet us with the children and also bring some local Sierra Leonean food for us. Of course, we got to the port and she came and we ate and met the wife with two children and thanked her very well. The second day we left, sailed for Tema and when we got to Tema, this same man says his wife is bringing food for us. So, this woman came with one child. And of course, we came to Lagos and this guy told us he wants to go and greet his family. But it is no longer like that because now you spend less than a day in a particular port.[42]

Many seamen kept pictures of their wives and children abroad hanging in their homes in Nigeria, and pointed them out during interviews. When asked about children abroad, one informant explained, "Well, the fortunate ones had [children]. Look at my wife in that picture on the wall. For the fortunate ones, they had children, but because they could not afford to bring them back to Nigeria, their wives stayed over there."[43]

Seamen's partners abroad were drawn from among the economically and socially marginalized underclasses of white societies in England and elsewhere. Testimonies revealed that many of the Liverpool wives were of Irish descent, but one seaman claimed his wife was an Egyptian immigrant to England.[44] As noted above, these relationships drew criticism from both local populations and government officials throughout the period under question. It is therefore significant that seamen's descriptions of their marriages abroad made little or no reference to official disapproval of interracial sexual relations. Quite the contrary, the narratives that seamen constructed around these relationships flew in the face of political and social constraints, and revealed a surprising sense of agency and entitlement. This is particularly evident in seamen's characterization of these women as wives. This classification is a significant indicator of how seamen viewed these relationships, and the role they played for them in their lives outside of Nigeria.

Although seamen were quick to identify their foreign wives and children as their families, seamen's "marriages" abroad stood in stark contrast to the commitments and responsibilities that accompanied their marriages in Nigeria. Seamen claimed that their salaries went in large part to their Nigerian wives, who maintained their households and raised their children while they were away. Many explained that half of their monthly allotment was collected by their wives at the shipping offices in Lagos in their absence, and this money was used to pay for food, rent, and children's school fees. Seamen did not recognize the same obligations to foreign wives and children. While conjugal ties to women abroad provided seamen with personal and social sustenance, seamen were forthcoming in explaining that they did not provide any support, financial or otherwise, for these families. After retirement, most were lacking in any resources to travel abroad, and the only long-term expectation the seamen seemed to have of these relationships was the exchange of greeting cards and letters around holidays each year.[45] From their testimonies, it seems that this was all their families abroad could expect from them in return. One informant disdained these relationships, claiming there was no correlation between the social and financial commitment to a Nigerian wife and a wife abroad:

> What happened was that when you go to the clubhouse and you meet a girl and there is sexual intercourse together and she gives birth to a child, but that does not make her a wife. These girls were prostitutes. A lot of these prostitutes and their children lived on government welfare fund, when they say such a child has no father . . . or they say the father of the child is a seaman; because seamen has no time to look for anyone. Most of these children, bore by these women of easy virtue, cannot be brought to Nigeria by these seamen. For instance, there used to be a nightclub in Hamburg, Germany, where we paid to watch nude ladies; the same club is in Bahia, Brazil. Do you call such ladies wives?[46]

Seamen interviewed saw no contradiction in defining their relationships with women abroad as marriage, largely because they employed a different set of rules for social conduct and responsibilities during their travels outside of Nigeria. Informants' descriptions of foreign marriages therefore provide important insights into the seamen's perception of themselves as a migratory and fleeting presence in the social landscapes they visited outside of Nigeria. The notion of "a seaman's life" was invoked over and over to explain the fluid and ephemeral nature of social and cultural ties that seamen exploited within the context of their sojourns abroad.[47] As one informant explained, "I have children over there that I can't claim because I am a poor man in Nigeria. I can't ask them to come over here. . . . I have those children in Liverpool. I also have children in Spain. You know seamen and their activities on duty. Seamen, generally, like to go out and make new friends."[48] Men acknowledged that their lifestyle made it impossible to expect or demand too much from their role as fathers on either side of the ocean, because, as one explained, "The seafarer's job is more of traveling from one country to another and if you have a young boy, probably, you left him and traveled, by the time you return, he may not recognize you as his father because you have been away for more than four to six months."[49]

Seamen's wives in Nigeria had little choice but to accept that their husbands led "a seaman's way of life." They acknowledged that this lifestyle included the nurturing of romantic relationships in various ports of call, and seamen's wives interviewed claimed that they were aware of the wives their husbands had abroad. While they might not have been enthusiastic about these relationships, those interviewed saw it as an inevitable consequence of the seaman's lifestyle. As one woman explained:

> I must surely ask him how his journey went, and he, too, is obligated to tell me. He brings pictures and wrote letters. We can only be jealous that he has girlfriends but we cannot go with them to sea in annoyance and protest. I cannot say he shouldn't have because for someone who has been on the high sea for months, he needs to get back to life and no matter what you do, a man will always enjoy himself. Once he takes care of me and if he did not bring his girlfriend into the house or if I did not see it myself, then there is no problem.[50]

Nigerian wives might have resigned themselves to their husbands' lifestyles because they had little choice. One seaman explained his Nigerian wife's attitude to his family in Liverpool: "She has no option, except if she wants me to throw her out."[51] Seamen's wives usually had no contact with these women abroad, but occasionally wives or children from abroad would visit, and Nigerian wives would have to welcome them. One of the wives interviewed claimed that she was expected to host her husband's Dutch wife while she visited Lagos, and she even assisted in the birth of this woman's child. In the process, she constructed her own notions of infidelity that allowed her to embrace her husband's foreign wife:

> Seamen generally get different girlfriends in all parts of the world due to the nature of their work. My husband is a classical example in this regard. As a matter of fact, he even brought back home a Dutch lady who got pregnant for him and gave birth to a baby girl called Maria. The woman even stayed with us in this country until she later left back to her country. While the woman was with us,

I took good care of her and her baby girl such that when the lady was going back to her country, her baby would not even allow me to leave her to her real mother. It was an experience that shows the true nature of most seamen. As for me when the situation happened, I just accepted my fate because there was nothing I could do to help the situation. Since I knew the working conditions of seamen, I tried as much as possible to cope with my husband's absence from home for a long period of time. For that period of time, it was a good job to do. I am proud of my husband as a seaman. It was compulsory for a seaman to have a wife. Whether the men like it or not, seamen must have a wife. For those that were not married, infidelity was very common with them.[52]

Living a seaman's life was both explanation and justification for seamen's ability to invent and reinvent their identities and allegiances in a fluid array of settings and encounters. When asked to recount something of his social relationships abroad, one retired seaman responded, "People had nicknames and they were called by that name and not their original names. So, we didn't really bother about our names."[53] The meetings and social attachments that seamen initiated in volatile and changing social and cultural landscapes reflected a present-based and utilitarian practice of latching on to individuals, groups, and communities that offered extant sustenance and support. Thus, musicians sought out others to play and perform with, Christians allowed missionaries to care for them at every port of call, and all knew where to go to share a drink.[54]

DEFINING HOME

Seamen ultimately honed an empowered worldview that enabled them to imagine a sense of community and belonging wherever they found themselves. As one seaman poignantly described it, "The fact was that anywhere the ship sailed to, that was where we were."[55] By making strategic use of local alliances on the one hand, and situating themselves somehow outside the political and cultural boundaries of any given local setting on the other, seamen were able to nurture a sense of belonging and proprietorship in many places that were, at least on an official level, unwelcoming. This is particularly evident in seamen's descriptions of Liverpool as home base. A seaman's sense of belonging in the city was far removed from official British immigration policies:

Liverpool city is second to Lagos in terms of Nigerian populace. In Liverpool, you don't feel that you were in a foreign land. After the harsh day's job, in the evening, you visited any of the clubhouses: Yoruba, Igbo, Sierra Leonean, and Black Star clubhouses. So, we felt at home because we saw our ethnic people, kinsmen, and so on. We were free.[56]

I prefer England. I prefer England because the people there care so much about the welfare of the other person.[57]

Liverpool is just like a home. Anything you want there, you can get it. For example, if you want palm wine, you can get it in Liverpool, if you want amala [local dish made from yams], you can get it. A lot of Nigerians are there.[58]

England is just my second home. I was in Liverpool.[59]

That [Liverpool] was our Lagos. We called it "New Lagos."[60]

Yes, I visited different clubs in Germany, Holland, England, and Liverpool is in fact a black man's home. I felt good everywhere because I am an international man.[61]

Seamen's descriptions of Liverpool made no mention of the historical, political, and cultural attempts to segregate, exclude, and repatriate black seamen from England to Africa during the colonial and postcolonial eras.[62] At the same time, the Nigerian seamen of this study defined Nigeria, and not Liverpool, as home. In explaining this choice, seamen did not make reference to political or social discrimination, but rather presented their choice as both personal and based on practical considerations. In explaining the choice to return to Nigeria, many cited the cold weather as a major factor determining that they could never live in England. One seaman interviewed said, "No, I can't stay over there. Firstly, I never liked staying over there because I hate cold, I can't even cope with it, if not for the cold I would have been staying over there a long time ago. After all, seamen dropped down and are staying over there. Even when I was abroad, I only went out when it was extremely important for me to do so, else I was always indoors watching TV. It was not as if I hated Europe, but what would I be doing over there?"[63] Another seaman explained, "If you are getting old, you don't stay longer in that place because of cold, or else you die for nothing. . . . I had to buy a coat, put on double socks, and I took coffee every minute, and there were cigarettes to warm up."[64] He claimed that he ate spicy food from home to keep warm, while another informant recounted that he always ran instead of walking whenever in Liverpool to combat the cold.[65] But more than the weather, informants most cited their families back home in Nigeria as the reason to return.[66] Seamen claimed they could not abandon their wives, children, and extended families in Nigeria, revealing that their strongest identification with family and community was grounded in Nigeria. Some claimed they could not settle in England because they were obligated to care for their parents back home.[67] Seamen's testimonies revealed that their foreign families did not engender the same kinds of commitments. This could be seen in the following excerpt of an interview: "In England, I had a woman that had a baby for me. She is still in England. The baby is now a big girl and she lives in Liverpool. . . . I brought the baby for a visit to Nigeria and I sent her back to England. The girl was born 1979; she is thirty-one years old now. I am in touch with her very constantly." When asked why he did not want to live in England, the man replied, "I love Nigeria so much. I have a wife and kids here also. I have a good relationship with my daughter in England but not with her mother."[68]

While seamen fashioned their decisions to return to Nigeria on personal considerations, testimonies recalling encounters with racism and other exclusionary practices perhaps reveal a more complicated reality. The seaman's way of life was clearly not immune to the frequent confrontations with racism and prejudice both on board ships and at ports of call. As seen in chapter 1, acts of discrimination and violence perpetrated by white crew members against black seamen were certainly not uncommon on board ships.[69] But just as seamen had little recourse for action against racism offshore, experiences in ports of call were also painful reminders of their status as black working-class men. One seaman recounted his first visit to Scotland: "When we got to the port after the closing hour, four of us went out to join a bus to go and buy something. When we were inside the bus, the little children on the bus kept looking at us strangely, they didn't sit beside us; maybe that was their first time of seeing a black man and there was a space for them beside us but they refused. I have experienced a lot."[70]

In confronting, resisting, and circumventing racism, seamen invoked the notion of the "seaman's way of life" to circumvent local hierarchies of power. This could be seen in the following account of the same seaman's visit to South Africa during the era of apartheid: "In South Africa in 1970s there was black toilet and white toilet. . . . Well, we always told them that we don't live here, we are from ships. I remember at the dock I didn't look at the notice, the sign on the wall; I just went in to ease myself. A white later came to me and said hey, this is not your toilet, go to black man's. I told him look at my ship, I didn't know. And the man heard and he said next time if you want to ease yourself, go to black man's toilet." The same seaman even imagined his own models of racialism: "You know Singapore is a country with mixed color. They are just like Pakistani or Indian people. Even a Singapore man is like a black man, it is just the hair that is different."[71]

THE TRANSNATIONAL TRADING
NETWORKS OF SEAMEN

As seen in the previous chapter, Nigerian seamen could not rely on the Nigerian Union of Seamen to serve as an effective instrument through which they could hope to improve their poor working conditions and compensation. Lacking an effective representative body, seamen had to devise alternative means and strategies to protect and improve their unfavorable conditions of employment. They quickly identified opportunities that could be developed and exploited for earning additional money beyond the context of their official work in seafaring. Within these pockets of autonomy derived from the context of seafaring, seamen initiated a profitable and unofficial trade that maximized benefits for themselves and their families back home in Nigeria. As will be seen below, smuggling can be examined as a measure of seamen's ingenuity and self-reliance. The flow of goods coordinated by Nigerian seamen across transnational networks provides important insights into the ways in which Africans devised creative strategies for combating their disempowerment in colonial and postcolonial labor regimes. At the same time, the narratives crafted around this unofficial trade provide a unique opportunity for understanding how seamen imagined their power to cross or circumvent the political, economic, and cultural borders that the British colonial regime attempted to secure.

While the lure to become seamen was linked to both imagined and real opportunities for an alternative lifestyle, the actual financial benefits accrued from the work were minimal, and Nigerian seamen used whatever resources they had to engage in independent trade and thus augment their low wages. Forty percent of wages for those employed by Elder Dempster was paid in England in pounds sterling, while the remaining 60 percent was paid in Nigeria. Seamen explained that their wives claimed their allotment in Nigeria, while they used the money they received in England to buy goods for resale.[72] Seamen interviewed maintained that everyone exploited the opportunity to trade, as this was the only way to offset the poor salaries. One seaman explained, "I was involved—and I am very happy to tell you that I really did a lot of buying and selling when I was working, and I did that because of our poor wages."[73] Trading was therefore a vital aspect of seamen's activities, and represented their ability to autonomously improve their financial standing. Money earned from the trade fostered a sense of self-reliance among seamen, and helps to explain why the ineptitude of the union was not more of a cause for unrest. As one man explained, "A lot of us traded on board the ship so as to have more money. And because we were involved in trading activities, we were slow to agitate for an increment in the salary. Even when the union agitated for such, it had no power to push harder. But the proceeds from our trade kept us going."[74] Trading provided a vital supplement to wages that seamen and their families became deeply dependent upon. Seamen and their Nigerian wives claimed that this extra income enabled them to pay their children's school fees and other household expenses that official wages would not cover.[75] One woman explained that the secondhand trade was essential for their survival, as her husband's salary would barely cover the cost of food.[76] Women took an active role in the trade back in Lagos, finding customers for the goods upon their husbands' arrival. A few of the seamen's wives even opened up stores where they sold the secondhand goods their husbands brought from abroad.[77] One of the seamen's wives reported, "On his absence I still continued to sell and he would bring more items. . . . Part of the money was sent to both our parents and the remaining I used to buy goods for my shop. I controlled the money from the shop. I paid for the children school fees from it and he never ask me to give an account because he trusted me."[78]

Seamen's trade involved the importing of secondhand goods from Europe to Africa, as well as the export of some Nigerian products to other ports in Africa and to communities in the African diaspora. In Europe, seamen would buy a wide variety of secondhand goods for resale in Africa, such as electronics, kitchen appliances, refrigerators, freezers, furniture, mattresses, ceramic goods, clothing, tires, and used cars.[79] Some of the items were purchased new in England and resold in Nigeria, where there was a strong market for them. One of the seamen's wives said, "I started trading in the items he brought such as shoes, cloth, wigs from the UK. The wigs were brand-new. I did not have a store, but before he even arrived, people would be demanding for them. And I was able to make money from this. I needed him to go and come back so as to have more goods to sell. There was a time he stayed about one year in India."[80] Seamen would also export Nigerian foodstuffs such as garri, yams, *egusi* (melon seeds), and *elubo* (yam flour), as well as palm wine and local beer.[81] Some also traded in wooden carvings on special order from customers in Europe or Brazil.[82]

One seaman explained, "Yes, there is no seaman who was not involved in the trading activities. If you have a house, as a seaman, you want to put chairs, table, television, stereo and so on, no matter how little it might be."[83] These purchases continue to serve as material reminders of their work and travels, as one retired seaman interviewed pointed out the imported items in his home: "Any old or fairly used items that were in good condition, we bought and sold them in Nigeria. You can see some of them in my living room, like the big mirror, the old pendulum wall clock, that flower vase, and the old stereo—were bought from Europe."[84] But once seamen filled their homes with these goods, they sold any duplicates they obtained on later journeys.[85] Seamen and their families were often the first in their neighborhoods to have luxury items such as televisions and refrigerators. This was sometimes the cause of jealousy among neighbors; one woman explained: "They felt we had everything in the world, so whether we eat or not, they do not know. So, in most cases, they feel we are very rich."[86]

While trading was described as a vital source of supplementary income, seamen's ability to engage in independent trade was dependent on a host of prerequisite conditions involving social, economic, and political relations. Changes in political or economic circumstances on board ships, at specific ports of call, or in customs policies in each country could result in the limiting or immediate cessation of seamen's independent trade. Thus, seamen had to successfully nurture and negotiate their personal relations with captains, immigration officers, customs officials, dockers, European retailers, African customers, and fellow crewmates in order to ensure their ability to buy, transport, stow, and sell goods from one continent to another, as well as continually adapt their activities to new circumstances not of their own choosing.

During the colonial period, seamen employed by Elder Dempster and other foreign companies were officially allowed to transport one to four items for personal use, depending on the specific vessel they were on. But seamen's testimonies revealed that there was considerable latitude in the enforcement of this policy under the Elder Dempster captains. Some captains were willing to turn a blind eye to seamen's activities, allowing them to transport items in their personal spaces, or even the cargo hold, space permitting. One retired seaman described the role of the captains in determining how much trade was permitted:

We bought, but we were not allowed to buy goods. Whenever you wanted to do that you will have to negotiate with the captain. If he were liberal and he will allow us to buy four items, but some captains never bothered, you could buy anything, hide it and keep it in your store. But some British captains will not allow you to do that, they would tell you that you have not come to the ship to trade, you have come to work in the ship. . . . The captain called the shots. . . . No captain will tell you to trade. . . . He would overlook whatever the seamen did as regards trade. But some captains will never allow you to do that. Even before the crew get on board, the captain would have pasted a notice on the board that "no one is allow to trade." . . . The notice on the board was boldly pasted by some captains while other captains never bothered.[87]

The incalculability of a captain's response could put seamen at great risk. For instance, one seaman claimed that he had invested tremendous time and resources after being contracted by a Canadian to carve and sell his wooden objects in Canada, but was later threatened with being sacked by his captain for conducting this side business.[88] Thus, the captain of the ship played a pivotal role in determining the extent to which seamen could engage in trade, as seamen could not bring goods on board without his knowledge or permission, and routine inspections were conducted. Captains who allowed the trade would often require seamen to pay freight charges to the company and on some occasions, customs duties. The use of containers led to increased surveillance of goods transported by seamen, as permission to use containers was required from captains, and this was at a standard freight fee paid to the company at the port of arrival. When this system was introduced, groups of seamen had to organize together to fill an entire container with goods to make the export trade economically viable for each individual.[89] But the containerization of shipping between West Africa and Europe began only in 1965, and it took several years before containers became the standard method for cargo transport on Elder Dempster Lines.[90] Thus, even in the period of decolonization, seamen employed by Elder Dempster still enjoyed the lower level of regulation associated with cargo transport in the pre-containerization era.

While captains served as the ultimate authority in determining how many items seamen could carry on board, seamen also had to establish and maintain solid relations with a complex mosaic of business partners and customers at each end of their operations. Seamen purchased goods from retailers across Europe and beyond, including in England, Holland, Germany, Spain,

Brazil, and the Caribbean. The immense distances between various locations, and the particularities of each place, made the trade unpredictable and risky. Customs officials could be whimsical, and seamen could face unexpected fees from officers practicing strict enforcement. This made the level of profit irregular and resulted in major losses for some.[91] Others complained that they themselves extended credit to customers, never to be repaid.[92]

To mitigate against risks and increase profits, seamen had to establish relationships of trust with a vast array of retailers. While most of the transactions were based on "cash-and-carry," some of those interviewed claimed that it was also possible to purchase items on credit.[93] Full payment could be rendered only on return journeys that were sometimes months away, and therefore the extension of credit was possible only once seamen developed relations of trust with retailers abroad. This can be seen in the following description of relations between one seaman and his German supplier:

> He used to sell electronic appliances, it was from there I met him and sometimes whenever I was in Germany, I stayed with him and his family. I also worked with him in his shop. Here he put my honesty to the test and he found me truly honest. I got to know him when the ship I was to bring to Nigeria from Germany was not ready and I went to Bremen to buy something to sell here, that was how I met him and because the ship was not ready for almost six months. When I was leaving he asked if I want to sell anything and I told him I was interested, he gave some goods to sell and I returned his money. He even told other crew members who were in the same business of buying and selling to give me their own proceeds for onward transmission to him. One day, someone among our crew that I cannot identify went and duped him when I was on leave. The fraudster ordered for goods in my name, worth five hundred thousand naira at that time, and he never returned again. When I went to Bremen, the man asked me of the goods he sent to me, it was a long list, I said no and when I saw the long list I wept. I told him I never sent anyone.[94]

This testimony revealed the extent to which personal relations were central to seamen's success as traders, and they prided themselves on their credibility as businessmen. As seamen did not rely on middlemen for purchases, transport, or resale, their success in the independent trade was the result of their personal initiatives and efforts, and those interviewed were quick to link their achievements to their upright reputations.

There were some seamen who, for various reasons, did not take part in the trade. For a few seamen interviewed, the secondhand trade was seen as a distraction to seafaring, and signaled a lack of professionalism. As one seaman charged: "Some people went there with the sole intension of making money. Some people even sold some portion of their food ration just for making additional money. All these I did not do and you could confirm this from other seamen and they will tell you the same about me."[95] Another seaman simply claimed that it was not worthwhile financially, and instead he opened side businesses in Lagos in order to supplement income:

> Look, you were paid for instance 5 kobo and you used that to buy something that you could sell for 10 kobo, which adds very little value. I don't call it trade because, after a trip back from Europe, before you could engage in this kind of trade again, it will take you about four to six months by which you could have spent all you had in the previous trade. I was not very keen about this, I already started a photocopy business in Lagos Island. In fact, I was the first person to have started that. . . . I bought the photocopy machine here in Nigeria, not abroad, and I did this business alongside as a seaman. And as I have said earlier, the seaman job was not a permanent one, so I needed something to [augment] my salary. More importantly, I already had children before I became a seaman.[96]

As much as seamen emphasized their honesty and credibility in their business transactions, there was a clear dissociation from the illicit activity that was frequent among seamen and commonly linked to them. Some worked in cooperation with dockers, breaking down company cargoes and selling them on the black markets.[97] Drug trafficking was also an extremely lucrative activity, and seamen claimed that many were lured to this business for its high returns.[98] Some crew exported cannabis from Nigeria and sold it in Europe, while cocaine was purchased in Brazil and the Carribean and sold in Europe and Nigeria.[99] Unlike the sale of secondhand goods, drug trafficking was conducted without the consent of captains, and required crew to hide the contraband somewhere on board. Small amounts of cannabis could be hidden among a seaman's personal belongings, with the hope that it would not be revealed in routine searches. The carpenters, known as shippies, were well known for constructing hiding spots in the woodwork of the common areas of the ship.[100] Drug trafficking by seamen required cooperation with dockers, who often sold them the drugs, and police or customs officials, who often acted as accomplices. Thus, similarly to the trade in secondhand goods, crew involved in the drug trade depended upon and fostered transnational economic networks.

It was not only the trade itself, but the narratives that seamen have reconstructed around the trade that also reveal an act of conjuring—a space within which seamen reiterate a former sense of innovation, empowerment, and influence linked to the trade. Time and again, seamen described their independent economic activities as deviceful and pioneering enterprises, and some claimed to have been the first to begin the importing and exporting of various items between Africa and Europe. Thus, one seaman interviewed claimed that seamen were the first to sell apples in Nigeria: "It depended on the items you had interest in. I, in particular, had an interest in apples. I bought apples. In fact, we, seamen, pioneered the importation of apples into Nigeria. We imported about from France, England, and so on."[101] He also attributed seamen with the start of the scrap metal import industry in Nigeria:

> The job was so attractive. We made casual friends in Europe who gave some of us these articles, including cars free without asking for a dime. Therefore, we didn't look into how much we earned. Our friends in Europe gave us these articles. We could bring in cars but because we couldn't afford the freight, so, we scrapped. Note that we, seamen, started scrapping cars to sell in Nigeria before different traders started it now. We scrapped the car into parts so that it wouldn't attract any freight.[102]

Seamen's trade also enabled an imagined redrawing of cultural boundaries between Nigeria and the Nigerian diaspora. The flow of goods from "back home" to places abroad played a role in extending a sense of familiarity and belonging, particularly in England. Thus, seamen identified the availability of Nigerian foodstuffs and alcohol in the social and cultural spaces of Liverpool and London as a factor contributing to their sense of proprietorship in the construction of those spaces. One seaman claimed, "[We sold] cartons of local beer [Star and Guilder] because our local beers are stronger than those ones brewed abroad. We sold all these items in Liverpool. People came to the ship and bought these items. . . . Sometimes, in those days in London, if you attended a party, Nigerian local beers were served."[103] The same can be seen in the quotation noted earlier in the chapter of a seaman who claimed that Liverpool was just like home because it was possible to find palm wine and amala in this British city.[104]

But while seamen might have fashioned themselves around these narratives as citizens of the world, a more critical scrutinizing of their trading practices reveals the resilience of some racial, cultural, and national border regimes that seamen's trade did not succeed in dismantling. Rather than reflecting a purely cosmopolitan enterprise, the circuits of seamen's unofficial trade were more reminiscent of what Paul Gilroy has described as the "Black Atlantic."[105] Thus, racial alliances and racial hierarchies played a pivotal role in directing the flows of goods and wealth within the context of seamen's trade. The following testimony hints at the role race played in mapping access to markets for seamen's trading activities: "Honestly, we never sold to any European, but we sold in different African countries like Dakar, Monrovia, Freetown, Lagos, Gambia [Bathurst], Accra, and so on. The people came to the dock and asked is there anything to sell? And we said yes; the transaction took place immediately, so no European bought the fairly used items and appliances from us—their country is good."[106]

This seaman's testimony reveals a keen awareness of gaps dividing African seamen, clients, and port cities on the one hand, and European citizens and countries on the other. The seaman's assessment of this difference is linked to race, class, and national consciousness, all of which played a significant role in shaping seamen's transnational encounters. Thus, while seamen's independent trade evoked moments of inventiveness and autonomy, they never fully overcame the hierarchies and inequalities enforced by the colonial context.

Indeed, rather than blurring notions of difference, some scholars have noted that transnational migrations and processes of globalization have in fact exacerbated historically entrenched hierarchies of race, class, and nation.[107] This fact is crucial for understanding seamen's engagement with nationalism in the era of decolonization. The innovations and inventiveness of their independent trade notwithstanding, it was seamen's encounters with exclusion and discrimination in the context of their work and travels in the late colonial era that ultimately aroused their nationalist yearnings. In the upcoming chapter, we will see that seamen initially saw nationalism as a remedy to their disempowerment and an opportunity to improve their lot.

Cargo on ship bound for West Africa. *Photo courtesy of Claes Thure Moberg.*

Krooboy. *Photo courtesy of Claes Thure Moberg.*

Group of Krooboys. *Photo courtesy of P. M. Bass.*

Cargo on deck. *Photo courtesy of P. M. Bass.*

Deck boys coming on board in Accra, Ghana. *Photo courtesy of Christopher Clark.*

Deck on a Palm Line ship leaving West Africa. *Photo courtesy of Christopher Clark.*

River Andoni, an NNSL ship. *Photo courtesy of Selim Sam.*

King Jaja, an NNSL ship. *Photo courtesy of Malcolm Cranfield.*

3 ⮑ From Citizens of the World to Citizens of Nigeria

At the end of World War II, a tantalizing array of ideological and political possibilities for protest and dissent began to emerge across the black diaspora and in Africa. New alliances and coalitions coalesced around demands for ending racial discrimination and colonialism. In Africa, the culmination of these processes was the dismantling of colonialism and the establishment of independent nation-states. But the paths to this decisive result traversed a complex terrain of competing visions and ideological stances that drew upon solidarities ranging from broad Pan-Africanist perspectives to localized ethnic chauvinism. The ultimate victory of nationalist movements was rooted not only in the dismissal of European colonizers, but also in the defeat of alternative visions for postcolonial political and ideological alliances that did not adhere to national entities within colonial borders. Leaders of nationalist movements were preoccupied equally with defeating competing notions of solidarity within local populations as they were with defeating European colonialism. Thus, their successful rise to power should be measured not only in terms of their anticolonial agitation, but also with regard to the effective silencing of rival ideologies of solidarity. Critical of the impact this trend had on the postcolonial political landscape, Fred Cooper summed up the era of decolonization in Africa as "a narrowing of possibilities."[1]

In the case of the Nigerian intelligentsia, Philip Zachernuk has argued that the processes of decolonization were characterized by a gradual move away from a Pan-African focus to a political agenda increasingly focused on Nigeria. Nigerian intellectuals educated in Europe were drawn to ideologies of Pan-Africanism while studying abroad. But returning home, they became entrenched in political activism and invested most of their energies in the internal affairs of Nigeria. Once nationalism became the main trope around which the political elite organized, the black diaspora offered far less ideological or organizational inspiration. Zachernuk argued that the turn inward was accompanied by increasing factionalism within this new Nigeria-focused group, as "they were pulled apart into factions representing the Nigerian domestic scene."[2] Thus, within the political organizing and ideological agendas of this intellectual elite, Pan-African ties played an increasingly minor role, and visions of black unity faded.[3] This process was not unique to Nigeria, as can be seen in Frantz Fanon's description of the rise of bourgeois nationalism throughout the continent: "We observe a permanent see-saw between African unity, which fades quicker and quicker into the mists of oblivion, and a heartbreaking return to chauvinism in its most bitter and detestable form."[4]

In the final analysis of Cooper, Zachernuk, and Fanon, the consolidation of power in the hands of political elites in the era of decolonization came at a price for everyday Africans. Leaders solidified their role in the local political landscape through conciliation with the colonial administration, and their co-option into the political establishment often led to ideological compromises. Pan-Africanism was largely abandoned, as were other radical agendas that challenged or disrupted colonial border regimes. The newly imagined nations were strictly confined to states adhering to colonial boundaries. In exchange for the gradual granting of political rights and powers within these borders, African leaders gave up on their militant anti-European rhetoric, and they moderated or even abandoned the more radical demands of their constituents. Michael Neocosmos claimed the very definition of the political underwent a narrowing in this process spanning the 1950s and 1960s, and popular expressions of political solidarity and protest were displaced by nationalist visions of politics. As he wrote, "African nationalism in that period had a particular conception of politics and the state that excluded popular-democratic self-activity. The writings and, even more so, the actions of most nationalists reflected an understanding of the state as the sole domain of politics."[5]

The history of labor organizing among Nigerian seamen in the era of decolonization largely mirrors this broader tale of emerging possibilities in the postwar era and their ultimate defeat to the nationalist perspective. In the previous chapter, it was argued that seamen's social and cultural lives in the postwar era reflected a lived Pan-Africanism. In what follows, we will see that seamen's political organizing and protests in the 1950s were also deeply influenced by Pan-African ideologies. The postwar protest movements of the black diaspora were an inspiration to seamen, and their organizing efforts throughout this era relied heavily on support from diaspora communities. But these transnational political solidarities became increasingly sidelined in the transition to Nigerian independence. In the final years of colonial rule, the leadership of the Union of Seamen insisted on a contracting of an ideological vision away from Pan-African perspectives and a turn inward to a political agenda focused on Nigeria. Although seamen's effective protests had ignited the process leading to recognition of union leadership as an equal negotiating partner with management, the new relationship based on cooperation and collaboration led the leadership of the union to abandon many of the demands and charges that were at the root of seamen's discontent.

This chapter focuses on the history of labor organizing within the seamen's union in the shadow of decolonization, and scrutinizes how the process of nationalization limited seamen's opportunities for forging transnational alliances. While organizing among seamen had historically relied upon and benefited from ties to black communities and ideologies situated in Liverpool and around the diaspora, the process of decolonization limited the potential for cooperative efforts between Nigerian seamen and diaspora working classes. A Nigerian perspective soon took the place of Pan-African perspectives, and seamen were gradually disciplined away from more radical visions of liberation. It will be seen that union leadership played a significant role in bringing about this shift following a change in the status of the union as an equal negotiating partner with shipping companies. As union officials secured more power and influence from British shipping officials seeking to cooperate with organized labor, power was consolidated around the Lagos-based union, and rank-and-file labor lost the ability to initiate spontaneous protests or to represent themselves in disputes on board ships. This had far-reaching consequences for ship-based organizing among seamen, and over the long run, contributed to their overall sense of disempowerment.

Two major incidents give life to these important transitions in the history of seamen's organizing. The first was the recruitment of Sidi Khayam, a new general secretary for the union, in 1958; and second, the strike that began on board the MV *Apapa* in Liverpool in 1959. The events and outcomes surrounding these two incidents provide important insights into seamen's organizing efforts and opportunities, as well as their successes and failures, in the shadow of decolonization. After examining the kinds of Pan-African ideologies that inspired and shaped seamen's labor organizing and protests in the postwar era, we will turn to the events that led to the consolidation of power in the hands of a subdued leadership, and the long-term impact of these events on seamen's political and ideological autonomy.

SEAMEN, THE BLACK DIASPORA, AND PAN-AFRICAN IDEOLOGIES OF LIBERATION

Africans who undertook transnational migrations during the colonial era were exposed to the denigrating experiences of racism and discrimination. But for many, mobility was also an empowering experience. Africans traveling to Europe and the United States in the postwar era came into contact with local black communities and with the protest ideologies and liberation movements emerging in them.[6] These colonial travelers became important conduits of knowledge and political mobilization linking blacks across the Atlantic World.[7] African seamen in particular played a central role as conveyers of news, ideologies, and trends across the diaspora as early as the slave trade, and they have thus played a central role in the historic evolution of the diaspora. As Jeffrey Bolster has argued, the work of seafaring was the catalyst for defining a new black ethnicity, as sailors embodied "a mode of communication integrating local communities into the larger community of color."[8]

Seamen were not only conduits of knowledge—they were also deeply influenced and shaped by their own transnational mobility. As targets of racism both ashore and on board ships, seamen were attuned to increasingly radicalized calls for change within black communities in England, the United States, and South Africa. Particularly in the postwar era, they were emboldened by the ideologies of liberation and the waves of protest that materialized across the diaspora at this time. As Michael Gomez has argued, "The dawn of African Independence included illumination from the Diaspora, and the effect of simultaneous conflict in Africa and the Diaspora were closer cultural and political links between the two."[9] In the following letter written to the Elder Dempster shipping company in 1958, we can see how seamen drew inspiration from contemporary struggles in England and the United States:

> Really, what I have found out is that what is happening in Little Rock, Arkansas, USA; South Africa; London and Nottingham in

England is happening on all the ships of the E.D. Lines in West Africa. . . . It is nothing but slavery, colour prejudice and racism. . . . African haters like the captain on board *"Egori"* are out to destroy our efforts. Personally, I still think it is high time that we tell the world of the truth about the E.D. Lines and their inhuman exploitations of us as Africans, i.e. apart from working between 12½ and 18½ hour days, we are exposed to the worst treatment and humiliations on earth. . . . I am now appealing to you to look into the case, for if they were punished because of the color of their skin, I am afraid the Union will have to share in the punishment since we are all black men and because injury to one of us is injury to all of us. We will also appeal to your country as a whole to help us fight this menace of colour prejudice which is the product of imperialism.[10]

Exposure to events in the black diaspora led to increasing militancy in seamen's protests, as can be seen in the following letter from the Nigerian Union of Seamen to Elder Dempster in 1958:

For your information, the African crews have long hesitated from retaliating not because they are cowards but because the Union has been continually telling them that they should obey before complaining. If by any chance you think that they are afraid of being defeated by the English offenders on board ships, you can refer to boxing history and see what Joe Louis and Sugar Ray Robinson did to their white opponents. Today, Hogan Kid Bassey, another black man, is showing the world how he can handle the white man.

· And while the [shipping master] sits back with his English friends from shipping companies, who carry away our raw material and minerals and enjoys this paradise of sunshine, our men — Africans and West Indians, are being slashed with knives and beaten with pokers in England.

Do the incidents which we have stated here not portray very clearly that the African are hated by their English co-workers and superiors on board the ships? Never are they only beaten by one at a time, but in every instant they are attacked by groups of English seamen. . . . Does this not prove conclusively that colour prejudice is rampant on all ships, particularly those of the Elder Dempster Lines? What is happening and what we have related here is no different from the incidents taking place in Little Rock, Arkansas, and London and Nottingham, England.

The E.D. Lines do not know that the African ministers who travel on the ships from time to time are aware of these facts and they will not shut their eyes to the fill-treatment and deaden their ears to the cries of their unfortunate brothers. The situation has now reached an intolerable point and we are no longer prepared to sit back and allow matters to run their own course while our men are being continually mishandled because of the colour of their skin. If the Elder Dempster Lines and other shipping companies continue to send the English seamen to beat up African crews, we will show them that Africans are no cowards.[11]

As the end of colonialism approached, seamen's protests became emboldened by the prospect of independence. Decolonization ushered in a new set of rules regulating relations between blacks and whites in Africa, and seamen were keenly aware that the balance of process had shifted. This can be seen in the following letter from 1958:

> You talk about bowing your head to an African Labour Minister as if it proves you consider Africans your equals. We know as well as you do that you did not bow your head to him because you felt like doing so but because you were compelled to by economic circumstances. . . . We are aware of the fact that the cause for which the shipping companies are fighting is that of super-profit, hence their inhuman exploitation of the seamen. . . . If fighting for your rights will make you recommend to the shipping companies that they should cease to employ Nigerian seamen, you should do it in time. . . . Time was when we would have been scared stiff hearing that type of threat from the Shipping Master, but fortunately for us, no nation has succeeded in stopping the forces of evolution. What we are trying to tell you is that the wheel of history is revolving in favor of Africans and against imperialism.[12]

Seamen warned the shipping company that changes were taking place throughout the continent, and the racial hierarchies that characterized the colonial era were being dismantled all over, and not just in Nigeria: "We are fully aware of the fact that we Africans are despised by the white man because of our race and colour but you should warn the captains and superior officers of your ships to refrain from showing their hatred of us when circumstances force them to work with us and moreover since these ships must call at ports in the west coast of Africa."[13] Shipping officials were also warned by insiders on ships that there were plans for forming a West African union of seamen, with Nigerians joining forces with seamen and dockworkers in Sierra Leone and Ghana.[14]

While union leaders in Lagos were the official representatives for seamen, crews on board ships did not rely solely on the union to represent them. In voicing grievances to the shipping companies, crews initiated autonomous onboard protests without the prior knowledge or support of headquarters in Lagos. These initiatives often mobilized support and drew upon resources available through their diaspora connections. Particularly in Liverpool, seamen relied heavily on the local black community and its leadership. As a meeting point for Afro-Americans, Afro-Carribbeans, and Africans, Liverpool evolved as a breeding ground for Pan-African political activism and ideology.[15]

With many of the black community of Liverpool engaged in seafaring, the plight of black seamen was high on the political agenda of local leaders and activists, and they took up seamen's causes and provided support on multiple levels. One notable figure dating back to the pre–World War II era was Pastor Daniels Ekarte, the founder of the African Church Mission of Liverpool. Ekarte was himself a former Nigerian seaman who settled in Liverpool in 1915. His mission became a center for all those in need in the black community, and Nigerians who visited the city knew they could turn to Pastor Daniels for help.[16] Ekarte's church established the Stanley House, a community center for the benefit of the local black community, and this became an important meeting place for West Africans, West Indians, and those of African descent who settled in Liverpool permanently.[17] The Stanley House provided seamen meals, lodging, and recreational activities. Another local figure, Mr. Akinsanya, took it upon himself to represent seamen in their conflicts with Elder Dempster. According to a 1959 report, Akinsanya was a committee member in Liverpool of the National Union of Nigeria, which "catered to the interests of all Nigerian workers and seamen in the U.K." Akinsanya met with shipping company officials to give voice to complaints among the African crews of Elder Dempster ships. He relayed complaints from the MV *Apapa*, where men were being asked to work excessive hours, and accused the second engineer of changing the hours "on account of his dislike of Africans." Shipping officials repelled these accusations of racism alleged by Akinsanya and other Liverpudlian blacks. As John Holt, the Elder Dempster official, reported: "I told him that I would be unable to carry on this discussion if he insisted on bringing an element of racial discord into it, and he withdrew his comments."[18]

Seamen relied on diaspora communities for support and leadership because the seamen's union in Nigeria had been largely ineffective in its role as the representative of seamen's rights. But the effectiveness of the union as an agent of change for seamen was drastically improved with the recruitment in April 1958 of a new general secretary, Sidi Omar Khayam, who replaced Franco Olugbake. Sidi Khayam, born in Nigeria, had lived, worked, and studied in England for nearly ten years before he was recruited by the Nigerian Union of Seamen to be their new general secretary.[19] Khayam was living in Liverpool when some local African residents and Nigerian seamen persuaded him to return to Nigeria and head the seamen's union. Khayam claimed to have studied economics and law, although he did not complete any degree, and had scattered experience with trade union membership as he worked in various factories and industries throughout England. The rank and file of the union believed that the recruitment of a Nigerian from abroad would improve the capabilities of the union, and perhaps help avoid the political competition and tensions that had plagued the union since its founding. Seamen suspected that the officers of the union were embezzling funds, and an auditor's report confirmed that there had been irregularities in the handling of dues. As representatives of crews docked in London wrote with regard to the elections of union officers in 1959: "Since the Nigerian Union of Seamen has been formed, we have tried several seamen, but they let us down. We collectively suggest to try outsiders by applications."[20]

As a recruit from abroad, Khayam was not recognized by the officers of the union—S. M. Ekore, T. Oguntimeyin, and A. Monday. In a public notice, these officers decided that following the ousting of Olugbake, A. Monday would act as general secretary until elections.[21] But rank-and-file seamen accused these officers of corruption, absenteeism, and antidemocratic practices, and rejected their executive decisions.[22] The shipping company reported to have very good relations with these men, a fact that might have fueled the rank-and-file seamen's distrust of them. These officers had their own faction in the union, but Khayam had the larger following, and, eventually, in May 1959, Khayam succeeded in leading a no-confidence vote, expelling them from the union.

From the start of his work as general secretary, Khayam made significant efforts to improve seamen's working conditions, taking actions that earlier officers had avoided. He boarded ships in port to survey working conditions, interviewed both African crews and European officers, and filed reports of abuses and complaints expressed by seamen. The shipping companies saw this as stirring up trouble.[23] Archival records reveal that Khayam's appointment to the position of general secretary strained relations with the shipping companies, particularly because of the confrontational manner he adopted toward the employers from the beginning of his term. Attempting to solidify his position, Khayam was initially uncompromising in his attitude toward the shipping company, making strong demands for salary increases, payment for overtime, and improved lodging for seamen on board ships and ashore. Previous officers of the union had avoided confrontations with the management, hoping that positive relations with shipping officials would lead to personal benefits for themselves. Khayam seemed to put seamen's concerns first, and he did not turn a blind eye to injustices. He reported instances of bribery on ships and in the process of recruitment, and insisted that seamen be recruited through a closed-shop system organized by the union. Khayam did not limit his scope to Nigerian crew members, but also made demands with regard to African seamen in general. In one instance, he filed a complaint with Captain Perkins of the SS *Winneba*. Khayam claimed that the captain was making unusually harsh demands against African seamen by demanding that they raise their mattresses during his inspections of crew quarters. Perkins told Khayam he had no jurisdiction over the Freetown crew, to which Khayam replied, "The Nigerian Union of Seamen concerned itself with the welfare of all African seamen, whether from Sierra Leone, Ghana or Nigeria."[24] At the end of his visit on the ship, he instructed all the African crews to refuse the captain's orders, and not to lift their mattresses for inspection. Khayam clearly was not deterred by the power of shipping companies, and it was reported that in meetings he became abusive and termed the shipping officials the "degenerate British."[25]

Khayam became involved in the broader trade union politics in Nigeria, and the shipping companies closely followed his activities. He was seen as a dangerous radical with ties to other agitators, and his moves were monitored and debated by colonial officials. Thus, the Department of Labour reported: "We have heard on the confidential wire that Khayam is in the meantime having regular contact with such people as Mrs. Ransome-Kuti, Imodou, and Goodluck. He is indeed running true to form."[26] They attempted to delegitimize him and looked for ways to condemn him: "Khayam wants the Union to purchase a car for his use. A rumour to this effect has also been heard previously and we are pleased to have it confirmed. Khayam's real intention is to gain control over the Union funds."[27] Shipping officials tried to build a case against him as an active Communist, and they solicited Tom Yates, general secretary of the National Union of Seamen in Britain, to do a background check on Khayam, to which he replied, "I am far from happy about the election of this young man. He has never been a seaman, or for that matter had any practical experience whatsoever, and although he claims to be associated with the Labour Party, he has visited Egypt, India, China and Moscow." Despite Yates's suspicions, he concluded, "I can not prove that he is a Commie, or that he will not do a clean job for the Nigerian seamen."[28] Khayam himself went to great pains to deny allegations that he was a Communist, but the shipping company was not convinced, as one official wrote, "He really wanted to impress me with the fact that he had nothing to do with the Party nowadays. Methinks he doth protest too much." The more vocal Khayam became, the more he became suspect and dangerous in the eyes of shipping officials, as the same official concluded, "In short, he is intelligent, clever, completely unscrupulous, has no regard for the truth and is willing to do anything to achieve his ends."[29]

But what was truly disturbing to the management of Elder Dempster was Khayam's habit of flying into a rage in his meetings with management, and frequently accusing them of racial discrimination. As one official wrote, "No doubt you have heard of the more recent activities of our friend Omar Khayam and the Nigerian Union of Seamen. It does seem as if he is continuing to stir up trouble mostly in Elder's ships, using the black vs. white theme."[30] Khayam often raised the issue of racism in his confrontations with union officials. He was particularly accusatory toward the Lagos crew manager, Colin Dyson. It was reported that Khayam told Dyson that "he did not know better than a lawyer merely because [he] had white skin." Khayam threatened Dyson that the pendulum of evolution was swinging in favor of his people and against imperialist countries. He accused the management of treating seamen as slaves, driving them with ships.[31] Sidi Khayam's presence had a galvanizing effect, drawing the entire union to a more militant position. The general secretary's activist approach forced the other officers to become more vigorous in their pursuit of the seamen's interests in order to maintain the support of the rank and file. It was only after Khayam's arrival that Ekore and Akpan Monday adopted an incendiary tone with management, and embraced the same confrontational discourse of racial oppression that they had previously avoided.

While the shipping companies were willing to enter into a dialogue with a legitimate representative of African labor to negotiate compromises with regard to pay scales or benefits, the employers were not willing to engage with a provocative racial discourse. Thus, Elder Dempster initially refused to recognize General Secretary Sidi Khayam, claiming that he was appointed illegitimately. Unofficially, they schemed to get him deported from Nigeria.[32]

But the changes in the balance and nature of power in the era of decolonization meant that simply deporting Khayam was not an option. Quite the opposite dynamic was set in motion. As general elections approached in Nigeria in 1959, shipping companies were instructed by government officials on "the paramount importance of employers recognizing trade union leaders and always negotiating with trade unions on all matters where difference of viewpoint exists."[33] As the elected leader of the seamen's union, any attempt to diffuse Khayam's influence would have to be more circumspect. Officials at shipping companies could count on the support of some key Nigerian politicians who were equally in favor of getting rid of Khayam. This group of Westernized elites owed their positions of influence to their proximity to colonial rulers, and they did not favor the radical approach of leaders like Khayam. These officials realized, however, that the legally elected general secretary of the seamen's union could be discredited and neutralized only through legitimate means. As Minister of Labor Nwokedi suggested to the Elder Dempter representative in Lagos in 1959:

> Khayam is unfavorable and it would be best to see him out of the country. But the Ministry would like the seamen themselves to get rid of Khayam and they consider that the only way to achieve this would be for Khayam to be shown up beyond doubt, on a wider screen than at present, as an irresponsible person not working in the seamen's best interests. The proposed method for "exposing" Khayam would be to have a "trade dispute" and for the Labour Department to appoint a conciliator. It could be expected that Khayam's behaviour during conciliation meetings would finally make clear to all his unreasonableness and irresponsibility . . . resulting in the seamen denouncing and dismissing him.[34]

Nwokedi's proposed strategy lays bare the broader changes set in motion in the era of decolonization. Despite their dissatisfaction, neither local politicians nor shipping companies could simply depose of Sidi Khayam. Both politicians and employers had to endure the controversial leader the seamen had elected to represent their cause.

As it turns out, Sidi Khayam's relationship to the rank-and-file membership of the union was no less antagonistic, and his approach toward them was equally belligerent. A few months after taking office, he issued a statement to the general membership, instituting an uncompromising expression of his rule over the organization and demanding unambiguous obedience from the seamen union members. The statement said:

Our plan is to run the Nigerian Union of Seamen on a pattern different from the gangster-tactics of yesteryears. . . . We have had enough complaints, some are true, some are not. But the damn truth is, that there is [an] absence of evidence that some of us are really serious seamen. From now [on] the union will take steps to rub in some discipline for those who are caught on petty-theft, underhanded business, smart rackets and fishy deals. It's none of our business to defend such mess.

. . . Any person whose acts will likely prevent all seamen from getting their rights and respect, who wants to clown around his job and shows us up as drones to shipping captains will get a fast punch out the union door. He will get a black eye from the union before the shipping company does it. Any guy who is feeling lazy can drop on shore to doze or booze about the place, but he is not going to pull down our prestige or weaken the effort the Nigerian Union of Seamen wants to put up for decent and hardworking African crews.

Members who feel a bit big or want to bluff their way by looking too sulky for instructions can just ask themselves how much they get for the same job white crews perform.

. . . And anyone who figures we don't mean business can start the stew and see how it tastes. We mean every damn decision we have put down here—that he will be thrown out of the N.U.S. picture outright.[35]

Khayam's sharp approach did not translate into significant gains for seamen, and each rebuff from management or the seamen themselves sent him into a new rage. His luck changed, however, in the aftermath of the *Apapa* strike of 1959, an event he played no role in initiating, but one that he masterfully exploited to his advantage.

THE MV *APAPA* STRIKE OF 1959

On 27 May 1959, the MV *Apapa* vessel arrived in Lagos. The crew met with General Secretary Sidi Khayam to complain of ill-treatment of the African crew during their most recent voyage. At the root of the seamen's grievances was what they identified as the systematic discrimination of black seamen on board Elder Dempster ships. They had several specific examples of this discrimination, claiming, for instance, that African seamen were limited to purchasing only Woodbines, Senior Service, and Capstan cigarettes, while the European crew was allowed to have any available brand. The seamen also complained that the bartender watered down the beer of Africans, but not the European crew's. They charged that the newly appointed chief steward denied Africans steak, chicken, and turkey, and instead served them only pork. The crew also suspected that the chief steward had ordered customs officers to perform in-depth searches of the belongings of crew members who had complained of the new arrangements regarding food, cigarettes, and beer. The most serious allegations were made against the second steward, who had become violent with crew, "pushing men about with his hands, cursing them and almost causing a physical fight." This same second steward demanded that the crew wash his car during working hours, and when the men refused he threatened to blacklist them from further employment.[36]

In the weeks leading up to the strike, Sidi Khayam was busy trying to oust the executive officers from the union, and organized a no-confidence vote at a delegates conference. In the midst of this turmoil, he met with the *Apapa* crew and heard their grievances, but he actually discouraged a walkout and persuaded them to sail again with the *Apapa* on 2 June for Liverpool.[37] The *Apapa* arrived in Liverpool on 15 June. On 17 June the Nigerian crew, represented by a local African resident of Liverpool rather than the seamen's union, submitted a letter to Malcolm Glasier, director of Elder Dempster, detailing their complaints and demanding the removal of the *Apapa*'s European chief steward, second steward, and chief storekeeper from the ship. Not surprisingly, the company refused this request. Some attempts were made at negotiating with the crew, but when the demand for removing the European bosses from the ship was refused, seventy-five members of the African crew walked off the ship on Wednesday, 24 June. They went from the docks to the Stanley House in Liverpool.

It was also reported on this day that a "shore-African" named Mr. Ogun went to the docks to collect men from five other ships to join the striking *Apapa* crew at the Stanley House. A meeting was called that night of all the African crews in port, hosted by a few local African residents of Liverpool, and with Ogun acting as chairman. Unable to force the crew back to work, Elder Dempster decided on Thursday, 25 June, that the *Apapa* would sail without her African crew. On Sunday, 28 June, the *Apapa* crew was repatriated to Nigeria via airplane, and the rest of the striking crews returned to their ships. The arrival of the *Apapa* crew in Lagos was followed by a mass protest along the marina in Lagos. Protesters included the returning *Apapa* crew as well as all Nigerian crews located in port, officers of the union, and many of the seamen's wives and children. Carrying placards calling for an end to discrimination and the payment of overtime, this group marched to the prime minister's house and demanded a meeting. Prime Minister Tafawa Balewa went out to the street to hear their grievances, and then invited a delegation of representatives, including Sidi Khayam, in for a meeting. In the aftermath, it was agreed that a committee of inquiry would be formed to investigate the seamen's grievances.

This strike that began in Liverpool was initiated by the seamen, but there were clearly influences from local Liverpool residents, including members of the Socialist Labour League, with both local British and African members in contact with ships' crews and representing their interests to Elder Dempster.[38] Elder Dempster's general manager, Glasier, later claimed that the local figures who had incited the unrest, including Mr. Ogun, Mr. Akinsaya, and Mr. Osa, were members of the Communist Party. As he wrote, "We have had information and knowledge that the matter has been fostered and followed up by a group of people in Liverpool and London whose activities I personally greatly deplore."[39] The role of diaspora Africans and British Communists in the inspiration, organization, leadership, and carrying-out of the MV *Apapa* strike is highly significant, particularly when compared to the inaction of the Nigerian seamen's union's leadership. Liverpool-based Africans, including Mr. Akinsanya, began meeting with representatives of Elder Dempster to complain about working conditions on board the *Apapa* one month before the strike. Two days before the strike, an anonymous telegram was sent from Liverpool to Elder Dempster Lines, warning of the impending walkout. When the strike broke out, it was members of the National Union of Nigeria in Liverpool that organized crew protests and rallied seamen from other ships to join in the walkout. As soon as the strike broke out, they also sent a written protest to the company, calling themselves the "African Defense Association." The letter declared that their group was made up of the "African Intelligentsia and Literary Detectives of this city" for the purpose of "protecting the socio-economic interests of our Nigerian Seafaring brothers" and was symbolically signed "Sojourner Truth." The authors drew direct links between the plight of the seamen on the *Apapa* and the situation of blacks in England, as they wrote that the crews "are victims of racial discrimination at sea just as we too experience the taste of colour prejudice in Britain ashore, both at work and at play," and they claimed that racism bred "British national malaise and trauma." In makeup and intent, the organization represented a solidarity bridging Nigerians across the diaspora, and reflected an alliance moving beyond the borders of the mother country: "In defense of Reason and In Honour's Cause, we speak of Africa and golden joys and as Nigerian Ambassadors of Goodwill we remain in friendships' garden always."[40]

Nigerian Seamen in the Aftermath of the Apapa Strike

As far as Elder Dempster was concerned, the strike on board the *Apapa* did not create any immediate disaster. In fact, the news of the ship that sailed without its African crew provided some comic relief for the British press, which recounted harrowing tales of *Apapa* passengers cleaning their own rooms and serving their own food. Elder Dempster contributed to the delegitimizing of the seamen's strike by publishing a press release that ridiculed the impact of the absent African crew on the journey, and applauded the ease with which European crews mastered the tasks normally taken on by African seamen:

> One quartermaster in addition to his normal duties on the 4 to 8 watch, and his helpers, have washed 70,400 knives, forks, spoons, etc. which he can now see in his sleep. It has been reported that he has kept a complete set as a souvenir. . . . The Chief Officer and his many Minions have been seen in the Laundry pressing the Cooks Whites and Aprons, to say nothing of Nappies and other unmentionables. . . . The Chef and his merry men (what a lovely bunch they are) can certainly slide food on to the plate even if on occasion a surreptitious thumb was used.[41]

The passengers themselves apparently approached the whole incident with equal amusement, and were duly pleased to receive "inconvenience compensation" from Elder Dempster at the end of the voyage. This compensation boosted everyone's spirits, as the captain reported, "Many passengers joked about 'house-keeping money' and, from the way they passed direct from Bureau to shop, I can predict an all time high in shop sales."[42]

While the company did not suffer any financial damages, the management of Elder Dempster did explore the possibility of initiating legal proceedings against the crew and local residents of Liverpool who were responsible for inciting crew members to breach their contract of service. The legal advice given to the company was to avoid such measures, and to focus on a swift return to routine sailings. In part, this counsel was based on an awareness of the political climate in the UK, as the solicitor wrote, "It has to be borne in mind that the Magistrates, and also the majority of judges, are desperately anxious at the present time to demonstrate clearly that they have no trace of political or racial bias, and in doing so are liable to lean too far in the opposite direction."[43] Following this counsel, the company dropped plans to prosecute the *Apapa* crew or any residents of Liverpool involved in the incident.

From the Nigerian government's perspective, the lingering threat of discontented seamen in Lagos was of deep concern. Prime Minister Balewa took a personal interest in the situation, as he feared that the incident would spread to other industries and incite broader unrest. He encouraged all the parties involved to find a negotiated settlement.[44] It was decided to appoint a committee of inquiry to investigate the incident and make recommendations to resolve the conflict. According to Fred Cooper, this was a typical response of late colonial regimes wanting to diffuse the impact of strikes: "Commissions of inquiry into major strikes were used to delineate . . . problem areas" and determine the "techniques and resources" that would be used "to set things right." Rather than formulating effective solutions for workers' grievances, these commissions ultimately contributed to the disempowerment of labor movements. Cooper claimed that investigations conducted in the framework of these inquiries and the final reports they produced "became apparatuses of surveillance, shapers of discourse, and definers of spaces for legitimate contestation." In bestowing all authority and judgment in the hands of a commission of inquiry, colonial regimes "were also saying that Africa's forms of knowledge were irrelevant."[45]

The establishment of the Board of Enquiry in the case of the MV *Apapa* set very clear boundaries for the terrain of the conflict, confining what was being discussed and who was being represented. "The Board of the Enquiry into the Trade Dispute between the Elder Dempster Limited Lines and the Nigerian Union of Seamen," as the investigation was called, was headed by two Nigerian conservatives: the industrial relations commissioner, Thompson Edogbeji Salubi; and the secretary general of the Trade Union Congress of Nigeria, L. L. Borha, a declared anticommunist. Also on the board was Alfred McClatchey, the secretary of the Employers Consultative Association.

Publicly, Elder Dempster supported the investigation, while privately the company was kept abreast of the committee's work directly by Chairman Salubi. Officials at Elder Dempster attempted to have the report serve as a firm condemnation of Sidi Khayam and hoped that he would be removed in the aftermath. In an attempt to win favor with the chairman, Elder Dempster officials made inquiries for his son, T. E. A. Salubi Jr., to be accepted to medical school at the University of Liverpool.[46] But despite these efforts of the company, the Board of Enquiry was not willing to make any resounding condemnations of the union's general secretary in their report, which was finally released in 1960. In fact, the report had the opposite effect, with the recommendations actually compelling Elder Dempster to fully recognize Khayam and to cooperate with him in the establishment of formal mechanisms for representing the interests of both the union and management. Khayam was now a full partner in any future negotiations. The union was to be the official channel for representing all seamen, and responsible for recruitment and registration of seamen, as well as for negotiating with management.

Following the publication of the report, Khayam marked his decisive victory by celebrating the *Apapa* crisis, as he reminisced: "It was this incident which led to the inauguration, to the setting up of specific machineries for negotiations and settlement of problems, to the real recognition of the Nigerian Union of Seamen, to more respect of Nigerian Seamen because they had proved they are not cowards but can stand up, protest and demonstrate and assert their views before management. We mustered our families, sons, daughters, wives in the most spectacular demonstration ever held in our country."[47] The Salubi report, then, had the unintended consequence of bestowing in Khayam a sense of proprietorship over the official narrative of the seamen's victory, and enabled him to boldly rewrite the history of his role in it.

Thus, the published report empowered Khayam, and he in turn reminded seamen of his new power: "From now own, we must devote all our energies in working harder, in improving our skill and mastery of the job, in maintaining respect for our superiors and preserving patience until we are on port to report our grievances to the union."[48] Over the course of two and a half weeks in July 1960, Khayam addressed the union four times, calling for seamen to end "tribalism, sluggishness," and he also spoke "on the need for efficiency, discipline, and consistent cooperation with their superiors."[49]

Sidi Khayam in the Aftermath of the Salubi Report

The Salubi report might have solidified Khayam's status as the undisputed spokesman for Nigerian seamen, but for shipping companies, this did not have the disastrous outcome they had feared. Much to the surprise of management, Khayam's improved standing led him to adopt a more conciliatory tone with Elder Dempster. This same outcome has been documented in the history of labor unrest throughout Africa in the era of decolonization. According to Fred Cooper, colonial powers commonly sought to mitigate dissent by establishing new channels for negotiations between union leaders and employers. Once union leaders were granted more power and influence with both management and the colonial regime, they shifted their focus to containing the demands of labor and maintaining order.[50] They moderated their tone, sought ways to cooperate, and ultimately abandoned the radical stances they had previously maintained.

The shift in Sidi Khayam's approach toward management following the Salubi report was immediate. He now sought reconciliation and collaboration with Elder Dempster officials. As he wrote in August 1960, "We can radically remove once and for all our present relationship from the wilderness of mistrust into mutual and common purpose."[51] The radical change in Khayam's attitude did not go unnoticed by management, but not everyone was convinced. One official wrote, "On the few occasions that I have personally met him, Khayam has always been well behaved. I still, however, subscribe to the view that leopards do not usually change their spots. It may well be that Khayam will reform and I am quite ready to give him this opportunity. I will not, however, disguise the fact that doubts still linger."[52] While Khayam did not immediately win their trust, shipping officials did recognize a shift in the general secretary's allegiances, and one Elder Dempster official wrote, "There is a very cordial atmosphere prevailing in our day to day relations with the Nigerian Union of Seamen. Several times in the past few weeks Mr. Khayam and other senior Union officials have been in contact with us on various subjects and a great deal of good sense and goodwill has been shown and without going into great detail there have been occasions when misinformed seamen making unreasonable demands have been sharply cautioned in our presence by the Union."[53]

The new proximity to management required that Khayam and the union give up the rhetoric of racial oppression. In a striking turnaround, he called upon seamen to abandon accusations of racial discrimination. Khayam now explained to union members, "We have a tendency of feeling that everything on the ship is colour bar while using this as pretext for escaping our responsibilities. . . . We must effectively learn more and more that it is not only colour. People cheat and oppress others because they believe in oppression which gives them profits, and whether black or white."[54]

Khayam's new position on race issues could be seen in the *Dan Fodio* incident of 1960, when allegations of racial tensions brought Khayam on board to investigate. Khayam claimed that his responsibilities in investigating the incident required him to be totally impartial: "I realized early that to make a success of the venture, I had to put myself in a dual position, so to speak, hold no brief for any seaman just because he is African."[55] Khayam asserted that the union wanted to avoid a racial discourse: "The Nigerian Union of Seamen is not interested in racial and social differences and is not anxious to promote any such ideas. . . . We admire white crews and black ones alike and consider some white crews very, very disciplined and social people."[56] Khayam's investigation led him to conclude that there was no racial discrimination on the ship, and that the real menace on board was "the pettiness of tribalism." His focus shifted to internal tensions among Nigerian crews, as he wrote: "The trouble right now is not between Africans and Whites, it is between the African and himself."[57]

For the shipping companies, the retreat from racial discourse provided security that conflicts with Nigerian labor would remain within a moderate range of disputes between employers and wage earners. As this was a prerequisite for securing his own position, Sidi Khayam was willing to make this compromise. Sidi Khayam's reconciliation with management was similar to the shift made by an entire sector of the Nigerian political and economic elite as they were slowly integrated into positions of power and influence in the process of decolonization. New avenues for advancement and integration of the educated elite into the power apparatuses of the government and economy resulted in a quick reversal of anticolonial attitudes among this elite. Armed with newly acquired powers, Zachernuk wrote, "the Nigerian leadership assumed a more cordial attitude toward foreign capital and expatriate experts."[58]

"NIGERIANIZATION" AND THE CONSOLIDATION OF POWER

In the aftermath of the *Apapa* strike and the Salubi report, Khayam also took steps to solidify his authority among the seamen themselves. This could be accomplished only by distancing Nigerian seamen from alternative influences within and beyond Nigeria. The Salubi report detailed the role played by diaspora Africans in the *Apapa* strike, and made it clear that Liverpool-based Nigerians offered to the union an alternative source of leadership for seamen. The *Apapa* incident only deepened this connection, and reports following the strike claimed that growing numbers of Nigerian seamen were using the Stanley House as their base in Liverpool.[59] Seeking the unambiguous loyalty of the seamen, Khayam wanted to redirect their focus toward Lagos and away from Liverpool. He began to portray Liverpool activists as bad influences, and worked with Elder Dempster to cut ties between seamen and the Nigerian National Union (NNU) based in Liverpool. According to an Elder Dempster representative in Lagos, Khayam was "repeatedly bothered by destructive advice given to his seamen from people attached to the N.N.U. . . . [He] is quite sure that much of the discontent which shows itself among his men is the direct result of advice from this organization." According to the report, Khayam opposed the efforts of the NNU to establish a "Nigeria House" in Liverpool, claiming that the members of the organization were Communists and would use the building to spread propaganda.[60] In blocking the development of a community center for Nigerians, Khayam was attempting to reduce the potential for Liverpool-based Nigerians to wield their influence with seamen.

Khayam also enlisted the help of the British-based National Union of Seamen in discrediting Liverpool Nigerians and their interventions in seamen's protests. The Salubi report had recommended that a representative of the British seamen's union be stationed in Lagos to advise the Nigerians on trade union organization and to help negotiate relations with management. At first, Khayam strongly opposed any intervention from the NUS, and he refused offers from Sir Thomas Yates of the NUS to mediate between the Nigerian union and Elder Dempster. He claimed that the Nigerian Union of Seamen had to be completely independent.[61] His ulterior motive was to block the influence of the British union on local processes, and he said that the seamen would not agree "to the introduction of someone from outside."[62] Despite Khayam's opposition, the NUS sent officer A. Paxton to Nigeria at the beginning of 1960. Khayam was ambivalent about Paxton's appearance at first, but he quickly warmed to him. As Paxton reported on the week of his arrival, "Khayam said he had kept me under close observation all day Monday and had decided I was a good man and recommended to his Executive that I should be accepted to give all the help I can to carry out Salubi report recommendations."[63] Paxton soon became Khayam's ally, and Khayam enlisted his help in blocking the ongoing influence of Liverpool-based Nigerians among seamen. Paxton reported to Yates in August 1960:

> Khayam has asked me to pass on his thanks for your assistance with telegrams to various ships in Liverpool. He is firmly convinced that the cable he received from crews of ships named was not the work of his own men. He reckons that words used in the cable would not be understood by African seamen and while the men may have knowledge of it he is sure that it was worded and inspired by somebody ashore in Liverpool. He also says that this is not the first time that elements ashore have tried to influence his members to take action against their own interests. . . . Khayam intends to visit the various ships concerned on their arrival at Lagos and advise his members not to be influenced by anybody abroad unless on the advice of his Executive.[64]

Khayam also sought to eliminate opposition within the seamen's union. He was particularly sensitive to the potential for Kru seamen based in Lagos to challenge his authority. Kru seamen were known to oppose organizing efforts of the Nigerian union, and they regularly broke ranks during strikes and onboard protests. Thus, following the publishing of the Salubi report, Khayam demanded that all Freetown ratings be removed from the Lagos registry. According to one Kru steward on the MV *Sekondi*, Khayam was angered by Freetown ratings who did not submit to his authority or join in protests called by the union. In a letter to Elder Dempster, the Kru seaman claimed that Khayam was attempting to run Sierra Leoneans out of Lagos, saying: "You Freetown people always make trouble for us Nigerian men who want to strike. He then asked me for me Union card stating that I would not get any more jobs off Elder Dempster ships unless I should go back to Freetown."[65] Starting in early October 1959, as the result of pressure from the Union, Freetown ratings were gradually removed from Lagos articles.[66]

The process of decolonization enabled these kinds of maneuvers, as Khayam drew upon nationalist rhetoric to consolidate his power. Under the banner of "Nigerianization," the union leadership was able to consolidate its power both vis-à-vis management and over the rank-and file membership. As soon as nationalism became the main trope around which Nigerians were organizing, it was easier for Khayam to sideline competing solidarities. The discourse of "Nigerianization" provided a justification for a turn inward, and a hardening of ideologies and identities around new political borders.

THE NIGERIAN UNION OF SEAMEN
IN THE POSTCOLONIAL ERA

As Sidi Khayam moved closer to the colonial power elite in the aftermath of the Salubi report, his autonomy, and that of the seamen's union, was compromised in the process. Khayam was not alone in this outcome, and trade union leaders across Africa experienced a similar loss of power as a result of political maneuvering in the era of decolonization. As Björn Beckman, Sakhela Buhlungu, and Lloyd Sachikonye have argued, trade union leaders who allowed themselves to be co-opted into positions of power ultimately lost the capacity to pursue an autonomous agenda.[67]

The transition to independence further weakened the seamen's union as an instrument of labor agitation and organizing in part because the Nigerian government adopted similar strategies to those of the British for dealing with the potential threat of labor unrest. According to Peter Waterman, trade unions in postcolonial Nigeria were regularly undermined and weakened by a process similar to the one seen in the aftermath of the *Apapa* strike. In times of unrest, union leaders were co-opted by the government, and awarded recognition, power, and influence in exchange for abandoning more radical stances. The effect was to prevent, undermine, or domesticate trade unionism: "Trade union leaders who were willing to ally themselves with one or another of the major parties were favoured with posts on government boards, parliamentary seats and memberships of delegations abroad."[68] Waterman claimed that these tactics served to moderate and tame the radical tendencies among union leaders.

Although Nigerian trade unions in the postcolonial era could count to their credit some effective initiatives, such as the General Strike of 1964, organized labor made very few actual gains for working classes following independence. As many scholars have noted, infighting within unions, caused largely by ethnic competition and struggles for limited resources, handicapped unions as effective advocates for labor.[69] Trade unions were also neutralized by state interventions aimed at keeping labor movements in check, and limiting industrial action and political resistance.[70] Thus, in 1968, under the pretext of the state of emergency necessitated by the civil war, unions were barred from initiating strikes. After the war, the ban was only partially lifted, with workers in several key industries prohibited from striking. In 1976, the state forced the dismissal of leading trade unionists such as Michael Imoudu and Wahab Goodluck from their leadership positions in their respective unions. Finally, the military government of 1978 dissolved all labor federations and existing trade unions, banned key leaders from holding office, outlawed affiliation to international labor centers, and instituted a new unitary national union structure, known as the Nigerian Labour Congress.[71] All of these offensives were debilitating for trade unions in postcolonial Nigeria, already engulfed in factionalism.

Ultimately, rank-and-file labor paid the price for the weakening of the Nigerian seamen's union in the transition to independence. The Nigerian seamen who had been accustomed to relying on a broad range of ideological and geographical solidarities across the black diaspora now faced a process of Nigerianization that limited opportunities for garnering support or inspiration from outside Nigeria. Many blamed Khayam for their weakened position in the postcolonial era, claiming that he had abandoned the seamen and manipulated his new position of power for his personal benefit alone.

Despite the broad-based support that Khayam had during his first two years as general secretary, following independence, seamen accused him of becoming corrupt like the officers who preceded him.[72] A report from an official of the Palm Line in 1963 claimed that Khayam was having a tough time with union members, and he could not account for union funds. Animosity against Khayam was so great that he reportedly had to flee from a union meeting.[73] Disappointment with Khayam was described by one seaman: "Our rights that we were supposed to get from both the Management of Elder Dempster Line and the Federal Government were not given to us, so, he failed in his promise." According to this seaman, Khayam put more effort into his own political career: "He was busy with other trade union activities because these people also wanted him and he abandoned us without fulfilling his promise to us."[74] Others were far more critical of Khayam, as can be seen in the following interview with a former seaman:

> R: A useless man . . . He was one of those people who stole Nigerians' money. . . . Khayam collected money from seamen's union and did not deliver as he was delegated to do. . . . All the benefits and percentage seamen's union were supposed to get, he collected all of them, everything.
>
> Q: Do you mean that seamen didn't like him?
>
> R: Never, how would they like him, a thief? Nobody likes a rogue! Someone steals from me and you expect me to like him? Some did like him because they were given part of the stolen money but as for me, I was always mad at them for stealing. You had to pay to the union. . . . This man, Khayam, we paid dues to him from our stipend. We didn't have a house of our own—no chair, no car of our own. He is a bloody rogue. For so many years, the union never had any property or office where it could operate from and we all paid our compulsory dues to him. These are people who spoilt Nigeria. Some goods like a freezer, a fridge, a bed, that he cannot ordinarily afford to buy, all he owned and yet he never did anything to develop the union. What! We placed [him] in position of authority and [he] didn't do anything![75]

For Nigerian seamen, the political and ideological currents favoring the strengthening of the union served to disempower them in their ship-based protests, and the union's insistence that crews rely solely on a "Nigerian" leadership rather than a fluid set of tools based in a multitude of locations represented a profound silencing. The imposition of Nigerianization severed the historic racial and class links that seamen had forged between themselves and others beyond the borders of Nigeria. The *Apapa* strike, and hundreds of incidents leading up to this action, grew out of a belief among African seamen that they could achieve the vision of justice they constructed for themselves. Their struggles were not limited to concerns over pay scales and clothing allowances, but expressed deeper and more fundamental wishes for color-blind camaraderie of men, perhaps similar to that enjoyed by black seamen in the Age of Sail. Crews fought discrimination through transnational alliances, and their sense of empowerment led to creative and forceful initiatives such as walkouts and demands for firing of their European bosses. The Salubi inquiry was a typical and effective tactic of the colonial regime and local Westernized elites to eliminate the radical and destabilizing creative force of African laborers that was so clearly evident in the *Apapa* strike.

In the era following the publication of the Salubi report, seamen continued to suffer racial oppression, but they also internalized the fact that they could no longer protest for themselves. This can be seen in the following letter from the crew of the MV *Apapa* at port in Liverpool in 1961:

> To our greatest surprise, when we arrive at Las Palmas this trip . . . the stewards who feel to buy drinks collect their money and give it to one man. The cleaners do likewise. On those men returning the ship, the captain was on the gangway himself and started to dump these drinks in the water before the passengers who were looking [at] the view of the town. Despite all the pleas by the head cleaner, he dump everything, including only one that Ibeji hold for himself. . . . Despite all the explanations to the captain, the drinks were dumped. The attitude so provoked our minds. Because none of that of the [white] sailors were dumped so we [took] it for another discrimination so an emergency general meeting was called and it last 20 minutes. We took a decision the two head men were delegated to the captain that we the entire crew want our drinks or he pay for them. . . . The captain promised to pay for the drinks. The headmen told him . . . that he cannot take it upon himself to accept the money for the whole crew . . . before we sail way on the Thurdsay [*sic*] the 20th we do not take any step either, we are just putting it to your knowledge at the same time we would like to know from you whether to receive the money from him or not. Reply not needed until our arrival.[76]

The seamen's letter is testimony to the entrenchment of the union's authority in the postcolonial era, and the recognition among seamen that they could no longer act for themselves. We have seen that Nigerian seamen successfully exploited opportunities arising within the context of colonialism to participate in globalized economies and cultures, exposing them to new solidarities and empowering them to seek an improvement in their lives. At the same time, political, economic, and ideological actions taken by union leaders in the era of decolonization sought to secure lasting power and influence for themselves through the manipulation of political institutions, and this occurred continually at the expense of seamen's autonomy. Thus, while able to engage with the globalized world, African seamen were prevented in the transition from colonialism to independence to secure for themselves positions of power and autonomy as an effective labor movement in the postcolonial context. As will be seen, the era of independence brought with it new contradictory and ambiguous experiences for Nigerian seamen.

4 ∽ The Birth of the Nigerian National Shipping Line

WHILE SEAMEN WERE AGITATING for better working conditions and an end to discrimination onboard Elder Dempster ships in 1959, the political elite of Nigeria were taking steps to strengthen Nigeria's position in the international system by creating a national shipping line. The establishment of a national line in 1959 was promoted as a vital step in Nigerians' march toward political and economic independence, and the clamoring for an indigenous shipping company was steeped in nationalist discourse and ideology. The vocal struggle of politicians calling for Nigerians to break free from the hold of colonial economic exploitation and to take control over their own national destiny through the establishment of a national line quite probably played a role in emboldening seamen in their struggle for rights on colonial vessels. For political and commercial elites, the Nigerian National Shipping Line (NNSL) aroused nationalist anticipation and optimism about the meaning of independence. As Okechukwu Iheduru described it, the historical struggle of developing nations over international shipping rights and ownership is one clear example of the ceaseless struggle between the haves and have-nots, and the efforts of the weak to change the international system in their favor.[1]

But beneath the surface of the nationalist rhetoric and aspirations, a far more complex reality emerges regarding the founding of the Nigerian National Shipping Line. The federal government of Nigeria lacked the capital to fund the shipping line, as well as the organizational and technical knowledge to establish and run the venture. The creation of a national shipping line in Nigeria could not have been accomplished without massive foreign backing in the form of capital investments, managerial expertise, and technical support. Moreover, the structural and financial disadvantages facing this indigenous line in the international shipping industry meant that the venture was doomed to fail in its goal of wresting control of Nigeria's economic destiny from the power of a disadvantageous international shipping regime. The Nigerian line could not operate outside the West African Lines Conference, and it was forced to join the very shipping cartel whose exploitative rates had inspired its establishment. Thus, it will be seen that what began as a strong expression of economic nationalism was soon revealed as a complex arrangement that only deepened Nigeria's dependence upon foreign capital and expertise.

The NNSL never evolved into a source of economic autonomy or a symbol of national pride, and the Nigerian national line ultimately represented a failed effort at economic empowerment and development in Nigeria. Scholars have debated whether or not indigenous shipping ventures established in the era of decolonization in Africa could have ever overcome the enormous asymmetries of the international system in order to succeed. Nigeria faced insurmountable disadvantages with regard to technological know-how and resources, and a weak position as a late-industrialized nation within the broader world economy. Against this backdrop, Iheduru has suggested that economic nationalism was a destructive force in the history of shipping in the postcolonial era. He argued that rather than attempting to go it alone, Nigeria should have pooled resources into a collective effort in the maritime sector with other West African countries.[2]

But while regional cooperation might have been the economically sound approach to take in West Africa, the political forces that led to the establishment of the Nigerian National Shipping Line were not primarily motivated by commercial success, or a firm commitment to the economic development of Nigeria. The NNSL was established first and foremost as a political project of the nationalist elite in the era of decolonization, and until its demise in the 1990s, it was continually exploited as a political tool of ruling classes rather than an economic enterprise. Thus, the history of the company cannot be divorced from the shifts, turns, and detours of the political developments dominating the day. The broader political context is reflected in every stage of the NNSL's development and decline, and the history of the national line therefore provides a window into the turbulent history of postcolonial Nigeria. The ruling elites of each era extracted the resources of the NNSL as they attempted to consolidate a base of support and reap the personal benefits of power. According to Iheduru, "State holders used their access to the state's economic prerogatives to create a subservient and dependent indigenous maritime class, and to enrich themselves or members of their own class or ethnic group."[3]

This chapter will examine the historical processes involved in the establishment of the Nigerian National Shipping Line, including the economic and political motives for its establishment, the terms by which the enterprise was launched, organized, and financed, and the relationship between the NNSL, British shipping lines, and international shipping conferences. We will review the management and development strategies in the first years of NNSL operation until the buyout of the British partners in 1961. It will be seen that the Nigerian line faced immense obstacles to success in a globalized shipping industry that favored former colonial shipping giants. The history of the NNSL raises questions about the significance and possibility of realizing an agenda of economic nationalism in a globalized industry such as shipping. What is the meaning of a "nationalist" venture that was made possible only through the investment of foreign capital and technical backing? It will be seen as well that the organization of the international shipping industry into shipping conferences also severely limited the autonomy of the Nigeria line, as the NNSL could operate only as a junior member of the West African Lines Conference that was dominated by former colonial firms. In broader terms, Nigeria's foray into shipping is a striking testimony to the complex relationship of dependency between postcolonial economies and the international system and the impossibility of economic autonomy for postcolonial Nigeria.

But while the NNSL was a doomed project of economic nationalism, this was not only because of the shipping line's weak position in the international system. Local political complexities in Nigeria played a significant role in shaping this history, and the regional competition, political volatility, and insufficient resources for development that had plagued Nigerian politics from independence also created immense obstacles to success for the NNSL. The fractures and weaknesses that characterized the broader political system of the postcolonial era were reflected in the establishment, development, and ultimate demise of the national line. From the very birth of the national shipping venture in Nigeria, the process of decision making, the allocation of resources, and the appointment of management all reflected a dangerous blurring of lines between economic and political interests. The Nigerian National Shipping Line provided politicians with a platform for promoting a political agenda, and political priorities often came at the expense of economically sound commercial practices. Public criticism of the founding of the NNSL, and the government response to it, foreshadowed the calamitous outcome of the mixing of political and commercial interests in postcolonial Nigeria.

The history of the NNSL is a window into broader processes that aroused popular criticism and disillusionment with ruling elites who failed to deliver on the promises of nationalism in the postcolonial era. It will be seen that public discontent fermented precisely in the gaps that emerged between nationalist rhetoric and the actual functioning of a commercial enterprise that was inextricable from a complex and unequal global economy. From its establishment, outspoken critics within and outside the government condemned the terms under which the company was created, and cast doubt on the potential for the national line to truly embody an agenda of economic autonomy. The heated debates surrounding the founding of the Nigerian National Shipping Line foreshadowed a deep sense of disappointment that civil society experienced following the unfilled promises of the nationalist elite. This review will provide important background to examine the ways in which the seamen experienced and interpreted the establishment and operation of the NNSL.

NATIONALISM AND REGIONALISM AMONG THE POLITICAL ELITE

The birth of the Nigerian National Shipping Line must be understood within the complex historical context of nationalist agitation that gained momentum in Nigeria in the postwar era. Following World War II, British colonial officials and the Nigerian political elite undertook the difficult and contested process of negotiations toward a self-governing Nigeria. While political leaders from across Nigeria engaged in determined efforts to establish Nigeria as an independent and unified nation-state, the negotiations between the British and the local leadership ultimately exposed the deep cleavages that existed between the multitude of regional and ethnic constituencies in Nigeria. There was a lack of consensus among the political leadership from across Nigeria regarding the administrative structures that would replace the colonial administration, particularly with regard to the balance of power between the central legislature and regional governments. The process revealed the absence of a strong Pan-Nigerian consciousness, even among the nationalist leaders themselves, as seen in the oft-cited remark of Obafemi Awolowo of the Western Region: "Nigeria is not a nation. It is a mere geographic expression." Awolowo was not the only skeptic, as

Tafawa Balewa of the northern legislature remarked in 1947: "Nigeria has existed as one country only on paper."[4] Divisions only grew over time, and the move toward national unity actually strengthened ethnic and regional affiliations throughout the 1950s. As Toyin Falola and Matthew Heaton wrote, "Nearly everyone recognized that, geographically, politically, economically, and culturally, Nigeria was an extremely diverse place, and a single unitary government was unlikely to please very many people for very long."[5] Over the course of deliberations and ongoing amendments to proposed constitutions, pressure mounted to maintain regional sovereignty. As Rotimi Suberu described this period, "Nigeria's leaders increasingly and persistently emphasized the need to grant the fullest autonomy to the country's component groups or regions."[6]

The federal structure that emerged in the final stages of colonial rule was thus the product of a long struggle between regional and federal interests. The Lyttelton Constitution of 1954 established a fragile balance of power between the federal government and three regional governments in the North, East, and West. The central administration had its own legislature, with half of the representatives from the Northern Region, and the other half divided between the Eastern and the Western Regions. Regional governments had their own legislatures as well, and each was controlled by a political party largely aligned with the dominant ethnic group of the region. Thus, the Northern Region was led by the Hausa-Fulani party, the Northern People's Congress (NPC); the Western Region was dominated by the Yoruba-led Action Group; and in the Eastern Region, the National Council of Nigeria and the Cameroons (NCNC) was generally associated with the Igbo. This division of power between the central administration and the three regions remained largely in place when Nigeria gained independence in 1960. The federal government had exclusive control over external affairs, defense, currency, mines, and minerals, and also the major forms of communication and transportation. The three regions maintained control over socioeconomic programs of health and education, as well as agriculture. Marketing boards, established in the colonial era to set prices and collect revenues from agricultural production in each region, also remained under the control of regional governments. Through the marketing boards, the regions maintained an immense degree of financial autonomy and significant control over resources. According to Akanmu Adebayo, the central administration entered independence in a weakened position, as the three regional governments together were more powerful than the federal government.[7]

The historic struggle between regional and national interests leading up to independence in Nigeria has been condemned by subsequent generations of scholars as the basis for ethnic competition, political instability, and corruption that have plagued Nigeria in the postcolonial era. Referring to the first decade of independence, Peter Ekeh wrote, "It is the sad history of a nation in which exaggerated loyalty to communities, ethnic groups, regions and religions overweighed the tenuous loyalties to state and in which the battle was for the control of state structures in the understanding that those who won such control would use state resources for the exclusive benefits of their primordial groupings."[8] Many scholars have claimed that elite interests have been at the root of these destructive ethnic tensions. It has been argued that the rise in regionalism and ethnic chauvinism in the era of decolonization was the result of the cynical manipulation of ethnic solidarities by elites seeking to protect their own material base. Thus, Rotimi Suberu argued, in the push for regional autonomy, the elite classes attempted to safeguard local resources from national distribution. Particularly for the political elites of the groundnut-producing North and the cocoa-rich West, federalism was seen as an instrument for protecting regional power and resources rather than a means for enabling national integration.[9] Okwudiba Nnoli has also charged that regionalism in the era of nationalist organizing was flamed by elite classes who used political machinery to amass wealth and privileges. As he argued, elites "used emotive ethnic symbols and played on negative feelings arising from alleged ethnic conflicts of interest as a means of mobilizing mass support for their own personal and class interests."[10] Some scholars have even accused the nationalist leadership of being primarily motivated by their economic grievances as an elite class, and charged that political agitation was merely the demand for "moderate constitutional demands as a means of finding a solution for the economic plight of the African merchant, producer and businessman."[11]

This political context provides essential background for understanding why nationalist projects, such as the Nigerian National Shipping Line, were ill-fated from their establishment. In a context where nation-building was fundamentally compromised and weakened by parochial interests, so, too, would the projects established in the spirit of nationalism suffer from a lack of real commitment. As elite classes continually exploited political power for their personal benefit and to the benefit of their constituencies, even those projects undertaken under the banner of nationalism have been fundamentally shaped by sectorialism. As Falola and Heaton wrote, "Efforts were made to promote a strong central state and a state-run economy that focused on development initiatives across Nigeria. All these efforts were meant to bring Nigerians closer together politically, economically and culturally, to promote commonalities and to downplay differences. Ultimately, however, these efforts failed, largely because of the overwhelming trend in the political sphere towards consolidating power at the regional level at any cost."[12]

While political competition and elite rivalries created immense challenges to nationalist projects in Nigeria, there were equally significant economic structures that prevented Nigeria from achieving economic independence in the postcolonial era. Decolonization signified the end to former British rule, but it will be seen that the march toward economic autonomy was far more complex and incomplete long after the departure of British colonial administrators. Despite the fact that economic independence was a critical element of the nationalist agenda in all regions, the transfer of economic power from foreigners to Nigerians was protracted and piecemeal far after the establishment of political independence.

Expressions of economic nationalism were seen in colonial Nigeria from the 1930s, as the business elite, particularly in southern Nigeria, began to make vocal demands for more participation of local interests in industry and trade. A significant growth in this trend could be seen in the postwar era, when there was a rise in the number of initiatives, described by Axel Harneit-Sievers as "politically-motivated trading enterprises" that were aimed at "self-reliance."[13] As Nigerian businessmen, traders, and politicians launched ventures in banking, commerce, industry, and agriculture aimed at economic and political empowerment and autonomy, they promoted a strong nationalist ideology as the rationale for their efforts. The spirit of these ventures is captured in the founding document of the National Bank of Nigeria, established in 1933: "No people can be respected or regarded as a nation unless it has its own national institutions, and the greatest of all national institutions is the financial institution in the form of a bank."[14] Economic nationalism had growing momentum in the 1950s, and politicians in the nationalist movement, particularly in the Western Region, developed elaborate economic agendas that reflected demands for more local control over economic growth and development. Obafemi Awolowo stated in the House of Representatives in 1952, "Nigeria's industrial progress should not be achieved by issuing invitations to foreigners to come in a large number into this country to exploit its resources but by allowing Africans to embark upon the industrialization of their country."[15] As local commercial interests in Nigeria sought a larger role for themselves in the local economy, the accelerating struggle against foreign capital and dominance led many to take up leading positions in the political struggles for independence.[16] Thus, as Robert Tignor has argued, in the final years of colonial rule, the lines between economic and political interests blurred, and Nigeria's major indigenous business groups became deeply embroiled in the political fray.[17]

But for the political and economic elite of Nigeria, the achievement of political independence was far more tangible than economic independence. The process of decolonization did not lead to the severing of ties between the local economy and British economic interests, and some critics have in fact argued that the power and influence of foreign investors has only grown over time. In the process of decolonization, Nigerians did succeed in expanding into areas that had been traditionally controlled by expatriate firms. But in doing so, they often had to rely on the capital or expertise of foreign firms, and these circumstances ultimately reaffirmed the influence of expatriates within the local economy. Foreign firms cemented their post-colonial involvement by drawing Nigerians into their companies, forming joint ventures with local actors, and by focusing on niches that were relatively safeguarded from nationalist attacks.[18] This is not to suggest that there were no significant improvements in the economic autonomy of Nigerian business interests in the process of decolonization. Indeed, according to Harneit-Sievers, several developments in the final years of colonial rule reflected a significant bolstering of African commercial and business sectors in Nigeria. These included the creation of the Department of Commerce and Industries, which was aimed at promoting development projects and maximizing the participation of Nigerians in them, and the gradual take-over of marketing boards by African producers. But European firms also maneuvered and adapted their business organizations and strategies to the approaching end of colonialism. Efforts were made to establish closer ties with African business elites, and cooperation became more widespread and entrenched. Thus, Harneit-Sievers argued, nationalist agitation of the postwar years ultimately gave way to a preference for cooperation between African and European business elites that carried over into independence.[19]

Economic nationalism that shaped postwar ideologies and political agendas did not successfully mobilize a Nigerian takeover of the economy, and many have argued that the outcome of decolonization was quite the opposite. Some have blamed the ruling elite for their complacency. It has been argued that the nationalist elite perpetuated colonial economic policies that preferred state-owned monopolies of industry, and discouraged the development of a strong indigenous entrepreneurial class.[20] Decolonization did little to break the hold of foreign economic interests over major sectors. As Björn Beckman has charged, "Nationalists have been co-opted by imperialism. They 'inherited' the colonial state, a state imposed by imperialism for its own purposes. The nature of the state itself therefore did not change fundamentally. The nationalists never really challenged the pervasive domination of the economy by imperialism. They were placed in a position where they were left to administer the state on behalf of foreign capital."[21] Similarly, Olasupo Ojedokun claimed that in the first years of independence, Nigeria's economic policy "oscillated between a benevolent acceptance and a selective rejection of the pattern of economic relations inherited at independence," and left intact the "Lagos-London economic axis."[22]

The ideal of self-reliance remained apparent in political discourse throughout the first decades of independence, and it was translated into periodic calls on the part of the government to "Nigerianize" the business sector. But while "indigenization" was trumpeted as the key to economic autonomy and national pride, the government failed to translate the pursuit of self-reliance into effective measures.[23] Nigerianization was limited to a cosmetic changeover from foreign to Nigerian hands in management positions of some industries and firms, but foreign interests still continued to dominate many sectors of the economy.[24] According to Adejugbe, the weakness of the economy in the 1960s made it impossible to forgo foreign investment, as seen in the National Development Plan for 1962–1968, which relied on foreign loans.[25] Others have seen the problem as a lack of commitment on the part of the government that remained largely procapitalist, and as Nwoke has charged, the Nigerian government was not orientated toward "doing serious battle with international capitalism."[26] Thus, Adejugbe claimed, the Nigerian political leadership in the early 1960s faced a dilemma: "Political leaders of an inherently capitalist outlook find that only through government can a private enterprise be created: the nationalism leads them to support ousting of foreign private enterprise while economic reality compels them to welcome expatriate capitalists."[27]

In the final reckoning, the process of Nigerianization in the early years of independence was of limited impact on the balance of power between Nigerian and expatriate economic interests. As Akinsanya wrote, indigenization "did not achieve much in terms of actually placing the control of the economy in Nigerian hands because majority equity participation by Nigerians does not necessarily imply or suggest actual control of an indigenized business enterprise. . . . [Expatriate staff] deal with critical and key issues of finance, management and production."[28] The frustration can be heard in Akinsanya's pronouncement: "It is an unpardonable naivety to assert that Nigerians are in full control or will ever be, of their economy."[29] In his view, the vast majority of Nigerians did not reap the benefits of indigenization. Rather, the policy further concentrated wealth in the hands of a very few, and widened the gaps and inequalities between the rich and the poor in Nigeria.[30]

THE NATIONALIST SHIPPING VENTURE IN NIGERIA

The creation of the Nigerian National Shipping Line must be situated in this broader history of political and economic nationalism in the era of de-colonization. Calls to establish the National Shipping Line were steeped in rhetoric espousing self-reliance, economic autonomy, and indigenization. In the final decade of colonial rule, some politicians targeted the colonial shipping industry as a persistent symbol of the economic injustices of the colonial era, and argued that independence could not be achieved without a national shipping line. Representatives from the Western Region were par-ticularly strong advocates of this position. Chief T. T. Solaru declared in a debate in the Nigerian House of Representatives in 1957, "We are tired of these shipping rings, . . . we do not want shipping lines to go on dictating us how much we have to pay in order to carry our goods."[31] In another debate in 1958, one representative warned that the ongoing dependence on foreign shipping spelled "nothing but sheer national ruin and economic suicide," and protested, "Are we emerging from political colonialism only to step into economic serfdom?"[32] This animosity toward colonial shipping lines was not uniquely Nigerian, and according to Iheduru, efforts to "Africanize" the shipping industry throughout the continent were part of larger programs of economic nationalism: "Just as the establishment of national armies, na-tional airlines, embassies, etc. were viewed as part of the trappings of mod-ern statehood in the 1950s and 1960s, the establishment of token national shipping lines was believed to add to the prestige and symbolic capability of the newly independent countries."[33] Ayodeji Olukoju has argued that rival-ries and competition for prestige between African colonies and postcolonies also played a role in the clamoring for national lines, as the launching of the Black Star Line in Ghana in 1957 added to the Nigerian sense of urgency in establishing the Nigerian National Shipping Line.[34]

But behind the slogans for economic independence and national pres-tige, a far more complicated picture emerges around the founding of the NNSL. From the very start, it was clear that a Nigerian shipping venture would not be purely Nigerian, and its establishment and running would re-quire cooperation with foreign capital and expertise. The question of which foreign entities would be involved was a highly contested and charged issue. The idea of forming a national shipping line was discussed in meet-ings of the National Economic Council (NEC) in 1956, and the council recommended that the federal government investigate the viability of such a venture. In January 1957, the council reviewed the federal government's memorandum, presented by the minister of transport, Amanze Njoku. The minister's report had concluded that Nigeria was not in a position to establish a shipping line. His initial inquiries revealed that the capital required would be at least £4.5 million—an astronomical sum for the government to expend, and a cost that had not been allocated in the current budget. The minister admitted that the preliminary investigation had been conducted with the aid of foreign shipping companies' expert knowledge, and to his admission, "these companies could hardly be expected to give assistance in establishing an organization which would compete with them."[35] Nonetheless, under these circumstances, it was concluded that there would be little point in proceeding to a more in-depth investigation, and Njoku suggested that the venture be held in abeyance until six months before the start of the next development program.

The Western Region representatives of the council were disappointed with these findings, and suggested that the government verify the possibility of establishing a joint overseas line with other West African governments. They also recommended approaching the International Bank for funding. The minister countered that there was little point in approaching other governments when Nigeria itself did not have the funds required, and the International Bank had already made it clear that it would not invest in the project. Moreover, he claimed that neither the Gambia nor Sierra Leone had the resources to fund such a venture, and the Gold Coast was shunning regional cooperation in general. But while the minister hoped to table the discussion for a later date, the council members from the Western Region prevailed. It was decided that the minister would send a semiofficial inquiry to the other West African governments to verify their interest in a joint overseas shipping line.[36] These inquiries did not turn up anything of significance, and in the following meeting of the NEC in October 1957, the Western Region once again expressed dissatisfaction with the government's position, and promised to raise the issue again.[37]

The pressure to establish a shipping line was undoubtedly influenced by the launching of Ghana's Black Star shipping line in 1957. Ghana's national line was a joint venture with the Zim shipping line of Israel, which provided 40 percent of the capital investment and undertook the management of the line and the training of Ghanaian officers and seamen. British colonial officials recognized that the establishment of the Ghanaian line might spur Nigerian efforts to establish their own line, as one official wrote in August 1958: "Since Ghana has established its own shipping line, Nigeria will feel impelled by motives of prestige or rivalry to establish one also (if possible bigger and better!)."[38] Recognizing that these African ventures would create competition for British shipping lines, this official recommended sending the Nigerians an official communication "pointing out objectively the actual disadvantages of such a proposal."[39] Colonial fears were not unfounded, as the Nigerians were undoubtedly motivated by the Ghanaian-Israeli partnership, and political pressure on the federal government in Nigeria increased with the launching of the Black Star Line. In September 1957, a resolution of the House of Representatives called for the federal government to make provisions for a national shipping line in the next five-year plan. Throughout 1958, popular discontent with the monopoly of European shipping companies mounted, and the issue of high freight rates was raised in the House of Representatives and the press, particularly around the rates for shipping timber. The National Economic Council in 1958 requested that the government conduct an investigation into freight rates set by the West African Lines Conference (WALCON) in comparison with other parts of the world. Notes from an August 1958 meeting of the council claimed, "There is unquestionably a very widespread feeling that West African Shipping Conference has established a monopoly or near-monopoly position which places the Nigerian economy largely at its mercy."[40] Both the Western and the Eastern Regions wanted renewed pressure on the government regarding a national shipping line. The Western Region wanted the federal government to establish an agreement with the Israeli line, Zim, similarly to Ghana. The Eastern Region was more militant, demanding that the federal government not conduct negotiations with any existing member of the conference. The government response to this was adamant: no potential partners would be rejected outright, and negotiations in the preliminary stage would be conducted with as many different interests as possible. The minister explained that technical experience and knowledge were of utmost importance in developing a shipping industry, and the federal government would not exclude the members of the West African Lines Conference from these negotiations. In fact, Minister Njoku revealed, proposals from Elder Dempster and Palm Lines had already been received and were under review."[41]

It seems that Elder Dempster and Palm Lines were also nervous about the Israeli incursion into West African shipping, and had hastily approached the Nigerians with a proposal for establishing the national line several months before. In a January 1958 letter to other members of the West African Lines Conference, the British shipping giants explained their motivation for initiating a partnership with the Nigerians:

In the last few days we have received information that made Elder Dempster and Palm Line think that an urgent move should be made with regard to a Nigerian Shipping Company, with a view to trying to ensure that no fresh Line is brought into the West African Trade. We have reason to think that some newcomer is about to approach the Nigerian Government, and, as we would naturally prefer that any Nigerian entry to Trade is accomplished with our assistance and participation rather than that of a newcomer, we have come to the conclusion it is urgently necessary for us to make a proposal of our own to the Nigerian Government. . . . After hurried but serious consideration between ourselves, Palm and Elder have decided to make a joint approach to the Nigerian Government that a new company should be formed in Nigeria with Nigerian Government and Palm and Elder participation, in a manner that we hope will prove attractive to the Nigerians and ensure stability in the Trade, and also ensure the minimum damage to the existing Line's interests. . . . We discarded the idea of a consortium of all Lines because such an approach might be thought to be an attempt by the Conference to get a grip on Nigeria's own shipping rather than a genuine offer of help.[42]

The letter makes it clear that the interest of Elder Dempster in the Nigerian national line was far from altruistic, and was aimed at blocking the Israelis and other parties from encroaching on their monopoly. Elder Dempster was highly aware of the negative image the company had in West Africa, and speculated that the inclusion of the Palm Line in the venture would be more palatable to the Nigerians: "We thought a partnership of Elder Dempster and Palm would be likely to be more acceptable than Elder Dempster alone, who were sometimes accused of being too big a single party."[43]

Negotiations with Elder Dempster took place over the course of 1958, and in fact had already been ongoing when the NEC representatives from the Eastern Region demanded that the government refuse to negotiate with any member of the West African Lines Conference, of which Elder Dempster was the undisputed controlling interest. Minister Njoku did not reveal this in the August NEC meeting, but the real surprise came to both the Nigerian House of Representatives and the National Economic Council when Njoku addressed the House of Representatives on 25 November. In this session, he asked the House to amend the 1957 decision calling for the establishment of a national shipping line within five years, calling instead for the establishment of a national shipping line "at the earliest possible date."[44] The minister explained that circumstances had drastically changed over the last year, and a worldwide recession had led to a dramatic decrease in the cost of ships. "Now is the time to float our national shipping venture. This is the moment for which your Government has been waiting, this is the moment when caution can be thrown aside, and Nigerian ships be launched upon the oceans of the world."[45] Njoku did not reveal any of the specific details of the negotiations, but claimed that he had spent the last three months scrutinizing proposals submitted to the Ministry of Transport and interviewing the fourteen foreign shipping firms or groups who had submitted them. He refused to provide details, claiming that "negotiations on this scale cannot be undertaken in the glare of publicity." But while the talks remained confidential, he assured representatives the final agreement would reflect three conditions that he had established for any partnership: (1) Nigerians would have the controlling share in the enterprise; (2) the technical partner would make a substantial investment of equity and do everything he could to make the venture succeed; and (3) Nigerians would both learn a new skill and obtain a fair share of the carrying trade to and from Nigeria.[46] Njoku explained the need for cooperation with a foreign shipping company:

> Let us not deceive ourselves. We Nigerians as yet know very little about shipping. A few of us have touched the fringe of the industry as shipping agents, dock-labour contactors or freight agents; some few hundred of us have gone to sea as deck-hands, engineers and apprentices. But let no one think for a moment that a few months or years in a shipping office or as a sailor qualifies one to run a shipping line. Ocean shipping is one of the most complex, diverse and highly skilled industries in the world. Large profits can be made, even larger sums can be lost in a surprisingly short time by over-ambitious people who lack both technical know-how and managerial experience. Do not mistake me. I am not suggesting for a moment that we Nigerians are incapable of ever acquiring the necessary skill and know-how. We can and are now acquiring them. But I am saying that if now we are to establish a national line on sound foundations, we must start in partnership with an experienced liner operator in whom we can have complete trust.[47]

Njoku's speech anticipated the public reaction to the surprising press release issued three weeks later, announcing the establishment of the Nigerian National Shipping Line. In what many saw as a highly controversial deal, Elder Dempster and the Palm Line were revealed as the technical partners "in whom we can have complete trust." In the agreement between the Nigerian government and the two shipping giants, ownership of the Nigerian National Shipping Line would be divided, giving the Nigerians 51 percent of the company's shares, while Elder Dempster held 33 percent and Palm Line held 16 percent. The technical partners committed to investing necessary capital into the venture, as well as training Nigerians for both seagoing and managerial jobs. The Nigerian government allotted up to £2 million. In addition, it was agreed that the NNSL would be positioned as junior partner in the West African Lines Conference.

What had led to the hasty agreement? It is clear that the federal government was at least partly motivated by a desire to counter regional autonomy. The federal government was likely alarmed by rumors of individuals and regional governments planning to establish overseas shipping lines. Autonomous initiatives had already given expression to the general discontent in the Western Region with WALCON's high freight rates. In the beginning of 1958, a local businessman from the Western Region, Patrick Osoba, set up his own shipping line, named the Nigeria Line. This was a joint venture with a Finnish shipping firm, Nordstrom and Co. Despite the company name, the ships were all registered in Finland, and, facing criticism, Osoba acquired two of the ships in 1959. Although the company could not withstand competition from the conference and folded in 1960, the initiative might have raised concerns for the federal government.[48]

Archival evidence indicates that the federal government and the British shipping lines were highly concerned about the Western Region's intention to form their own shipping line, following reports and rumors that representatives of the region had already been in contact with the Israelis about a joint venture.[49] A conflicting report from the UK Board of Trade in January 1959 claimed that the Western Region had already closed a deal with the London & Kano Trading Company.[50] In the January 1959 meeting of the National Economic Council, following the announcement of the newly formed NNSL, the Western Region protested that the federal government had finalized the negotiations without consulting the NEC. That same month, Elder Dempster and Palm Line offered the Produce Marketing boards up to 25 percent of the founder shares (of which Nigeria held 51 percent), hoping that this would induce the Western Region to drop their plans for their own shipping line.[51] Apparently this move did not appease, and in July 1959, one month after the first voyage of the NNSL's *Dan Fodio*, the Western Region threatened to join a boycott of WALCON. According to a report by Minister Njoku, the boycott began with the Electricity Corporation of Nigeria, which had given WALCON six months' notice of termination of its freight agreement "in protest against the alleged monopoly of the Conference Lines in the Nigerian trade." The Nigerian Railway Corporation also announced that it would give preferential treatment to Nigerian shipping companies in transporting its imports from overseas because of the monopolistic practices of the conference. Following these moves, the premier of the Western Region government announced that his government would not ship produce with WALCON in protest against the shipping combine.[52] According to Njoku, at the time of the announcement, the Western Region was still investigating the option of its own shipping line.[53] The aspirations of the Western Region to establish an independent venture, along with the establishment of Ghana's Black Star Line, undoubtedly played a role in the decision of the federal government, and in particular Minister Njoku, to close the deal with Elder Dempster and the Palm Line.

CRITICISMS AND PUBLIC DEBATE CONCERNING THE NIGERIAN NATIONAL LINE

The announcement of the Nigerian National Shipping Line was celebrated by the federal government as a historic milestone in Nigeria's march toward independence. In a speech to the House of Representatives on 19 February 1959, Minister Njoku praised the agreement with the technical partners as the best option available to Nigeria in the current circumstances:

> We must recognize that at the moment we Nigerians simply have not got the technical experience to run an International Shipping Line on our own. We must rely on the best and most experienced liner operations we could find to help us during the first years of the Company's life. . . . Because we intend this should be a truly Nigerian project, manned and managed as soon as possible by Nigerians, we must therefore learn to walk before we run. The line will therefore start in a small way with one owned and two chartered cargo vessels.
>
> We are starting in a very small way because we are determined to build on firm <u>Nigerian</u> foundations with the help of the best technical partners it has been possible to find. But we are not going to remain small. The Nigerian National Line is going to grow with all possible speed into one of the biggest and most important Companies in Nigeria. Indeed it will take a proud place among the Shipping Lines of the world.[54]

Despite Njoku's enthusiasm, a review of the public outcry that followed the announcement indicates that not everyone was pleased with the negotiated deal. The press took the lead in this protest, and already in February 1959, editorials appeared in local newspapers regarding the terms under which the national line was established. In a *Daily Times* editorial titled "The Shipping Muddle," the general sentiment was conveyed:

> People are baffled and shocked with an agreement which ostensibly seeks to establish a "truly Nigerian project" and yet allows itself to be completely swallowed up by two giant foreign firms which are members of a shipping monopoly, the West African Lines Conference. . . . New ships can only carry 50,000 tons of shipping worth a mere £250,000. This means that the country's new shipping line will be limited to about 2½% of the nation's cargo whilst the rest will be handled by the monopoly!
>
> Two facts emerge: The new shipping line is completely impotent; it will give no effective competition to the monopoly the country seeks to break up! . . . No steps are being taken by the Federal Government to encourage the indigenous shipping enterprise.
>
> What Nigeria needs is a true "national" shipping line or none at all. The project announced by Njoku is an insult to the national aspirations of the country.[55]

In an editorial appearing in the *Daily Service* on 7 May 1959, there is skepticism regarding the good intentions of the technical partners, Elder Dempster and the Palm Line:

> There is considerable public disquiet about the line-up between the Nigerian National Line and the foreign shipping monopolists. It is inconceivable, for example, that a shipping organisation operating 83 vessels will allow the interests of these 83 vessels to suffer in favour of a National Shipping Line operating on line three vessels with whom it professes to be in partnership. The logical conclusion, therefore, is that the foreign shipping monopolists are in the National Shipping Line not only to protect their own vested interests in the trade but also to defeat the national desire to establish an indigenous shipping trade.

The paper demanded that indigenous shipping interests be permitted full opportunities with the National Shipping Line, as this would ensure that the shipping sector remained competitive.[56]

Another source of criticism was the planned membership of the National Shipping Line in the West African Lines Conference. An editorial from the *Daily Service* called this a "Shameless Surrender":

> The West African Lines Conference is the monopoly combine of shipping lines which all nationalists wish to see broken. It was for this reason that the agitation for a national line was carried out on the floor of the House of Representatives. But not only did Mr. Njoku betray the nation by inviting members of this conference to control and manage the so-called national line, his nominees on the Board of Directors have now gone one step further to throw the national line altogether inside the jaws of the monopolists. . . . The interest of the nation has been sacrificed to foreign monopolists and the country has been badly let down. The agreement to join the conference is a shameless and cowardly surrender to evil to which there can be no excuse.[57]

According to the *West African Pilot*, the NNSL agreement with Elder Dempster and the Palm Line was evidence that power had corrupted the nation's leaders. In an editorial titled "Nationalists in Office," it was charged that once Nigerian nationalists held public office, their views and mode of thinking became corrupted. The proof of this was the "sell-out" of the nationalist government, which had "auctioned away our economy to British interests" by establishing the Nigerian National Shipping Line in cooperation with Elder Dempster. The editorial reflected the depth of disillusionment and anger the shipping deal had fostered:

> No matter how hard those responsible strive to convince us that they have acted in our own best interest, the practical facts belie them. A few days ago, as if to add insult to injury, we were told that the Nigerian National Line had joined the West African Lines Conference. . . .
> FOR TEN YEARS WE HAVE BEEN SHOUTING AND GROANING ABOUT THE MENACE TO THE ECONOMY OF THIS COUNTRY POSED BY THE CONFERENCE LINES. WE DID SAY THAT THEIR MONOPOLY OF OCEAN TRAFFIC AND OF GOVERNMENT PRODUCE WAS INIMICAL TO OUR INTERESTS. Federal legislators picked up the cry and forced the Government to safe guard our interests by

starting our own Line. But in doing so, the Government merely allowed itself to become an appendage of the mighty Conference Lines. We sold out to the High Priest of the monopoly.

. . . We set out to stand on our feet and found ourselves being taken care of by the very people we said would want to bleed us to death. Surely, political independence will come next year. But when do we have economic independence? Our nationalist Government has made certain that we will not win both together. We shall have to fight for economic independence after the first round. This would not have been necessary had the Federal Government been made of sterner stuff and if the men at the helm were real national-ists and not just drum beaters. What a pity![58]

Njoku's response to these criticisms came in August 1959, in another statement to the House of Representatives. In this speech, he accused his critics of having sectarian interests rather than a nationalist outlook. This was a subtle reproach of the Western Region's aspirations to launch their own shipping venture:

The National Line is a national enterprise affecting the well-being of the thirty-five million people of Nigeria whose overall interests must prevail over the interests of a few Nigerians personally inter-ested in shipping, as well as over the interests of any section of this country. I can assure the House that in the establishment of the National Line the overriding factor was not what would please cer-tain individuals or a certain section of the country but rather what would be in the best interests of the nation as a whole.[59]

Njoku claimed that the goals of the federal government remained the same: to give Nigeria a foothold in the shipping industry, to train Nigerians to manage and run the enterprise on their own, and to ensure the technical and financial support of the NNSL from the technical partners. With regard to membership in WALCON, Nkoju explained that the international ship-ping industry was organized around the conference system, and Nigerian membership in the conference would ensure a regulated shipping schedule and cargo sharing. He claimed that the Nigerian national line was follow-ing in the footsteps of other decolonizing nations, such as Ghana and India, whose shipping lines had also joined the conference systems. Njoku assured House members that the conference membership would enable the NNSL to turn a profit already in its first year.

Njoku was particularly critical of those who claimed that the national line was not truly Nigerian, and cast doubt on other ventures that claimed to be "Nigerian." He claimed that anyone could open an agency in Lagos and claim it was Nigerian, but a closer inspection would reveal that the ships were registered abroad, and the controlling interests of these companies were also foreign. Njoku explained that the national line was a "genuine Nigerian Line," as Nigerians held the bulk of capital, the ships were manned by Nigerians, and all final decisions rested with the board in Nigeria. And unlike other ventures, the NNSL was represented by all regions of the country, as the regional marketing boards were also shareholders in the company.[60]

It was not only the Nigerian press that was highly skeptical of the arrangement between the NNSL and the Elder Dempster and Palm Lines. In fact, the most virulent critique of the partnership came from one of the members of WALCON, the Norwegian firm Leif Hoegh and Company. In January 1958, Elder Dempster informed WALCON members of their intentions to pursue the joint venture with the Nigerians. In their reply to this announcement, the Norwegians cast doubt on the motives of Elder Dempster and the Palm Line. Hoegh expressed deep skepticism and disdain for the British companies' maneuvers, and forecast doom for the Nigerians:

> It would be a peculiarity for West Africa that already existing Lines should help the underdeveloped countries in the Liner service. . . .
> It is hard for us to judge how wise a move this is, and you seem to be in a hurry so we have no time to investigate or even consider it. As you want an immediate reply, you put us in a difficult position, and we really have no choice, . . . but I do not really like that you will educate the Nigerian government in the Liner trade. We must presume that the Nigerian venture is kept within narrow limits, and that a possible further appetite is staggered. . . . We take it for granted that you will not help the Nigerians to run their ships, so that the mistakes they make in this field they will in all fairness have to take themselves. . . . For us it is, of course, unpleasant news that another line in addition to Black Star Line should enter the Conference on better terms than we have ourselves.[61]

While Leif Hoegh's protest can hardly be detached from his own company's interest in keeping competition at a minimum, his criticism of the deal between Elder Dempster/Palm Line and the NNSL echoed the same skepticism that was voiced in the Nigerian press toward the underlying motives of the technical partners. Hoegh made it clear that there was no altruism at work, and Elder Dempster could easily agree to the minor loss of cargo share that would result in the NNSL joining of WALCON in exchange for the preservation of the monopoly. But for Leif Hoegh and Company, and the other smaller members of the conference, this could have a more significant impact. The Norwegian's protest revealed the complexities of the conference system for the smaller carriers, and the mix of increased benefits alongside increased dependency of smaller shipping lines on the industry giants once they joined the conference.

For the Nigerians, the pursuit of WALCON membership might have posed an ideological or even sentimental problem, but the NNSL also had little choice but to join the conference. The West African Lines Conference was a cartel formed to regulate shipping schedules and freight rates between Europe and Africa. Throughout the twentieth century, conferences were formed on most international trade routes in order to regulate competition between the various lines involved in any route. The heavy investments and heavy risks that characterized the shipping industry led shipowners to embrace this regulation in order to ensure profits. The West African Lines Conference was established in 1924 with three members: Elder Dempster, Woermann Line, and Holland West Africa Line. Following World War II, two more British shipping companies joined in the conference—Guinea Gulf Line (1951) and Palm Line (1949). In the 1950s, two Scandinavian firms joined, SWAL (1955) and the Hoegh Line (1957). Ghana's Black Star Line became a member of WALCON in 1957.[62] With the addition of the NNSL in 1959, the conference membership reached nine. Within the conference, cargo share was determined by fleet size, and this gave a clear advantage to Elder Dempster throughout the entire history of WALCON. Thus, from the end of World War II until the end of the 1960s, Elder Dempster controlled 50 percent of all tonnage to West Africa, and the rest was divided among the other members of the conference.[63]

There were many benefits to the conference arrangement, both for shipowners and for shippers. The organization of shipowners into this conglomerate was insurance for shippers that there would be regular, scheduled services, as well as stability in freight rates, equal treatment of all "loyal" shippers, and a high quality of services. In short, the WALCON arrangement enabled shippers to know with relative certainty that ships would arrive in ports on set times and dates, and that rates would remain stable. For shipowners, the conference helped members to weather economic recessions and periodic declines in shipping by setting freight rates at a level that compensated for the ebbs and flows of supply and demand.[64]

For shippers, however, these benefits were often shadowed by an overall sense that freight rates were too high, and the conference system erased competition from the industry. The system was shrouded in secrecy, as freight rates within WALCON were never publicized. Shippers lacked vital information in order to determine if shipping services had been supplied at reasonable prices.[65] The system increased a sense of powerlessness among shippers by tying them to the conference through what were known as "loyalty rates." These were rates that offered shippers a 10 percent discount, provided they did not ship with nonconference members for up to one year after shipping with WALCON. Thus, for shippers, the benefits of regular schedules and rates were largely offset by a frustrated sense that there was no alternative to WALCON.

For the press and some politicians in Nigeria, the decision of the NNSL both to join ranks with Elder Dempster and to become a member of WALCON did seem like a gross betrayal. Both the shipping giant and the conference it dominated had been the very symbols of economic exploitation and disempowerment for Nigeria in the colonial era. Joining the conference was a political liability for the NNSL, a situation bemoaned by one Elder Dempster official: "An agreement and organisation for rationalizing the West African trade must of course continue, but must it continue to carry the liability of a name that is now so dirty that all connected with it are tarred with the same brush?"[66] But the organization of the international shipping industry left the NNSL founders little alternative. In joining the conference, the Nigerian National Shipping Line was guaranteed a share of the cargo to and from Nigeria, and the opportunity to join the ranks of decision makers and profiteers from which they had been historically excluded. As a member of the conference, Nigeria could take part in decisions regarding shipping rates, port traffic, and shipping schedules for all fleets involved in the trade between Nigeria and Europe.[67]

There was, however, an unsettling irony in the arrangement. In joining WALCON, the Nigerian National Shipping Line lent legitimacy to the conference and had voluntarily agreed to subscribe to its policies. This had a potentially detrimental impact on the evolution of an indigenous shipping industry in Nigeria. The Nigerian federal government and the regional marketing boards, as part owners of the Nigerian National Shipping Line, had become members in an organization that was determined to keep competitors in the shipping industry at bay. As members of WALCON, the Nigerian national line would naturally want to discourage ventures into shipping by other Nigerian interests. Already in April 1959, the NNSL had argued to

WALCON members that the Nigerian line needed a larger share of cargo in order to prevent the Western Region from developing their own shipping company.[68] As Elder Dempster executive John Joyce wrote in April 1959 regarding plans for additional indigenous lines: "If such a line came into being it would be inevitably followed by similar Lines and similar requirements of Board cargo from other Regions. Mr. Ojukwu and the Federal Government wish to see one successful Nigerian National Line and not a number of other Lines supported by the Regions."[69] Thus, the government-controlled national line occupied an irreconcilable position of wanting to discourage competition locally, and worked to block efforts to develop an indigenous shipping industry that could offer some competition to the much-resented cartel.[70] According to Larry Diamond, this was part of a broader problematic in which the establishment of state monopolies ultimately discouraged the growth of local enterprises.[71] This is just one of the incongruences of the mixing of nationalist politics and business, to be examined in the following section.

THE POLITICIZATION OF BUSINESS

The federal government of Nigeria was originally reluctant to jump into the shipping industry, and despite public pressure, attempted to delay the enterprise until after independence. Political and economic circumstances led to a sudden turnaround in this position, and the Nigerian National Shipping Line was established in 1959 with much celebration and fanfare. The national line was quickly touted as a powerful symbol of decolonization and independence, and the activities and successes of the company were promoted as the lifeline of the new nation of Nigeria. Thus, news of the delivery of the first ship to Lagos was greeted by Minister Njoku: "The arrival of the *Dan Fodio* marks the opening of a new trading venture but it also has a deeper significance. Today marks the entry of Nigeria among the mercantile fleets of the world. We have taken our place amongst them, owning our own ships and carrying the exports and imports by which our country lives."[72]

While the NNSL provided opportunities for grandstanding the nationalist agenda, the actual running of the company mirrored the ambivalence with which the government had initially approached the entire venture. It soon became clear that the successful operation and development of the shipping line required more than ideological commitment and enthusiasm, and the government would have to dedicate significant resources to the company beyond grandiose speeches. The business of shipping was a complex enterprise that required technical expertise, massive capital investment, and a strong commitment to withstand the pressures and challenges of succeeding in a highly competitive and specialized industry. Yet, from the very start, the federal government's management and input into the NNSL reflected an unhealthy mix of political considerations and an inconsistent regard for proper business practice. Rather than developing the company into a viable and successful enterprise that would be the pride of Nigeria, the federal government used the NNSL again and again as a tool to advance a political agenda. As a result, decision making among management of the Nigerian National Shipping Line often reflected an approach that was politically savvy but economically ruinous.

The first chairman of the NNSL, Louis Ojukwu, was a successful businessman who had warned against the dangers of mixing government and enterprise. In 1956, he testified to a government commission investigating corruption among politicians: "I told government that they cannot be the government and be businessmen. The only thing I would like the government to do is to encourage African people to get on their way and later on withdraw. I will never like government to interfere in business. In fact, I will not like to share a company with government. It is just like a lion and a lamb sharing business."[73] Despite this unequivocal position, three years later, Ojukwu accepted the offer of Minister Njokwu to serve as the first chairman of the board of the Nigerian National Shipping Line.[74] Ojukwu had built his fortune in construction and transport. A leading figure in the business community, he served as the chairman of the Eastern Nigerian Marketing Board, the Eastern Nigerian Development Corporation, and the Nigerian Produce Marketing Company.[75] He was also a board member of the Nigerian Coal Corporation and the African Continental Bank, and the founding president of the Nigerian Stock Exchange. This impressive list of responsibilities raised the concerns of critics who felt that Ojukwu would not give the running of the NNSL the time or attention it required.[76] According to Robert Tignor, Louis Ojukwu was not even aware of all the companies that had appointed him to their board. Thus, when he saw his name on the letterhead of the Nigerian Engineering and Manufacturing Company, "he ordered it removed because he had never been approached about serving on the board." Ojukwu could not fulfill all of his obligations on the various boards he served, and Tignor claimed that although he collected payment for participating in board meetings, he could not in fact recall afterward if he had actually been in attendance.[77] It could well be that Minister Njoku was fully aware of this situation, and perhaps recognized its advantages. Meetings of the board of directors in Lagos were only periodically scheduled, and many of the major debates and decisions of the management of the NNSL took place in monthly meetings in London among executives of Elder Dempster and the Palm Line.[78] In Lagos, the day-to-day running of the NNSL was in the hands of the expatriate general manager, Donald Tod, who came to the NNSL from Elder Dempster. With very little familiarity with shipping, Louis Ojukwu might have been the ideal chairman from the perspective of the technical partners—a figurehead with little inclination or time for becoming too involved in the daily operations of the company.

The appointment of Louis Ojukwu as chairman of the board undoubtedly served the political interests of the minister of transport, as well as the managerial agenda of the technical partners. But the choice of Ojukwu also came with a certain price. With his extensive influence across a broad range of major corporations and deep ties to the political and business elite of Nigeria, Louis Ojukwu became accustomed to a level of influence and privilege. During his tenure at the Nigerian National Shipping Line, he deemed that his position as chairman of the board of directors should afford him certain benefits from the NNSL. In one incident, Elder Dempster officials in Lagos wrote to Liverpool following the arrival of two dogs Ojukwu had purchased from England and shipped to Nigeria. The official wrote, "I think he was somewhat surprised at the size of the bill." The letter explained Mr. Ojukwu would be extremely grateful if Elder Dempster charged him the freight for only one dog instead of two, though he expressed willingness to pay for the gratuity on both.[79] In another incident, Ojukwu stormed into the Calabar offices of Elder Dempster to file a complaint concerning the "poor treatment" and "discourtesy" he received while traveling on the *Oron Ferry*. On his journey to Calabar, Ojukwu was approached by the ship's purser and asked to present a receipt for his fare. Ojukwu told the purser to go look for his driver to get the necessary paperwork, and became outraged when the purser replied, "I do not know you, how is it possible for me to go down and collect your fare from an unknown driver?" In his report concerning the complaint, the agent claimed the purser who had mistreated the chairman would be fired.[80] Incidents such as these, as minor as they might appear, reveal a more troubling pattern. Political appointments came with a price, and from the very establishment of the NNSL, the functioning of the company was colored by the personal ambitions of the management, who did not prioritize the economic interests of the shipping line over their own personal needs.

Poor business practices resulted not only from personal ambitions of specific individuals, but also from a conceptualization of the NNSL as a political project rather than an economic one. Gerald Chidi wrote, "It could be said that profit motive, though implied, was not the motivating factor for the company's establishment. One has to understand the mood of the major political players at the time to appreciate why 'showing the nation's flag to the world' was a major focus."[81] From the outset, the development and growth of the NNSL was framed by politicians and management primarily in ideological terms. This could be seen in debates surrounding the issue of fleet expansion. The Nigerian National Shipping Line would have to acquire a significant number of ships in order to play a substantial role in the trade with Europe and beyond. In its first meeting of February 1959, the board of directors authorized the purchase of two ships. Three months later, Chairman Ojukwu asked the technical partners to provide funding for a third ship, arguing that the expansion of the fleet would help to dispel public criticism of the company. But Ojukwu's request for more ships was framed in political considerations: "I would like to see us take steps as quickly as possible to acquire our third ship. We already have the *Dan Fodio* with her Northern Regional name association and the *Oduduwa* to satisfy the pride of the Western Region. We have decided that the third ship will be named *King Jaja* and the Eastern Region will be thus identified. I appreciate, of course, that it will mean our calling up additional capital. . . . I trust, however, that with so much politically involved, Elders and Palm will be able to make the money available."[82] Similarly, political benefits were prioritized when weighing the option of opening branch offices outside of Nigeria: "Apart from the prestige value to the Line and to Nigeria of our opening offices in other West African ports, and this is of international importance in itself, there are other perhaps more tangible advantages."[83]

From the beginning of the company's history, there was a lack of determination on the part of the government to invest in the NNSL. Modest profits were made in the first year of operation, with earnings of £155,000, and the company expanded to five ships owned and three ships chartered.[84] This success fueled the aspirations of the management, and plans were made for the acquisition of more vessels to maximize Nigeria's cargo-carrying potential. According to the agreement with WALCON, the NNSL could operate up to six ships in 1959, eight in 1960, and ten in 1961.[85] Fleet expansion would enable the Nigerian line to capture a larger proportion of the cargo, as allocated by the WALCON agreement. But fleet expansion required massive investments from the Nigerian government, and this was not forthcoming. Throughout 1960, discussions between the management of the Nigerian line, the minister of transport, and the management of Elder Dempster and the Palm Line concerning NNSL fleet expansion revealed that political enthusiasm for the national line in Nigeria was not matched by the necessary material support for the shipping line. Time and again, the rationale for expansion was framed in political rather than commercial terms. In May 1960, Minister Njoku wrote, "I feel that the time is right for further expansion because of Independence and because of Ghana's fleet expansion."[86] Chairman Ojukwu also used the approach of independence to argue for more ships: "It is my conviction that with the realization of Independence on the 1st of October, Nigeria will have to rely on her National Shipping Line more than any other economic asset. In case of war or other emergency we would be helpless without our National Line. . . . In any real emergency after the 1st October we would have to rely on our own vessels to carry essential imports and exports. We must therefore build up our National Line as swiftly as possible."[87] But despite the political significance of fleet expansion, Njoku explained, the government would not allocate funds to buy these new ships: "Unfortunately the Federal Government has not got all the money it needs and due to the NNL's modest original plan there is no provision in the current Capital Programme. Extra expenditure now means either a widening of the gap between approved projects and available cash or the deletion of some already approved projects."[88]

The technical partners argued that the time was right for buying new ships in 1960, as a global recession had led to a significant drop in the prices of vessels. Elder Dempster officials made a very strong recommendation to Njoku to try to persuade the government to invest an additional £2 million for the expansion.[89] But independence came and went, and the government had not committed to purchasing new ships. By the end of 1960, Njoku conceded that there would be no additional government funding for the new vessels, and he suggested that the management of the NNSL purchase the ships on deferred payment terms. But here again, political considerations played a part. Njoku instructed Chairman Ojukwu to invite tenders from shipbuilders and to award the contract to the one offering the best value, "but when assessing the 'best value' it is important that you should have regard to the value of the financial terms offered as well as to other factors. I would like your invitations to include all those firms which have taken the trouble to make offers to Nigeria (e.g. Inter-States Economic Developments, Mr. Comis and Sofindus)."[90] In fleet expansion as well as other aspects of commercial development, ideological and sentimental considerations were continually set against best business practices.

The reluctance of the Nigerian government to invest in the National Shipping Line put a strain on relations with Elder Dempster and the Palm Line. At the start of 1961, the cost of two new ships was £2 million, and the NNSL had only £400,000 available, so the purchase of the new ships would leave the company short of cash. Ruling out additional funds from the government, Njoku proposed that the technical partners loan the NNSL the funds.[91] He presented them with calculations demonstrating that the NNSL could pay back the loan and still make a profit, but conceded that these calculations were based on a highly positive economic forecast and the risky assumption that freight rates would rise.[92] Elder Dempster and the Palm Line were not in favor of taking such risks, and recommended that if possible, the Nigerian National Shipping Line should avoid taking out loans in order to buy new ships. But Elder Dempster officials recognized the pressures facing the NNSL. Joyce wrote in January 1961, "The two ships have to be built for political reasons," and the technical partners recommended a compromise of purchasing the ships and then chartering them to the NNSL.[93] Elder Dempster assured the Nigerians that the Nigerian flag would be flown on the charters. But this solution was unacceptable to the NNSL, and the management of the British shipping firms continued to plead with Njoku to seek the necessary funding from the government, to no avail.

The Elder Dempster officials forecasted that there would be a political price to pay for refusing the Nigerians the loans, as Albert Hoffman of ED Lines wrote in January 1961: "I think our general attitude is that we want to be firm—on the other hand we do not want to fall out with our Nigerian colleagues if an acceptable solution can be found. I do not consider an acceptable solution to be one which in itself would be known beforehand to be uneconomic, but undertaken purely for the sake of prestige of Nigeria. This creates a difficult situation, but there are perhaps means of dealing with it without a break."[94]

The fears of Hoffman were not unfounded, as the aspirations of the Nigerian government and those of the technical partners regarding the Nigerian National Shipping Line could never be fully reconciled, and two months later negotiations began for Nigerians to take over full ownership of the NNSL. The federal government acquired 100 percent of the company shares from Elder Dempster and the Palm Line in September 1961, making the Nigerian National Shipping Line an enterprise fully owned by Nigerians. This buyout was seen by many as a rash decision motivated by "either the euphoria of political independence or the selfish interest of the Nigerian management of the company."[95] Bolaji Akinola wrote, "There was no rational justification for the acquisition. The shares were acquired out of sheer zeal to take control. The move by the Nigerian government was premature and was the first major bad policy of Nigerian leaders concerning the shipping sector."[96] Elder Dempster and the Palm Line had continually promoted a conservative program for expansion and development, and advised against taking on too much risk or debt. According to Gerald Chidi, a former managing director of the NNSL, the buyout of the technical partners removed a vital safeguard against the total politicization of the shipping venture. Chidi claimed, "The absence of [Elder Dempster and the Palm Line] denied the NNSL the privilege of being run as a pure commercial concern."[97]

While regarded as an imprudent business decision, the political motivation for buying out the foreign investors was clear. The public outrage toward the partnership with Elder Dempster and the Palm Line embodied all the emotion and anticipation that accompanied a nation moving from colonialism to independence. The process of decolonization generated a sense of hope and optimism about the meaning of autonomy and self-reliance on the one hand, and optimism that soon Nigerians would be free from the oppressive and debasing status of colonial subjects on the other. The deal struck with the foreign monopolists incensed those who had invested hope in the prospect of decolonization, and the ongoing presence of foreign management in the national line threw into question the very meaning of independence. Politicians and the press wondered what was indeed Nigerian about a national line that was half owned and fully run by foreigners. The level of emotion could be seen in the 1960 remarks of J. A. Akinyemi, a member of the House of Representatives from the Western Region, regarding the foreign face of management of the NNSL. Akinyemi alleged that Leslie Passage, the head office manager of the NNSL, was a South African: "I refer to the head of the shipping line—the notorious shipping line. No wonder there has been a lot of confusion and a lot of mis-management in that section of the country's undertaking, when we have a South African at the head of affairs to advise the Permanent Secretary. Who will in turn have to advise the Minister himself. I think this man, called Mr. Passage, should be given his passage back home!! (Hear, hear!)"[98]

Akinyemi also named the foreign managers of the Electricity Corporation and the Nigerian Broadcasting Corporation, and claimed, "These three people are negrophobists, and there should be no room for them in this Government." Leslie Passage was deeply disturbed by the allegations. In his response, he asserted that he was British and not South African, but nonetheless, he was fully committed to the Nigerian nation: "I have never visited South Africa nor am I remotely connected with that country but on the contrary have worked and lived in Nigeria amongst its people in amity and accord for over twenty years and have found much happiness here. I am certainly not a negrophobist and had I been anything but sympathetic and enthusiastic to the ideals and aspirations of Nigeria I would not have remained in the Country for so long a period of time."[99]

The incident surrounding Leslie Passage revealed the extent to which politicians were rallying around "Nigerianization" in the political and ideological buildup to independence. The Nigerian National Shipping Line was born out of an aspiration to Nigerianize the economy as a vital step toward autonomy, and the call to replace foreign managers with Nigerians provided an opportunity to see a tangible result of decolonization. But while the notion of Nigerianization was rhetorically powerful, it had far less potential as a practical operation. The history of the founding of the NNSL gives shape to the complexities of realizing the agenda of economic nationalism in an industry such as shipping, where foreign capital and expertise were fundamental to the successful founding and running of the company. Public critique undoubtedly played a hand in the buyout of the technical partners, and critics have argued that this move was ultimately detrimental to the enforcement of proper business practices in the national line.

But while public outcry led to the removal of the British face of management ashore, it was far more difficult to replace the foreign officers and captains on board vessels. The Nigerianization of ships was a process largely removed from public scrutiny, and one that faced a unique set of challenges, implications, and outcomes, particularly for seamen themselves. The following chapter will examine the establishment of the NNSL from the perspectives of seamen. It will be seen that the NNSL provided an opportunity for seamen to engage with a nationalist agenda, but similarly to the broader political process of Nigerianization of shipping, seamen on board NNSL vessels confronted a more complex reality than they had imagined in their embrace of nationalist rhetoric and the idea of a national line. The broader political processes propelled by economic nationalism came to bear on the Nigerianization of ships, and in the working lives of seamen.

5 ↜ Nigerianizing the Sea
Cultures of Work on NNSL Ships

ON 11 MAY 1959, Derek Bailey joined the crew for the maiden voyage of the *Oduduwa*, the second ship purchased by the Nigerian National Shipping Line (NNSL) following the *Dan Fodio*. Appointed as fourth engineer, Bailey sailed under the command of Capt. F. Sam Weller, a man he described as "one of the gents of this world." Bailey's first trip on the *Oduduwa* "turned out to be one of the most unusual and entertaining voyages" he had ever been on. The ship left Rotterdam en route to Lagos, stopping at West African ports along the way. From port to port, the crew was feted and celebrated by local crowds, all exhilarated at the sight of the first Nigerian-owned and -operated vessel to arrive at their port. As Bailey recalled, the festivities began in Freetown, where the ship's captain was whisked ashore by local dignitaries. He returned several hours later, Bailey claimed, "a little the worst for wear and dressed in the regalia of an African Chief!" The celebrations continued at each port of call, increasing with intensity as the ship approached Lagos. Bailey recalled the surprise and disbelief of the crew: "It should be understood that we had no prior knowledge of these celebrations which became more and more elaborate as the hitherto unremarkable ex-tramp steamer (now a LINER) continued her triumphal progress down the coast, interrupted only by the occasional breakdown."[1]

The reception the *Oduduwa* received across West Africa required extra work from the crew because at each stop, the ship had to be cleaned and readied, but as Bailey recalled, this was "well worth the effort, considering the parties laid on for us." Alcohol ran freely at each port, and elaborate meals, called "small chop" by locals, were prepared by the chief steward. The ships were boarded by large crowds of those with official invites, as well as dockworkers, deckhands, and passersby who were happy to join the party: "Anyone who happened to be passing took up their imaginary invitations with alacrity, so the tables were soon cleared. 'Like a swarm of locusts,' as the Chief Steward gloomily observed." The climax came in Lagos. There, representatives of the Yoruba Oduduwa Society arrived at the ship and carried all the officers away in a fleet of limousines. Not having any idea where they were headed, Bailey recalls, he was delighted to eventually find himself seated under the stars in a green pasture outside of Lagos, where each man was given a roasted chicken and a bottle of scotch. Immersed in the food and drink, he could not recall what all the speeches were about.[2]

Derek Bailey's memorable voyage on the *Oduduwa* embodied the deep complexities that characterized the newly founded Nigerian National Shipping Line. His account exposes the profound disconnect between public anticipation of the NNSL and the actual materialization of the venture. The NNSL was born in the nationalist fervor taking hold over the Nigerian political and business elite in the final years of colonial rule, but when the Nigerian ships finally set sail, they were largely indistinguishable from the Elder Dempster vessels that had dominated the West African trade since the nineteenth century. Minister Njoku glossed over this complexity as he celebrated the ship's arrival in Lagos: "On the *Oduduwa*, out of a crew of forty-four, twenty-nine are Nigerians, two of them being cadets."[3] The minister's political grandstanding concealed an uncomfortable truth: the colonial division of labor was largely preserved on the Nigerian ships. British captains and British officers commanded the vessels, and African crews continued to provide labor as greasers and firemen in the engine room, catering staff and deck ratings. It would take nearly a decade before Nigerian captains and officers would begin taking command over Nigerian ships, and European officers remained visible on NNSL vessels into the 1980s. While the *Oduduwa* was hailed as a symbol of decolonization throughout West Africa, the European officers actually manning the ship did not identify with, or fully comprehend, the ideological significance of the national line for the decolonized masses.

For Nigerian seamen, there were also significant disparities between the anticipated national line and the ultimate manifestation of the Nigerian National Shipping Line. Slogans of economic nationalism paved the way for the establishment of the Nigerian national line, but the outcome of this political and ideological history was lived very differently "on the ground" by the seamen. An examination into seamen's engagement with the NNSL demonstrates that while the broad strokes of history are largely written by politicians and the economic elite, there are equally significant agents of interpretation and change to be found among the working classes. In the lead-up to the founding of the NNSL, Nigerian seamen invested their own hopes and aspirations in the possibilities of working for a Nigerian line. While politicians linked the establishment of the NNSL to the broader po- litical, economic, and ideological struggle for decolonization, for Nigerian seamen, the meaning and significance of the establishment of the NNSL, and their later experiences and reflections as employees of the national ship- ping company, were largely based on their own personal experiences and aspirations as seamen. As will be seen, the establishment of the Nigerian National Shipping Line had far-reaching consequences for those previously employed on Elder Dempster ships. The allure of the national line was inseparable from historical experiences of discrimination and exploitation on colonial vessels. At the same time, seamen's identification with nation- alism seems to contradict their ongoing reliance on mobility, fluidity, and cosmopolitanism that had characterized their transnational migrations in the colonial era. It is therefore important to unpack seamen's identification with the promise of nationalism, and attempt to understand more precisely the underlying political, ideological, and economic aspirations seamen invested in "becoming Nigerian." This chapter will describe the ways in which Nigerian seamen interpreted the changes brought on by the creation and operation of the NNSL, and the ways in which they portrayed and made sense of their participation in this ill-fated venture. The discussion will pro- vide rich insights into how everyday Africans lived and responded to broader historical processes of decolonization and nationalization.

The process of "Nigerianization" was both anticipated and lived by sea- men on ships in the founding years of the NNSL. For seamen, the move to work for the national line held the promise of better working conditions. Seamen were lured by guarantees of better pay and fair treatment by the management, but they were also stirred by the opportunity to feel a sense of ownership and "home" on board the NNSL vessels. The initial manifesta- tion of these dreams was largely a disappointment, as there was nothing very Nigerian about the NNSL ships apart from their flying the Nigerian flag. But as will be seen, ships of the NNSL with time did undergo a process of Nigerianization. We will examine what was "Nigerian" about the ships of the NNSL, and what the process of Nigerianization entailed and signified in the working lives of seamen on board ships. Historians and political scientists have studied the processes and outcomes of indigenization in postcolonial Africa as part of broader investigations into nationalist politics, statecraft, and development.[4] In the context of postcolonial Nigeria, indigenization has been interrogated and evaluated with an eye to public policy and political ideology.[5] An examination of how shipboard hierarchies, labor relations, and working cultures evolved over time and became "Nigerian" will enable a view "from below" and provide significant insights into how working classes lived through, interpreted, and shaped the history of Nigerianization in the postcolonial era.

SEAMEN AND THE POSSIBILITY OF NATIONALISM

A full appreciation of seamen's engagement with the Nigerian National Shipping Line must take into account their experiences as colonial subjects on British merchant ships. As seen in chapter 2, seamen's transnational travels enabled them to develop a cosmopolitan consciousness, and they nurtured social, cultural, and political ties that cut across national and racial boundaries. At the same time, Nigerian seamen suffered from discrimination on the basis of race and class both on board ships and ashore, and these experiences primed them for embracing nationalist ideology. The establishment of the Nigerian National Shipping Line (NNSL) presented seamen with an opportunity to express a nationalist allegiance. The transfer of Nigerian crew from Elder Dempster to employment in the NNSL was negotiated at the level of management as part of the founding process of the NNSL. In the aftermath of the Salubi inquiry, the National Maritime Board was created to organize and regulate the recruitment of seamen for shipowners, and seamen were directed to employment by the NNSL through the Maritime Board.[6] Nonetheless, the majority of Nigerian seamen interviewed described the move to the NNSL as their own decision.[7] This is because, while the opportunities and choices seamen had in choosing to work for the NNSL were not fully of their own making, seamen's engagement with nationalist ideologies and policies led them to embrace the NNSL as the answer to their frustrations and hopes. Seamen's expectations of the national line reflected a unique engagement with nationalist discourse, framed in the context of their working lives.

Many of the men interviewed claimed that they chose to move to the NNSL as an expression of their nationalist sentiment following the end of colonial rule. The declaration of independence was remembered as a time of great celebration, and Nigerians on board ships organized parties for their entire crews. One seaman recalled that European captains also joined in the festivities, having cakes baked and allowing the crew free drinks: "Oh yes, a man to a bottle of brandy, two cartons of beer, stout, everything was free on that day. Anything you asked was free, you didn't pay for anything on that day."[8] Seamen were proud to have their own shipping company and claimed that they came to work for the Nigerian National Shipping Line as an expression of their patriotism. As one said, "I was very happy to work with national line because I was ready to serve my country."[9] Another replied, "It was our national carrier, so we must be happy working for it. It was our national flag!"[10] Others simply assumed that it would be better to work for a Nigerian line: "Yes, we were happy. Because it was an indigenous company, so we assumed it will be okay once it is established. Like conditions of service, welfare—like what took place in the Congolese shipping company, where their seamen were taken care of."[11]

As soon as they went to work for the Nigerian National Shipping Line, seamen were issued Nigerian passports. This was hailed by some informants as a sign that Nigeria had joined the ranks of independent nations. In their work as colonial seamen, men were issued seamen's certificates rather than international passports, and these identity papers limited their options for mobility at various ports of call. In 1960, when seamen began working for the NNSL, things changed for the better: "Yes, everyone of the crew had an international passport and with it we could go to anywhere in the world without any problem. An international passport is better [than a seaman's certificate]. We used the international passport to enter Russia, Korea, and other areas including Europe—Germany, Holland, Belgium."[12] Seamen's satisfaction with their new status must be understood against the backdrop of the colonial era, when they were issued a form of identification they viewed as second-class. Seamen's experiences of mobility in the colonial era and their encounters with border regimes fostered a longing for national status and the benefits it could bring. As Craig Calhoun has argued, the turn to nationalist identification among cosmopolitans is often linked to a longing to "join the ranks of those with 'good' passports."[13] Thus, the identification with patriotism was often linked to tangible benefits that national status could bring.

In the same way, seamen's enthusiastic embrace of the NNSL was rooted in the hope that conditions of work would be better under the national lines. The enthusiasm with which Nigerian seamen greeted the creation of the NNSL was a direct reflection of the discrimination they had suffered at the hands of white officers. As one said, "I remember that one of the chief officers, a white man, often made racist comments addressing us—we blacks, and then I knew him to possess the South African white man's attitude, a racist attitude. . . . Do you know why they wanted us to work for them? It was because of cheap labor, we were so cheap, that was why they kept on doing business with us."[14]

While seamen hoped that employment for the national line would mean an end to discrimination, they were specifically drawn to the prospect of better salaries. Following the Salubi report, the National Maritime Board formulated new rates of pay for seamen. At its founding, the NNSL promised Nigerian seamen to adopt the new pay scale and to begin paying for overtime. This was a benefit they did not receive on Elder Dempster ships and a long-standing point of contention between the Nigerian Union of Seamen and Elder Dempster management throughout the 1950s. Many seamen interviewed claimed that they were attracted to the promise of overtime pay, but this financial benefit was also linked to an overall sentiment that they would be treated with more dignity on board the Nigerian ships. Seamen's hopes (and ultimate disappointment) can be seen in the following seaman's testimony regarding the move to the national lines:

> It was my choice to be paid off [the ED Line] because we Nigerians now had our own ships and we left the European shipping line and joined our local line. It was because the national line paid us a lot of overtime, but there was nothing like overtime in the ED Line. We came because of this and also with the intention to serve our country, but later we suffered and regretted our action, joining national line. Really, apart from the money, we had this patriotism in us, but it was unfavorable to us.[15]

The issue of overtime pay was central to most seamen's preference to work for the national line, but another issue that played a prominent role in seamen's recollections of the move to the NNSL was that of food served on board. For many seamen, the possibility of being served Nigerian food was an important drawing point for joining the national line, as it was inseparable from deeper desires for belonging and a sense of home on board ships. The issue of food played a prominent role in seamen's detailed descriptions of life on ships, first on board Elder Dempster vessels and later on vessels of the NNSL. Many of those interviewed complained bitterly of the food they were served on the British vessels; one seaman recalled: "We ate English food, ate a lot of rice, they did not give us African food. No pepper on the food. The food was not really suitable for us, but we ate it like that."[16] The memory of food on board colonial vessels reflected the symbolic significance of food for the Nigerian crew, as another seaman recalled: "The European stewards didn't know how to prepare or cook African food.

We carried most of the burden, carrying passengers and cargoes to London. But each time they wanted to serve us, they gave us chicken! No! No! No! Everybody wanted to eat *fufu, eba, garri*. . . . In the cold weather we wanted that! Ti o ba je eba wa laagun! [Yoruba expression: When you eat *eba* you will sweat]."[17] This same seaman claimed that labor disputes on the Elder Dempster Lines were related to the issue of food: "It was about pay and the food. Because of the food they were serving us, we didn't like English food; rather we wanted *garri, eba,* that will make us feel warm, not *edie odindin kan bayi ti o jinna* [Yoruba: one big half-done chicken]. Sometimes, the chickens were not well cooked . . . and it irritated us whenever we ate them because there was no pepper."[18] Many claimed to bring their own food on board, or to prepare food in the kitchen in off hours:

> Nigerians bought their own food like *garri*, pepper, and so on. We traveled with this. Anytime we signed for any ship in Lagos here, some of us used to buy some African foods and we kept it in our cabins because the menu that the kitchen officer made is for the whole crew in the ship and most of the food on the menu was European food. For instance, chicken and chips, baked bread, eggs, and so on. Most of Nigerians did not like this food so they want to cook their own food in the galley. After the chief cook finished from the galley, we then went into the kitchen with our own pots and cook our own food. Africans, sometimes, would say that they didn't want fish and chips, "I want *garri*, give me *garri*!" Most Ijaw men were fond of this because we didn't believe in this baked bread and eggs.[19]

While most seamen recalled that the food on the British ships did not suit the majority of the ratings, the situation on the national line was completely different. Seamen often framed their satisfaction with the move to the national line in terms of the Nigerian food served on board. For example, one seaman recalled that the issue of food was the only difference between the Elder Dempster and the NNSL ships: "It was the same thing I was doing at the ED Line that I was also still doing at the NNSL, but the diet and food changed. The ED Line had European types of food, whereas the NNSL supplied us with Nigerian types of food like *garri*."[20] Another claimed that the only significant difference between the British companies and the NNSL was the food served: "There was not so much difference except on the feeding aspect."[21] One seaman who worked in the catering department explained that on the national line, there was more consideration for all the crew's culinary tastes, whether they were European or Nigerian:

In the morning we wrote a menu: sometimes custard, Quaker oats, fried egg, omelets, scramble eggs, and so on. In the afternoon, we prepared rice and stew. Whenever we had Europeans among the crew, we prepared them European food differently. We sometimes prepared salad and so on for the Europeans. . . . In the evening we prepared *fufu* with *egusi* [melon soup] or *ogbono* [gumbo soup]. This was the food menu of the national line but in the ED line, we ate only European food, whether the African crew liked it or not.[22]

The seaman's testimony regarding the diverse menu on NNSL ships hints at a deeper claim with regard to the Nigerian National Shipping Line. Through the description of menus designed to suit both Nigerian and European tastes, the former steward intimated that NNSL ships were more inclusive and tolerant of the differences among crew members, regardless of their national background.

While employment with the Nigerian national line initially satisfied seamen's longings for fair and equal treatment through better salaries, the payment of overtime, and availability of Nigerian food, there was a sense of disappointment among seamen regarding the unanticipated continuities between colonial and national ships. Despite their initial enthusiasm for the nationalist enterprise, seamen soon discovered that they continued to occupy the lowest rungs of ship hierarchies, and the racial division of labor remained intact. As one seaman recalled: "Working with national shipping line, we were going to be free because it was our ship, but still when the ship came, we were the crew members. But the top, like captains, were white: chief engineer, chief mate, and boson were all white people, even second and third engineer, second and third mate were white, . . . the carpenter, the shippie, used to be white but later we had a black person as carpenter. All white people from the beginning."[23]

The presence of European officers on board made it harder for Nigerians to feel that the ships were their own. Changes in the conditions of service also took time to implement, only increasing seamen's frustrations. Archival records regarding the first few voyages of the *Dan Fodio* and the *Oduduwa* recount the mounting discontent of seamen as they confronted a transition that was overly smooth and nearly seamless for those who had invested much hope in the changes that would come with the NNSL.

On the early voyages of the *Dan Fodio*, despite initial promises, payment for overtime work had not yet been implemented when the ship first set sail. According to officials at the Palm Line in Liverpool in September 1959, the Nigerian crew became agitated and unrest stirred around the issue of unpaid overtime. As the chief officer claimed, "The crew work up to 8 hours and when called to put in more work, outside this period, without some overtime allowance, they naturally feel demoralized. They are inclined to grumble and murmur and do the job without a tang of cheerfulness." Seamen threatened to walk out, and to appease them, the management quickly organized an "ex gratia payment."[24] In another incident, which took place in Rotterdam during the ship's second voyage, it was reported that the Nigerian crew threated to walk off if the mate was not removed. The crew would not tolerate unfair treatment on Nigerian ships, but despite their protests, the mate was signed on again. The crew agreed to sail only when a federal commissioner from the United Kingdom convinced them "that it would be shameful as well as illegal to abandon their ships in a foreign port."[25] The situation came to a head on the *Dan Fodio* in August 1960, when five European officers resigned from the ship. They claimed that the Nigerian crew "had become unruly and chaotic because of the spirit of nationalism."[26] With the unrest among the NNSL Nigerian crews a growing concern, Sidi Khayam decided to board the *Dan Fodio* to conduct an investigation into the European officers' claims that nationalist sentiment had made the Nigerians intractable: "The situation came desperately in need of investigation when, with the march of events, five engineers automatically resigned from the service of the same ship, on the basis of a particularly peculiar pretext, which seems pathetic at first blush, that the Nigerian crew, was fishing around for chaos and was becoming more systematically difficult to handle, inspired by what they regarded as the feeling of their national ownership of the ship in question."[27] Khayam wrote, "If it's true that this tendency exists, it would do a world of damage."[28] His final report dismissed the allegations of the European officers and reported that relations between the races on the ship were in fact harmonious. Indeed, subsequent reports from the *Dan Fodio* indicated that tensions had been largely dispelled. But similar dynamics were also seen on the *Oduduwa*, according to a report of the operational manager in Lagos. He claimed that the police in Hamburg had to be called in during the ship's second voyage because "the crew behaved so disgracefully." The agent claimed that the potential for unrest remained high on the ships, and he feared the long-term consequences of this situation: "If Nigerian seamen continue to behave in such a manner we will find difficulty in getting good officers to serve on our ships."[29]

The unrest seen on the ships of the NNSL in 1959 and 1960 is poignant testimony to the impact nationalist ideologies and organizing had on working classes. Far removed from the centers of power and decision making, seamen nonetheless internalized the ideological currents that shaped the era of decolonization, and became inspired to hope for change. Unfortunately, the pace of change did not satisfy the seamen's longings, and their frustration at the status quo was evidenced in onboard protests and threatened walkouts. Despite their dissatisfaction, the presence of European officers on NNSL vessels was a sight that seamen would have to endure for nearly two decades more. As will be seen in the following section, the ideological commitment to Nigerianization would have to confront the lengthy process for training of Nigerian officers and captains for the NNSL ships.

NIGERIANIZING THE STAFF

From the very founding of the Nigerian National Shipping Line, plans were made to train personnel of all levels for positions both ashore and at sea. As Njoku explained to the Parliament in August 1959, one of the main factors leading to the decision to sign a deal with Elder Dempster and the Palm Line was the issue of training, as the British companies had in place the facilities and expertise necessary to prepare Nigerians to eventually take over all aspects of the shipping enterprise. The agreement between the technical partners and the NNSL called for the employment of Nigerians in managerial positions, and the training of Nigerians in seagoing jobs as officers and crew. With the arrival of the *Dan Fodio* at Lagos, Njoku reported on the quick pace of Nigerianization, to the approval of Parliament members:

> On the *Dan Fodio* during its maiden voyage, out of a crew of forty-five, thirty-one were Nigerians (applause), including the Second Mate, two Engineer Officers, a Writer and two cadets. . . . The Nigerian National Line has undertaken as a primary duty the training of Nigerians as navigating and engineering officers (applause), and shore management staff. The operational Agency Agreement will, in the first instance, run for six years, but may be terminated therefore and may be renewed only from year to year so that our hands are not tied at all. (Applause.)[30]

The efforts toward Nigerianization continued throughout the early years of the Nigerian National Shipping Line, but it would be a long while before Nigerians would command Nigerian ships. This was because the training of officers and captains spanned several years, including periods of academic training along with thousands of hours logged at sea. While ads were placed for candidates in the local press, only a small percentage of those who responded met the minimal academic requirements to begin courses for officer training. Thus, among 323 respondents to newspaper ads in 1959, only 77 were found to meet the necessary educational standards.[31] Despite these obstacles, the policy of Nigerianization remained a priority. The importance of the process to the company was emphasized in the Annual Report of the NNSL in 1962: "Particular attention is being given to the question of Nigerianisation in the company's expansion program so as to reflect the company's national character while maintaining, at the same time, the international nature of our trade. The training of management personnel as well as marine engineers is being vigorously pursued and there is no doubt that this will yield ample dividends in time to come."[32] By 1963, Nigerians could be seen in various positions of command on board ships, and the Annual Report claimed that the national line was operating with twelve deck cadets, seven engineer cadets, and five radio officers and trainees. Of the seven vessels owned by the company, six were manned by Nigerian chief stewards and had Nigerians in charge of the purser's departments. The policy of Nigerianization remained a top priority: "This aspect of our policy is being pursued with the utmost vigour. It is our hope that with the training being given to the trainee managers and other personnel it will not be too long before our key posts in our company are Nigerianised."[33]

The efforts paid off, and by 1968, only eighty-two jobs were still held by foreign employees. But here the statistics are very telling, as the top positions of ship hierarchies were still dominated by foreigners, with 9 masters, 12 deck officers, 9 chief engineers, 39 engineers/electricians, and 9 radio officers. While many Nigerians had begun training for these positions with the establishment of the national line, at the end of the first decade of operation, NNSL ships were still largely controlled by foreign captains and officers. With the very founding of the company, efforts to recruit Nigerians for these positions had to focus on educating potential candidates about the benefits and advantages of a career at sea. The NNSL focused recruitment efforts for management on recent university graduates.[34] For seagoing positions, it was decided to advertise to dispel any prejudices regarding this line of work: "Very few Nigerians knew neither the types of training necessary towards fitting themselves for a sea career or the prospects available to a qualified Master Mariner. It was felt that a brochure or booklet, providing information on a sea career, for circulating amongst suitable young men through the Schools would remove the misconceptions which many of them hold of the training and standing of a Deck Officer."[35]

For Nigerian seamen, the process of Nigerianization was long overdue. Seamen lobbied for more opportunities for crew seeking to advance in the shipboard hierarchy. Most ratings lacked the educational background to become officers themselves, but they strongly supported policies for training Nigerian officers to command the ships upon which they were employed. From both personal and organizational perspectives, seamen believed that the process of Nigerianization would improve the atmosphere on NNSL ships, as was claimed by Sidi Khayam in a letter to management in 1959: "We would be immensely impressed, if you accept the application of Nigerianisation and set out a plan for qualified boatswains, Carpenters, Second Stewards, Chief Stewards, Officers and Engineers to eventually take over. This will definitely strengthen the confidence of African Crews towards your company and give us a feeling of more security."[36]

Khayam's request reflected a deeper belief that Nigerian officers would be preferable to Europeans for the Nigerian ratings. African crews undoubtedly imagined that the replacement of European officers with Nigerians would spell an improvement in their working lives. But once the national line was established, Sidi Khayam went to great pains to emphasize that European captains could be just as fair and respected by the crew as Nigerians. In his report on race relations on the *Dan Fodio* in 1960, he claimed that Capt. J. C. Salvidge was "colour-blind," and his command of the ship reflected this: "His basic preoccupation is how to build more and more harmony among his crew, how to achieve efficiency in the style of their work, how to remove and solve the problems of all seamen under his care. He has in fact a burning impatience against quarrels and misunderstandings. His life is dominated by tolerance and discipline. This explains his irresistible attraction and prestige before all the seamen who worked with him."[37] Khayam claimed that Captain Salvidge was living proof that racial tensions could be overcome: "The man has shattered the misconception that the crew of all national origins cannot work in harmony devoid of strain and mistrust."[38] According to Sidi Khayam, Nigerians took pride in their ships, even with a British commander, as he described the greasers and stewards on board: "I saw them pick up some waste or rubbish even outside their working time. When I asked them why they bothered doing this while not on duty, they said the ship was after all their own. 'Besides, the master or old man wants the ship to be kept clean and we want to help him.'"[39] Khayam reported that the British captain organized games and competitions "to provide diversions and combat the loneliness that was often a problem with seamen." He even reported that Captain Salvidge taught some of the African crew English and arithmetic.[40] Khayam said: "He was worked side by side with European and African seamen and frankly contrasting both, he feels the Africans are as good, some of them better than some Europeans and can compete with seamen anywhere."[41]

Khayam's report emphasized that European captains could be fair in their treatment of all seamen regardless of race, and some even became the object of deep admiration and respect from Nigerian seamen. Thus, the racial identity of the officers could not guarantee either a positive or a negative relationship with the crews and the running of the ships. Some seamen claimed that once the Nigerian National Shipping Line was established, seamen got more respect from the British officers, as one explained: "After 1960, I observed that we seamen had a more cordial relationship with our white bosses but before 1960, whenever any seaman had an argument with the white, either he was right or wrong, when the ship got to Lagos, that seaman was paid off." After independence, he claimed, British captains encouraged them to see the national line as their own: "Most times, the captain called us under National Lines, and advised us to endure whatever our condition [of service] was, and after a while, we were going to benefit. He said the ships were our own and they had only come to work and earn some money, and they were bound to leave at any time but we would remain, he urged us to always do the right thing."[42]

Indeed, seamen invested their hopes in the changeover from British to Nigerian officers, but it soon became evident that racial solidarity did not guarantee harmonious working conditions on board ships. In the following sections, we will examine the impact that the Nigerianization of captains and officers had on working relationships on NNSL vessels. This discussion will be largely based on an examination of ship's logs from 1960 through 1985. These daily logs written by captains offer a rare view into the dynamics on board the ships. A review of the entries provides an excellent opportunity to examine day-to-day happenings, including technical difficulties, personnel issues, and disciplinary problems. The captain's logs contained detailed information related to incidents on the ship, but they were often reflective of the captain's perceptions. Therefore, the reading of the ship logs must be juxtaposed against interviews with seamen. Taken together, we can gain rich and valuable insights into the Nigerianization of work regimes and cultures on the NNSL vessels.

SHIP CULTURE AND NIGERIANIZATION

For Nigerian seamen, the Nigerianization of personnel played a significant role in providing seamen with a sense of belonging, and even ownership, on ships. The appearance of Nigerian captains and officers was much anticipated by seamen, and contributed to seamen's sense that the ships were "our own." Over time, the replacement of European officers and masters with

Nigerians did have a noticeable impact on the working cultures, labor hierarchies, and the overall running of the ships. Some Nigerian captains established less distance between themselves and the rest of the crew. Capt. Alao Tajudeen described it this way: "Family. We were all one family. Although our training required that cadets should not mix with ratings, in Nigerian ships, this was never so."[43] A seaman interviewed confirmed this lack of distance between Nigerian officers and crews: "They were all okay. Unlike the British, the Nigerians officers intermingled with the crew."[44]

Ship logs reveal that the Nigerian captains and officers often took on a fatherly role with the crew. At times they approached their role not only as commanders, but also as caretakers. This could be seen in an incident on the River Ogun in which a trainee carpenter had insulted the chief officer "with dirty words and refused to work overtime." The carpenter explained in his defense that he did not insult the chief officer, but that he indeed had refused to work overtime because his previous overtime was not approved. The ship's logs reported, "The Captain stated that from the carpenter's bar bill, he could see that he drinks too much. He further reminded Mr. Familun that he is merely a trainee carpenter and if he carried on in this manner, he may not succeed in becoming a full-fledged carpenter. He therefore warned him to be of good behavior from now onwards."[45] Nigerian officers also attempted to provide guidance and support to seamen, as can be seen from a 1973 logbook of the King Jaja. In this incident, Assistant Engineer L. Adio refused to go on watch "as he was found to be drunk and using swear words" to his senior officers. In a letter to the captain, the chief engineer wrote, "In my own way I did try very hard to give him sympathetic advices repeatedly to change his behavior because he was already demoted to Asst. Engineer on the vessels of this company."[46] On the Oduduwa in 1973, the second engineer pleaded with the captain to not take disciplinary action against two seamen who had missed the sailing time in Warri in September and had to catch the ship in Sapale a few days later. As reported in the log: "The 2nd engineer having said that they are good workers, both men were severely cautioned and made to understand that any such subsequent behavior will result to severe penalties."[47]

Logbooks from the NNSL ships also reveal that Nigerian captains were able to develop a kind of dialogue with the crew that was grounded in a shared cultural background. They could often speak to crew in vernacular languages and made themselves far better understood by seamen. The logbook of the River Majidum from 1983 recounts one incident involving a seaman, A. Disu, who could not perform his duties in the galley because of excessive drunkenness. The captain was called in to handle the situation and ordered the unruly Disu to rest in his cabin, but the seaman refused and "poured a torrent of abuses and insults on the Master." Disu was later called to the captain's quarters, and in the presence of the catering officer and crew spokesman, he was charged with "being absent from his place of duty, excessive drunkenness on board, disobedience of lawful order and command and action prejudiciary to good order and discipline." The captain read the charges and asked Disu if he understood. When the insolent seaman replied that he did not understand, the captain translated to him in Yoruba. At that moment, Disu "prostrated and begged for leniency and forgiveness, that he [did not know what he was doing or saying, or] what he was charged for."[48]

Another logbook offers transcribed dialogues from the *River Benue* in 1974. From these records, we see how Capt. E. Olu Ogunsiji encouraged a dialogue between Junior Engineer Ajonu, who was being charged with negligence, and the chief engineer and the fourth engineer, who were also invited to express their views on the allegations. The junior engineer had been caught sleeping while on duty in the engine room, leading to the leakage of five tons of fuel. Despite the severity of the charges, the chief engineer encouraged the captain to take a lenient approach with the offender:

> Master to C/E: Why is this J/E here before me?
>
> C/E to Master: He is here to be warned officially because his carelessness is becoming too much.
>
> Master to C/E: Can you expatiate on this word CARELESSNESS?
>
> C/E: Yes. On several occasions he has been caught sleeping in the engine room while on watch; and on one occasion he lost 5 tons (to be precise) of diesel oil while on duty because of his sleeping.
>
> Master to J/E: What have you got to say in order to defend the allegation leveled against you, as I consider same to be a grave offence?
>
> J/E: This is my first time of hearing the loss of 5 tons of oil while I was on duty in the engine room.
>
> 4/E in attendance.
>
> C/E to 4/E: Tell me of what happened?
>
> 4/E explained: When I came down to the E/R, I found the J/E dosing off while the purifier lost oil into the bilges. The 4/E then stopped the purifier and woke up the J/E to tell him what he observed when he entered the E/R.
>
> Master to J/E: From the evidence before me, I am convinced that the 4/E's statement confirms the C/E's allegation that you were

found sleeping while on duty and as such I should have dealt with your case with all seriousness but since the C/E would like to warn you I have got to give him benefit of the doubt. You are therefore warned to be of good behavior in performing your duties diligently and to conduct yourself in a sober manner while you are in this ship or otherwise drastic and disciplinary action which may lead to summary dismissal from the company might be taken against you in any future occurrence for negligence of duty in the E/R. What have you got to say?

J/E: I am sorry sir and it will not happen again in the future.

Master to C/E: In view of his "SORRINESS" would you like to pardon him?

C/E: A change is badly needed if he is to survive on this boat.

J/E: I thank you for pardoning me, sir.

Master: You are pardoned. You can go.[49]

Records indicate that Nigerian crews on NNSL ships also petitioned European captains in instances when disciplinary action was to be taken against one of the crew. Thus, on board the *River Adada* in 1982, Capt. T. Pienkowski reported that Fourth Engineer Kolawole requested to be sent home because one of his family members was dying, but the captain refused. Kolawole later had an argument and threatened the shore watchman with a knife. A delegation of officers, including the chief officer, the radio officer, and the chief steward, came to the captain to plead for the fourth engineer "because of his psychological condition." The captain finally agreed to fly him back to Lagos.[50]

The process of Nigerianization onboard NNSL vessels was experienced not only by Nigerians but also by the British seamen and officers who worked on NNSL ships. British seamen engaged with Nigerians from a wide array of cultural backgrounds, and they told stories that revealed their wonder at many of the situations they encountered as part of NNSL crews. For example, a British captain on the *River Ogun* reported that a seaman on board had complained of illness: "He had in his possession, a 'native preparation' which he procured from an undisclosed source. He had taken a dose of this native preparation the previous day. Since taking this medicine, he had in addition to other discomfort, been constipated." The captain assumed he was suffering from indigestion, but the next day, he experienced swelling all over his body, and within a few hours, the seaman died.[51]

For British seamen, voyages on NNSL ships were memorable experiences that exposed them to cultures and traditions quite different from their own, and their bemusement remained with them many years later. This can be seen in the following testimony of Derrick Bailey:

> On NNSL's *"Oduduwa"* there was an engineer's steward, Sam (weren't they all) a young, twentyish healthy young man. He took his leave in Lagos and rejoined the ship a worried man. He told us that his family's enemies had put a *juju* on him and that he would die. There was no way that we could accept that, he was too full of life, a really nice guy. We left Lagos for Port Harcourt and anchored at Dawes Island waiting for a berth. Sam spent the morning giving the engineer's cabins a good going over then went and lay down in the tonnage well and died!! Please explain.[52]

Working for the NNSL, British seamen also became unwittingly entangled in the politics of postindependence Nigeria as this affected the NNSL ships. This could be seen in the testimony of a British seaman who worked for the NNSL during the Biafra War: "When we arrived in Lagos the Nigerian civil war was on and we were conscripted into the Nigerian army. We appealed to the British Consulate to try to get off the ship but as we were on Nigerian articles they did not want to know. We took part in two invasions in Biafra. We eventually got home and I left the ship at Immingham never to go to sea again. I am sure but for that trip I would have stayed at sea for much longer."[53]

A SENSE OF HOME AND ENTITLEMENT

For Nigerian seamen, the move to the national line was a kind of homecoming and fostered a feeling of belonging on the ships of the NNSL. Particularly in the early years following independence and the establishment of the Nigerian line, seamen's identification with the NNSL ships as their own fostered a clear sense of entitlement with regard to their status on the vessels. This sense of entitlement found expression in the working cultures on board, and was apparent in the emboldened attitude seamen took with European officers and captains. Particularly in the early years, seamen were empowered by the notion that they were Nigerians on Nigerian ships, and several incidents reflected a shifting balance of power away from colonial relations. This could be seen in an incident reported on the *Yinka Folawiyo* in 1976. In this incident, the second officer found a crewman, P. Ige, banging on the door of the chief officer's cabin:

The 2nd officer found that P. Ige was trying to force the door of the chief officer's cabin and calling him to come out. The 2nd officer asked P. Ige what he doing. Ige answered that he was celebrating Nigerian Independence Day. Then P. Ige started shouting abuses at the 2nd officer and calling him names: white bastard, you are not our brother, this is a Nigerian ship. The 2nd officer shouted: please keep away from me because you are drunk and don't know what you are doing. Ige then stated that the 2nd officer takes Nigerian money and therefore, when Ige talks, the 2nd officer was to shut up. Ige then hit the 2nd officer in the shoulder with the bottle once and after this with his hands. Whilst hitting the second officer who did not strike back Ige called him a white bastard and other foul words.[54]

Following this incident, the chief officer refused to sail with the NNSL, but it was not only the British officers who became targets of crew empowerment. Nigerian seamen's sense of entitlement on Nigerian ships could also be seen in exchanges with Nigerian officers and captains. Seamen's sense of ownership on board NNSL ships was apparent in the logbook from the *River Ogun* in 1970:

> T. Morron, Able Seaman, entered the chief officer's cabin shouting and complaining about the cleaning of hatches. Mr. Oyewumi, Chief Officer, ordered him out of the cabin and back to work and he replied "fuck you, this cabin doesn't belong to you, it belongs to the whole staff of the National Lines" and continued using abusive language towards the Chief Officer for several minutes. Mr. Fanto, 2nd officer was present throughout. T. Morron is hereby fined one day's pay for using insolent and contemptuous language to the chief officer.[55]

Particularly when docked in Lagos, the seamen's sense of home and entitlement was more pronounced. This inspired them to initiate bolder protests against commands that they found unfair. In Lagos, seamen would simply walk off ships and rejoin their families when the captain's orders were deemed unreasonable. This could be seen in an incident that took place days before Christmas in 1974. On their approach to Lagos, Capt. F. Lemessurier informed the crew of the *Oranyan* that they would be given no time off for the Christmas holiday. But once the ship anchored in Lagos on 23 December, several seamen and some officers simply walked off the ship; on 27 December, the captain reported that he was still awaiting their return.[56] In another case, it was reported that Chief Officer Ali of the *King Jaja* protested against the ship's captain by disembarking each day in Lagos rather than taking part in the running of the ship. According to the ship log, the captain called Mr. Ali in to inform him that he would be deducted five days of pay for failing to participate in the running of the ship, and this deduction would continue until Ali returned to work. The captain read out the log entry to Mr. Ali and asked him if he had anything he wanted to say in his defense, to which Ali responded, "Since the 2nd June, 1975, I have come to a conclusion and decided that I cannot work with you and I have already given you a notice to pay me off. I always go out about 0900hrs and come back to the vessel about 1700hrs."[57]

The atmosphere on board NNSL vessels reflected seamen's level of comfort, at times leading to a lack of discipline. Rules were slowly relaxed, and general discipline began to decline on board ships. The lack of discipline was seen among officers who disregarded regulations regarding uniforms, requiring the NNSL management to publish a reminder to all officers: "We have observed in the past year a decline in the standards required and/or a neglect on the part of some of our officers to wear the correct company uniform whilst serving in the fleet both afloat and in port. It is, of course, appreciated and accepted that on occasion dirty or uncomfortable work in the course of their various duties necessitates that officers wear boiler suits or other protective clothing. We accordingly advise reasonable cognizance of this fact, but not to the extent it becomes an item of permitted uniform for unjustified purposes."[58]

Incidents of insubordination were frequently linked to excessive alcohol consumption, and the insolence and fighting reported in logbooks often involved drunk crew members. These incidents are revealing for what they can teach us about the roots and the nature of conflicts on board Nigerian ships, and the ways in which crews framed their discontent. One noteworthy journey in this regard was that of the *Ahmadu Tijani* in 1978, where multiple incidents of drunkenness, fighting, and insubordination were reported in the captain's log. One greaser in particular, Dosunnui, was involved in several incidents that threatened the safety of the ship. In a log entry in May, it was reported that Dosunnui demanded a cash advance from the captain, and when he was refused, he became violent toward the captain and needed restraining. Efforts to calm him down were unsuccessful, and he refused to be removed from the captain's private quarters, "claiming he is not a slave and had the right to sit anywhere."[59] The captain ordered the crew spokesman to reason with him, but apparently this had only a temporary influence on

Dosunnui, and one month later, he was again the subject of the captain's log. It was reported on the night of 21 June that the head greaser, Medieros, barged into the wheelhouse, shouting that he was fed up with Dosunnui and he was being pushed to the point of murder. It was clear to the officers present that the headman was drunk and had encouraged drinking among his men, and he was therefore sent away. Minutes later, Dosunnui entered the wheelhouse, demanding medical attention for the injuries he sustained while being struck by Medieros. Dosunnui was also ordered to leave the room, but he refused to do so. According to the log, "Mr. Dosunnui jumped into the pilot's chair in the wheelhouse and continued to obstruct the duty officer in carrying out his lawful duties—an act and misconduct which was likely to endanger the navigation of the ship." The greaser was not deterred, and he remained in the pilot's chair for the rest of the night, waiting for medical care.[60] Following these and other incidents, Captain Tsiquaye decided to limit the alcohol allocated to the crew. He posted a notice explaining the matter:

> You are aware of all the efforts I have been making to persuade and convince the crew to live in peace and harmony as brothers. You are also aware of the many incidents that have taken place due to drunkenness and certain members of the crew refusing to work, others going out of their way to fight and pursue unnecessary quarrels whilst others threaten to kill one another. It would appear from the cases mentioned above that certain people have the intention to commit murder or harm others and want to use alcohol as the means to achieve this. Since it is my responsibility to safeguard the interests and well-being of all the crew . . . it has been decided that from today the 21st day of June 1978, the Issue of Spirits to the crew has been cancelled and only half a case of beer will be allowed to each crew member as contained in the company's Standing Instructions and anyone getting drunk on these will have his beer stopped altogether.[61]

Apparently, the ban was not fully successful, as two weeks following the ban, a drunken cook chased several members of the crew with a chopper, and was discharged from the ship.[62] But the captain seems to have been generally satisfied with the return to order, and on 28 July 1978, he lifted the ban on beers, and allowed each crew member a "docking bottle" at the time of discharge.[63]

The sense of home and entitlement that Nigerians felt on board NNSL ships could also translate into a relaxed sense of fun. Unfortunately for

Nigerian crews, European captains did not often share in this playfulness. This can be seen in an incident from the *River Ogun* in 1978, in which Radio Officer A. K. Oke had delivered the following message to the captain: "Please be informed that the general manager of the company is dead, hence all our ships requested to anchor for 3 minutes at sea at 1200 hrs 1-4-78 to honor the dead man. Nigerline Lagos." The captain eventually discovered that this was merely an April Fool's prank, but only after he had ordered the work stoppage. According to the ship's log, the captain was not amused by the radio officer's explanation of what happened: "He was very sorry and his assumption that it would be understood today being April 1st could not be accepted because of the seriousness of the message, and effect on organization of vessel. Steps had already been taken to stop ship at 1200, and work to stop for 3 minutes in commemoration when at 1140 the Master realized it was a fake and informed all Heads of Departments."[64] According to the log, the captain noted that he was worried about Radio Officer Oke's future conduct and he was severely reprimanded for delivering a false message.

The nonchalant attitude of the Nigerian seamen could infuriate the European officers, as seen in an exchange between Fourth Officer Imonikhe and the captain of the *River Benue* in 1976. The officer had ignored the captain's orders to keep anchor watches on the bridge, and was found instead in the saloon eating breakfast. The captain reprimanded him, telling him that if he did not act and behave like an officer, he would be demoted. According to the captain's log, Imonikhe "laughed and asked if he was being threatened. He was told that if being reprimanded constituted being threatened, then he was indeed."[65]

Insubordination could also be seen in the interactions between Nigerian officers and the captains. Captains frequently recorded full conversations that took place in the process of disciplining junior officers, and the replies of officers to the disciplinary actions taken against them reflected a disdain for the captains' authority. For example, the logbook of the *King Jaja* from 1973 reads, "The above offences were read to the 2nd engineer—Mr. S. R. Azmi, and when asked if he had anything to say, he replied 'I do not agree with the statement put on because the captain's behavior was insulting to me.'"[66] On the MV *River Ngada* in 1980, Chief Officer Bob-Foues repeatedly disrespected the captain and disregarded his orders. The logbook records incidents in which the chief officer refused the captain's orders, threatened him with violence, and spit on him in the saloon in front of other crew members. The insubordinate officer had come to dinner wearing shorts and bathroom slippers, and the captain ordered the steward to not serve him until he went to change. Bob-Foues responded by rushing into the pantry and grabbing food, shouting, "What do you call proper dressing?"[67]

In many incidents, seamen challenged or disregarded the authority of captains when they felt that the working conditions promised to them at the founding of the NNSL were not being upheld. Seamen were aware of the official terms of their employment, and they refused to carry out orders that violated their contracts. For example, on the *River Ethiope* in 1980, the captain's log details a dispute between himself and the deck crew. The captain had complained to the bosun about the lack of work being done by the deck crew, claiming they were working only on the derricks and hatches and refused to do any other work. The master claimed that according to his experience, the crew could take on other jobs as well. In the ship log, the captain reported a protest meeting with the deck crew that took place in his cabin:

> One of the crew was demanding to change the whole crew if the Master was not satisfied. Another, Thomas, stated if the Master wanted other work, then to hire a rigging gang. In the Master's opinion this was disorderly conduct on behalf of the crew and would make no more entries until he instructed the Chief Officer who was presently ashore, as it appeared there was complete indiscipline amongst the deck crew. At approximately 1930hrs, the Chief Officer reported to the Master and the master stated he wished to discuss the matter of discipline amongst the crew, the Chief Officer replied that he would prefer to take a shower before discussing the matter and the Master replied to the Chief Officer to come up immediately after he had had a shower. At 2130, the Chief Officer reported to the Master and stated that in his opinion there is no indiscipline amongst the deck crew. The Master replied if so, then by tomorrow 5-10-1980 there had better be a different attitude amongst the deck crew.[68]

An entry from the *River Oshun* in 1981 further demonstrated the lack of regard the crew could display for the captain's orders when they felt rules were arbitrary or wrongly enforced :

> Crew were boarding cases of beer on board from this morning. I summoned all departments to officers' smoke room and tried to find out who owned these beers. They all claimed to have certain amounts of cases. I appealed with them to discharge the beers as

these were contraband goods and explained to them the possible problems the V/L might face arrival Lagos. The crew refused to carry out my instructions. Some threatened to be paid off immediately and some became very hostile. In order to prevent any possible delay to the ship in port I requested them to submit to me a signed protest also stating how many cases of beer each individual had purchased. At this time of this entry 1800hrs 15/4/81, this written document has still not been received.[69]

Seamen made unilateral decisions to ignore or amend the captain's command if they felt it violated their rights, even if this compromised the safety of the ship or cargo. This could be seen in an entry from the *River Benue* in 1974. In the incident under question, the captain reprimanded the second officer, who had not reported for guard duty because of the rain, and in his absence, a container had been broken into. The captain demanded that the officer explain why he did not show up for duty, and the officer replied, "The supervisor would not probably need me because it was raining heavily and I intended to be around as soon as the rain ceased." The exchange that followed reflects the brazen attitude of the second officer toward the captain:

> Master: Is that a reasonable answer to my statement?
> 2/O: Regarding cargo work it is.
> Master: If I put it to you that your answer is unsatisfactory and it tantamounts to negligence of duty and unconcerned attitude towards the safety of the ship and cargo as a result of which the container in question was tampered with. As a prudent duty officer you should have made yourself available to the supervisor etc. on duty with you in case of any events on board. Have you got anything to say to my preceding statement?
> 2/O: I have nothing more to say as my defense has already been declared unsatisfactory.[70]

In another incident on the *Oduduwa* in 1973, crew members were called to duty to assist in covering up the hatches during a storm. They refused to do so, claiming they were not given the required oilskin jackets. As a result, rain entered the hatch and damaged the cargo. The seamen were fined and cautioned by the captain.[71] In another incident occurring on the *River Oji* in 1981, the captain had declared a state of emergency due to an oil spill on deck. He reported that the oil spill presented a fire hazard and could also pollute the water around the dock. The declaration enabled him to demand overtime hours from the crew. Despite the declaration of emergency, the deck crew refused to carry out the order to clean up the spill, and the captain called them for a meeting to explain their refusal. He wrote, "They unanimously said that they disregarded the emergency declared as well as refused 2nd Engineer's orders because they feel neglected in respect of compensation for cleaning the oil. They assumed the sailors had compensation promised before cleaning the ship-side and I told them that this was not true." The captain decided to fine each of the men one day's pay, and denied them overtime hours for the previous day as well.[72]

These incidents reveal that crews were not simply insubordinate, but mobilized onboard protests and work stoppages when they felt that their rights were not being protected by captains on the Nigerian ships. As in the previous case where the crew refused to clean up the oil spill without being assured overtime pay, the crews of the NNSL were aware of the conditions of work promised to them and agitated to ensure that these rights were indeed protected. On board the *River Niger* in 1971, Captain Vittle reported that the crew refused to clean out the oil tanks unless they were paid "fifteen hours pay at the tank clearing rate agreed by their union for seven men plus the bosun and headman." The captain claimed that this job should normally take three or four hours, and told the crew that their demand was unreasonable. Nonetheless, in the face of the crew's refusal to do the job, the captain had little choice but to hire shore labor. The tanks were subsequently cleaned out by four men employed for two hours.[73]

DISAPPOINTMENT AND DISEMPOWERMENT

While ship logbooks describe incidents of insubordination and protest among crews, these records do not document the widespread abuses of power by captains and officers on Nigerian ships. Oral interviews with seamen revealed a pervasive sense among rank-and-file seamen that despite their hopes that Nigerian ships would provide a sense of belonging and security, the reality of employment with the NNSL was a great disappointment. Seamen came to work for the NNSL with great anticipation, but the Nigerianization of ships eventually came to represent violated agreements and unfulfilled promises. Crews on Nigerian ships complained that Nigerian captains rarely abided by the conditions of work established in agreements between management and the seamen's union, and instead made arbitrary or self-serving decisions that left seamen feeling exploited or mistreated. Increasingly over time, seamen were exposed to the whims of captains and officers and required to work under conditions that were in direct violation of official employment policies. Seamen charged that over the course of the 1970s and 1980s, until the liquidation of the NNSL in 1994, Nigerian captains and officers frequently exploited their positions of power and disregarded seamen's rights and entitlements.

The deterioration in working conditions on board NNSL ships was directly linked to the broader fate of the NNSL as a failed political project, and the incidents of authoritarianism and arbitrary command on board Nigerian ships must therefore be situated against the backdrop of the broader political history of postcolonial Nigeria. This history is one characterized by ongoing political and economic instability that over time led to increasing authoritarian tendencies and corruption on the part of ruling elites.[74] Some scholars, such as Eghosa Osaghae, have argued that colonialism introduced a system of law and order based on coercion and authoritarianism, while others have claimed that authoritarian regimes had deep roots in precolonial societies in Nigeria.[75] Despite disagreements over the roots of the phenomenon, scholars largely concur that the postcolonial period has been characterized by increasing hegemonic tendencies among ruling classes. The demise of the First Republic in 1966 signified an end to the democratic experiment in Nigeria, and gave way to a succession of military rulers for the next three decades, with the exception of the Second Republic lasting from 1979 to 1983. Military rule increased the abuses of power by ruling classes. As Augustine Ikelegbe argued, the succession of coups and military dictatorships institutionalized "authoritarian rule, hegemonic agendas, patrimonialism, clientelism, and repression."[76] Against the backdrop of diminishing resources and growing uncertainty, those in power increasingly turned to draconian methods.[77] In the face of narrowing options, working classes experienced increasing vulnerability and disempowerment.

This broader history was reflected in the working relations and hierarchies of power on the NNSL ships. The enthusiasm and anticipation that characterized crews' moves to the Nigerian line from European vessels soon gave way to bitter feelings of exploitation. Seamen's descriptions of everyday incidents on board ships reflected an overall sense that Nigerian ships were not properly run. There was widespread sentiment among seamen that European ships were well organized, predictable, and offered more security. On Nigerian ships, there was a sense of instability and arbitrariness to the rule of order, and crews complained that captains and officers had little regard for maintenance of ships or crew welfare. Seamen's assessment of their working lives on Nigerian ships soon became a metaphor for what was wrong with Nigeria in general. As one man said, "There was a problem with the NNSL. Although I did not quite understand the nature of the problem, I do know that there were problems that led to its collapse. I left the NNSL because in this country we have a lot of dictatorship. This was exactly what the problem was all about that made me leave. This affected the NNSL because sometimes you could bring about a very good idea but it would be rejected afterward without implementation."[78] For the crew, life on ships became a microcosm of the disappointments and disempowerment they experienced in the postindependence era.

The organization and payment of overtime on Nigerian ships provides a useful example of these broader dynamics. The issue of overtime payment on board ships was one of the strongest drawing points for crews to the NNSL. The rules regarding the payment of overtime on NNSL ships were established and institutionalized through agreements between management and the seamen's union at the founding of the national line. But while seamen greatly anticipated the benefit of overtime that had not existed on European ships, the reality ultimately did not meet their expectations. According to labor agreements, captains had full discretion in determining the compensation for overtime. This opened the way to bitter disputes between the master of the ship and the crew. According to the Conditions of Service formulated in 1960, seamen would be paid for hours of work that surpassed the standard eight- to nine-hour workday (depending on the seaman's job) during the week. Overtime would also be paid for all work that exceeded the six-hour workday on Saturdays, and four hours on Sundays. The regulation gave the master much discretion in determining overtime work and compensation. First, seamen were required to work overtime at the master's command, and thus could not refuse to work extra hours. In addition, overtime was not calculated in emergency situations "affecting the safety of the vessel, passengers crew or cargo (of which the Master shall be the sole judge) or for safety or emergency boat and fire drills." As seen in the incident above, the declaration of an emergency could be disputed by the seamen, who resented working overtime without compensation. Other points of contention arose around the form of compensation that was paid for overtime work. According to the regulation, the ship's commander was to keep a record of the overtime hours worked by each seaman and then determine the compensation they would receive. Compensation was not always in the form of salary, and overtime that was accumulated on sailing days, when the workload was heavier, could be paid in time-off duty in port. As the regulation stated, "Under normal circumstances, but subject always to the Master's discretion, compensating time-off in port will be limited to overtime hours earned on days of sailing and arrival."[79]

The agreement therefore gave NNSL captains full discretion in determining what was considered overtime, how many hours would be paid, and how it would be paid. This opened the door to many abuses. Seamen interviewed complained that in fact, Nigerian captains had little regard for adhering to the hours of a normal workday. Seamen often remarked that the British officers kept to a strict schedule and discipline. One remarked, "The European captains never give us problems. There was time for everything—there was time for work, food and so on."[80] Alternatively, in many testimonies, seamen complained of being asked by Nigerian officers to work at odd hours without being compensated: "[European captains and officers] are all good.... Everything have normal time and hours. When it is your time, you go and work, and when you finish, nobody worry me. I do not know about any other person, but they are good to me. Elder Dempster followed the line while the NNSL had no rules and regulation.... We often work at ED line for eight hours, but in the NNSL, you are called to duty with no specific time and at any time."[81]

Seamen claimed that the arbitrary and unregulated hours of the working day on Nigerian ships led to negligence and compromised safety. One seaman claimed that he was often forgotten while on anchor watch, and he was forced to spend hours outside in the bitter cold: "Because of this terrible freezing cold I often faced in arrival, they have me three bottles of rum to drink."[82] He claimed that this type of negligence would never be seen on European ships: "In ED line, this never happened because they are very careful."[83] Seamen complained of their subjugation to the whims of officers, and expressed a feeling of betrayal by their compatriots:

> When we were in national line, Nigerian people, captains and officers, made the work very boring for us. For example, there is time for work and time for food, but when everyone had eaten, Nigerian captains, chief engineers, and second engineers always came for their own meal at odd hours, for example at night, they woke up the steward at the wee hours of the night to warm food for them and their girlfriends. They bothered the steward a lot. This was not so under ED line; work time was work time; mealtime was mealtime for the white men, but Nigerian officers called at any time. We worked with national line as if we were slaves.[84]

Overtime was just one of the areas in which officers and captains attempted to exploit their positions of power. Increasingly, seamen on NNSL ships experienced a deepening sense of injustice as work regimes and hierarchies of power reflected a diminishing regard for the safety and well-being of the crew. The following protest letter included in the logbook of the *King Jaja* in 1972 reflects the feelings of despair the crew experienced on board:

We the above mentioned crew of this vessel have deemed it fit to submit our grievances of all what we have encountered during the voyage . . . with the captain manning the ship Mr. F.O. Olatunji.

1) On leaving Lagos for Port Harcourt on the 6th of May 1972. We began to experience the shortage of beer from May 21st 1972.

2) while on our way to Dakar for bunker we notice the shortage of foods running down gradually. On leaving Dakar, for two days we were given horse-biscuits for consumption in place of bread but yet we did not make any noise or report to anyone. On getting to Rotterdam, Holland the 10th of June 1972, the captain of the ship drew the attention of the crew saying the company have introduce a new formula saying no one should be given cash advances exceeding £5 from each port. This we refused saying we suffered enough during the voyage since we left Lagos and so long we have got our money in the bank, we must have any amount we ask for provided we are not in red. We do not ask the purser of the ship to give us what we do not have in the bank but what we have.

We feel to bring to your notice also that before the vessel left Apapa wharf for Port Harcourt the crew have worked many hours over time and on reaching Sapele and Port Harcourt most of our crew have put in for same few pounds which they were quite sure they have in bank. The captain refused and cut it down.

As a seaman, we work with our lives in hand to face any danger confronting the ship at all times and we must be given the chance to enjoy ourselves before eventuality.

While the vessel was at Port Harcourt we notice there was no beer onboard for 3 days before the vessel sail out and this was before the captain and the rest of his officer have consumed the beer for a party being sponsored by the Captain.

. . . We are sure the explanation we made in this letter to you is enough and if the captain fails to give us the money we ask for we demand the company should repatriate us home without further delay.[85]

The captain's log refuted many of the claims as false allegations and took no action but to ensure that the crew was being fed. According to seamen interviewed, it was instances such as these, in which there was unfair treatment at the hands of some officers, that led to the decline in discipline in the NNSL ships. The following description of the abuses of power reveals the bitter disregard seamen developed toward some Nigerian officers:

One Nigerian captain told me that he wanted a crate of beer and
he told me to carry it for him. I told him I don't work for him and
I can't carry it because he didn't pay me. He told me to clean his
room for him, I abandoned it. . . . One chief engineer (then we had
both white and black men), when we were serving, he asked for
water, I replied that water is there and he said put some in the cup
for me. There I was very angry and I told him that if you are waiting for me to put some water in the cup for you, I will not do it. He
insisted on water, I was just looking at him. All other officers who
were there laughed and the white captain shook his head.[86]

Another seaman claimed that abuse of power was commonplace and
widespread, and fostered deep-seated anger among the crew:

The only trouble that came is usually from the officers. This often
happen when most of the officers want to show off in front of their
girlfriends by directing some rating to go and wash their underwear.
When some rating now say no, it became the source of conflict.
Some officer also have good relationship with the ratings while majority were bad. So, we know how to treat them because the Bible
said that by their fruit, we shall know them. You, if you are good,
we would be good to you and if you are bad we do the same to you.
This problem has nothing to do with the management.[87]

For some, the experience with Nigerian captains was so disappointing that
they ultimately preferred the British. The disappointments with the NNSL
were linked to Nigerianization: "When our people took over, there was relative peace, a short-lived peace, because the way and manner our Nigerian
officers spoke to us was forceful, so either you liked it or not, we must do
whatever we were told to do, obey first before complaining." When asked if
Nigerian bosses were better than the white captains, he said, "I can't say they
were better because they were both educated in the act of seamanship, but
the patience the white bosses had, the Nigerian bosses never had it."[88]

Seamen who had formerly imagined themselves as "workers of the world"
were now, in no uncertain terms, workers of Nigeria:

Under the British, we usually sailed to Germany, Liverpool, Spain;
if by chance, they improvised and sailed to India, the British captains paid us for such improvisation, it may be little, but that was
not so with Nigerian captains. . . . ED line has improved the salary

of its workers according to international standard but we, in the national line, still remain the same. . . . In ED line, we worked according to the law and when you do that you are better off, but in the national line anything could happen. Lack of discipline. . . . Even British ship officers used to taunt us that between British officers and Nigerian officers, who is better? Really, we were happy that we had our fellow Nigerians as captains and ship officers, but they maltreated us.[89]

As seen in this review of working conditions and labor relations on NNSL ships, the appearance of black captains did not necessarily bring lasting harmony to NNSL ships. Conflicts with Nigerian captains and officers, and a deep disappointment with working conditions on NNSL ships, led to a longing for employment on colonial shipping vessels. Some seamen came to romanticize the relationships they had with the British officers, but these testimonies are in fact powerful indictments of the National Shipping Line as an anticlimax to seamen's aspirations. This disappointment was only to grow over time, and evolved into a general critique of the postindependence era in Nigeria. As will be seen in the next chapter, resources of the NNSL became increasingly scarce over time, and all those associated with the Nigerian National Shipping Line, from seamen to captains and officers and management, manuevered to maximize opportunities against the backdrop of growing insecurity. The optimism that accompanied seamen's testimonies of decolonization ultimately gave way to images of corruption and decline.

6 ∽ Seamen in the Shadow of the NNSL Decline and Demise

IN AN INTERVIEW CONDUCTED in Liverpool in 2009 with a former Elder Dempster executive, the topic of discussion was the decline and demise of the Nigerian National Shipping Line (NNSL). At one point in the conversation, Kenneth Birch suggested that the process of establishing the NNSL was too hasty, and the buyout of the technical partners happened too early. Birch was critical of the politicization of the enterprise. He acknowledged the pressures that led to the Nigerian government's decision, but he suggested that "they weren't ready yet."[1] The sentence stayed with me throughout the remaining course of my research on the NNSL. These remarks suggested that the fate of the NNSL could have been different had there been institutional, structural, or political changes to the ways in which the Nigerian line was established and run. Throughout the interviews and archival research, I have spent much time speculating about what political, structural, or economic conditions could have or should have been in place so that the Nigerian National Shipping Line would have succeeded.

But in an interview in Lagos two years later, a former engineer with the NNSL provided a very different perspective. According to Olukayode Akinsoji, the failure of the shipping line was not linked to political interventions or institutional deficiencies, but rather to the cultural distinctiveness of Nigeria. As he explained it, "Shipping depends on some elements of culture. You have to have the right culture to keep abreast in shipping, and if you don't have that culture, it will be difficult for you to sustain shipping." When I asked him what specifically about "Nigerian culture" put Nigerians at a disadvantage in the shipping industry, he spoke about the "time consciousness" that was lacking from Nigerian society: "Time consciousness, which shipping is all about. Time consciousness is very important. Take it from a point of view that a ship has a life span and it is operating in a competitive environment and you must optimize from the vessel within its life span in a competitive environment. Whoever does well under these circumstances often has the advantage. Based on that, everything has to fall in place. It is about a lack of time awareness."[2]

The differences in the perspectives of Birch and Akinsoji are reflective of broader academic debates regarding the political and economic history of Nigeria in the postcolonial era. Confronting a history of extreme political instability, economic failures, vast disparities in the distribution of wealth, and massive, endemic corruption, scholars have debated the roots and causes of Nigeria's postcolonial predicaments. Debates such as these are not limited to scholars of Nigeria, and recent years have seen significant contributions to academic deliberations regarding the economic and political difficulties faced by postcolonial states in Africa. On the one side of this debate are those who identify external influences, particularly colonialism, as the cause of institutional weaknesses leading to political instability and economic stagnation in the postcolonial era. Mahmood Mamdani, for example, has argued that the institutional legacy of colonialism remained intact following independence in Africa, and as a result, there has been little change in the nature of power in the postcolonial era. While some variations exist, Mamdani claimed that throughout the continent, the preservation of colonial institutions of rule resulted in the continuation of centralized coercive authority, nepotism, and corruption. Postcolonial elites continue to reap the benefits of despotic rule inherited from the colonial state, while the masses fail to organize any meaningful resistance to authoritarianism.[3] Proponents of underdevelopment or dependency theories focus on the economic legacies of colonialism and claim that political independence did not translate into economic independence. As Alois Mlambo wrote, postcolonial states "inherited non-viable, mono-cultural economies," and remained marginalized and disadvantaged in a "generally disabling global economic environment."[4] With regard to Nigeria specifically, Eghosa Osaghae has argued that colonialism introduced an "extractionist" state to Nigeria, whose sole purpose was to facilitate the smooth exploitation of resources and expropriation of resources, without investing in social services or development schemes. The postcolonial state, he argued, was the direct descendant of this colonial model.[5] Abonyi Nnaemeka claimed that colonialism introduced a form of statehood that lacked cultural roots in Africa, and the state therefore became an "amoral entity" that was carried over into the postcolonial era.[6]

Alternatively, recent years have seen the appearance of critiques and theories that attribute postcolonial political and economic predicaments to cultural norms and social systems deeply rooted in local African societies. Patrick Chabal and Jean-Pascal Daloz, for example, claim that culturally entrenched social systems based on patrimonialism and patron-client networks centered around "Big Men" have survived and thrived in postcolonial societies, hindering the development in postcolonial Africa of democracies based on Western notions of individualism.[7] In the context of Nigeria, there is a large body of literature on the role of what Richard Joseph has called "prebendalism" and its deep roots in Nigerian politics. According to Joseph, in the system of prebendalism, politicians see their office as a means of exploiting resources of the state for their own personal wealth and aggrandizement.[8] Prebendalism underscores how and why Nigerian ruling elites use public office to parcel out national resources to their inner circles, but as Chudi Uwazurike wrote, it is a system "whose ethos now permeates down through the culture."[9] The patronage associated with prebendalism also has deep roots in many local political traditions. As Isaac Albert has argued, patron-client relations were the basis of political, economic, and social life in the precolonial cultures of the Hausa, Yoruba, and Igbo. Hierarchies and inequalities were personified in "godfather" figures, who were gatekeepers to power and provided resources and security to subordinates and loyalists. Present-day godfatherism, Albert wrote, "is a primordial tradition taken to a criminal extent."[10]

Thus, scholarly explanations for the "failures" of the postcolonial waver between institutional/structural perspectives on the one hand, and more culturally centered explanations on the other. But whether coming from the institutional or the cultural perspective, it seems that the notion of "failure" drives the literature on the postcolonial Nigerian state. How might the failure of the NNSL fit into this larger debate of politics and economics in Nigeria? The history of the Nigerian National Shipping Line follows broader trajectories that characterize postcolonial political and economic developments in Nigeria. What began as an ideological venture to symbolize Nigerian independence soon deteriorated into a breeding ground for economic waste and corruption. At all levels, from management to captains and officers, and finally seamen, those who took part in the history of the NNSL attempted to navigate a complex political and economic terrain and to turn any circumstance into an opportunity. This bleeding of the company resources meant there were no resources for maintaining ships, paying bills, and upholding contracts. By the 1990s, the NNSL was in a deep financial crisis. Ships were seized abroad for unpaid bills, and the periodic injections of funds from the government disappeared along with the rest of the company resources. The NNSL was finally shut down in 1994 by the head of state, Gen. Sani Abacha.

The NNSL decline toward the misappropriation of resources and blatant acts of illegality must be seen against a broader backdrop that is full of complexities. Daniel Smith's work offers a useful model for taking into account the multitude of structural and cultural factors underlying the demise of the NNSL. In a study of contemporary Nigeria, Smith set out to understand what he described as a society plagued by corruption. Smith argued that corruption is neither solely institutional nor solely cultural, but rather rooted in "the complex intertwining of popular morality, contemporary social processes and postcolonial statecraft."[11] Nigerians have had a complex and contradictory relationship to corruption, as they engage in the social reproduction of corruption "even as they are also its primary victims and principal critics." Thus, while Nigerians frequently condemn corruption, they also participate in behaviors that enable and even glorify it. But corruption is not experienced in the same ways across class, and it is essential to pay attention to what stories are being told about corruption and who is telling them. According to Smith, the focus on discourses and practices of corruption can provide rare insights into the aspirations and frustrations of Nigerians, but it can also reveal the enormous inequalities that characterize postcolonial Nigerian society.

Following the suggestion of Daniel Smith, this chapter will examine the complex set of factors that led to economic insecurity and inequality in the NNSL as the backdrop for understanding the decline to misappropriation, illegality, and, finally, liquidation. It will be seen that the NNSL, which began as a political endeavor, was underfunded and mismanaged by politicians and their networks of clients, who had little understanding or interest in developing a successful shipping company. Instability was exacerbated by a lack of committed leadership, and in the absence of authority, all parties involved attempted to seize opportunities as a safety net in a climate of immense uncertainty. The examination of the demise of the NNSL demonstrates that material inequalities become a breeding ground for corruption, and corruption can therefore not be understood in isolation from inequality and injustice. It will be seen that the turn to illegality, in the forms of theft or drug trafficking on the part of seamen, or misappropriation of company resources on the part of officers and management, cannot be divorced from broader political and economic contexts.

The troubled history of the Nigerian National Shipping Line has been documented by several scholars. From the start, the endeavor faced disadvantages rooted in the inequalities of the political economy of the international shipping industry. Political and economic circumstances in Nigeria also greatly limited the potential for the NNSL to succeed: There was a lack of sufficient resources to operate and expand, a profoundly unstable political climate in Nigeria that led to a revolving door of management hirings and firings, and an acute lack of the managerial and technical expertise necessary for running a successful shipping venture. This list of insurmountable challenges brought debilitating instability to the NNSL over time, leading the way to abuses by those who had little vested interest in the growth and success of the company over the long term. The NNSL thus became an easy source of revenue for politicians and their networks of clients who lacked both the knowledge and the commitment necessary for nurturing a successful shipping venture. Over the course of the 1970s and 1980s, economic booms added lifelines to the company that were quickly exploited or wasted, only prolonging the inevitable outcome of liquidation that came in 1994.

As seen in chapter 4, the establishment of the NNSL was primarily an expression of economic nationalism, and had great symbolic significance for a nation on the eve of independence from colonial rule, but the viability of the venture as a successful shipping business was given little consideration. Gerald Chidi wrote, "The ships were indeed expected to play the role of 'Ambassadors' for the emerging independent country."[12] Beginning with the hasty buyout of the technical partners in 1961, political agendas shaped the history of the NNSL until its demise in the 1990s, and ideological rhetoric was continually invoked by politicians and management to explain company policies.

From the start, appointments to the management of the NNSL were political, resulting in the selection of company directors and board members who had little knowledge of the shipping industry. Already in 1962, Elder Dempster officials were concerned by the impact that this politicization would have on the NNSL, as seen in the following correspondence regarding the appointment of Kolawole Balogun, an NCNC politician with close ties to Nnamdi Azikiwe, to replace Louis Ojukwu: "The new Chairman is by background a politician and there is no doubt that his appointment as Chairman of the Nigerian National Lines is entirely a political one. In these circumstances, Chief Balogun will no doubt associate himself with the type of publicity to which the Nigerian press is always very willing to listen in relation to the National Shipping Line."[13] The fears of this Elder Dempster official were not unfounded, and Balogun did indeed use his new position to unleash a virulent critique in the press of the global shipping industry and the disadvantages faced by developing countries aspiring to ship their cargo at reasonable rates. As *Lloyd's* reported in 1962, Chief Balogun took over the chairmanship of the NNSL by declaring "The Battle for Cargo":

> The Nigerian National Line must have its own share of cargo and we will not be brushed aside by all sorts of formulae worked out with no other intention than to keep developing countries in their place. We do not ask to be pampered but we do ask to be given our own share of trade. We propose to expand. Nigeria will build new ships. We are aware that many shipbuilding yards all over the world are now offering reasonable prices and easy terms. Naturally, we are tempted to secure the best ships, pay reasonable prices and securing the most favourable terms having regard to many commitments of a developing country like Nigeria. First, we would naturally look forward to doing business with our old friends, but if we are taken for granted we would look further afield.[14]

Despite Balogun's antagonistic rhetoric, he did not succeed in significantly increasing the percentage of cargo carried by the NNSL during his three-year tenure as director of the national line. As seen in the charts below, the NNSL controlled only a minuscule share of the total shipping volume in the first ten years of its existence:

Shipping Activities at the Nigerian Ports by Nationalities
(Selected Years)

Nationality	Number of Vessels Entered at the Nigerian Ports							
	1960/61	%	1962/63	%	1965/66	%	1969/70	%
Nigerian	150	3.2	364	8.6	156	3.6	152	4.6
British	1,959	42.3	1,260	29.7	1,156	26.4	607	17.8
Liberian	466	10.1	325	7.7	352	8.0	233	7.2
Norwegian	403	8.7	430	10.1	462	10.6	220	6.8
Dutch	352	7.6	403	9.5	247	5.6	262	8.1
West German	255	5.5	298	6.9	396	9.1	231	7.1

continued

Shipping Activities at the Nigerian Ports by Nationalities
(Selected Years) *continued*

Nationality	Number of Vessels Entered at the Nigerian Ports							
	1960/61	%	1962/63	%	1965/66	%	1969/70	%
French	155	3.3	94	2.2	272	6.2	101	3.1
Ghanaian	56	1.2	131	3.1	127	2.9	42	1.3
Others	837	18.1	940	22.2	1,206	27.6	1,475	44.0
Total	4,633	100.0	4,245	100.0	4,374	100.0	3,323	100.0

Source: Bassey Udo Ekong, "Survival Opportunities and Strategies of a Marginal Firm in a Cartelized Oligopoly: Case Study of the Nigerian National Shipping Line" (PhD diss., Michigan State University, 1974), 77.

West African Lines Conference (WALCON) 1962/63

Member Lines	Nationality	Fleet Strength	Gross Registered Tonnage	Percent of Fleet Strength
Elder Dempster Line	British	54	353,301	19.7
Guinea Gulf Line	British	36	280,141	13.1
Palm Line	British	24	145,863	0.8
Holland West African Line	Dutch	63	369,529	22.9
Dal Deutsche	German	14	131,135	5.1
Scandinavian West Africa	Danish Norwegian Swedish	68	852,537	24.8
Black Star Line	Ghanaian	10	54,182	3.6
Nigerian National Shipping Line	Nigerian	5	29,292	1.8

Source: Bassey Udo Ekong, "Survival Opportunities and Strategies of a Marginal Firm in a Cartelized Oligopoly: Case Study of the Nigerian National Shipping Line" (PhD diss., Michigan State University, 1974), 81.

In order to achieve a significant increase in the cargo share of the NNSL, Kolawole Balogun would need to acquire more ships and renegotiate WALCON agreements determining the tonnage allocated to conference members. But Balogun did not have any expertise in the shipping industry, which would have been necessary to truly wage his "Battle for Cargo." Moreover, fleet expansion required massive capital investment, and this was not forthcoming from the federal government. Two ships were purchased in 1963, but these did not have a significant impact on the NNSL carrying capacity. In any event, Kolawole Balogun's tenure was cut short in 1966, when he was replaced by Otunba Adekunle Ojora. Ojora was a member of the royal family of Lagos, and the NNSL directorship was only one of several directorships that he held, including the United Africa Company and chairman of AGIP Oil. Ojora's appointment, like those who came before and after him, was political, and he had no expertise in shipping. Political appointments such as these had grave consequences for the running of the company over the long term. Bassey Ekong wrote, "Except for just a few cases, most board chairmen have been anything else but practical businessmen, versed with shipping techniques. . . . That political factors are allowed to influence board appointments can never ensure neutral influences on the managerial and operations staff of the company. Thus appointments and rewards of such staff may not be by pure merit alone."[15]

The political instability that plagued Nigeria during the lifetime of the NNSL only exacerbated the situation. According to Okechukwu Iheduru, Nigeria had twenty ministers responsible for the transport portfolio between 1952 and 1994.[16] Constant changeovers in the political leadership over the years led to endless volatility and unpredictability; former managing director Gerald Chidi recalled, "Regular changes in the headship of the Federal Ministry of Transport and the company brought inconsistency in the focus and vision of the company. For instance, during my tenure as the managing director of the company from 1990 to 1993, I worked under four ministers of transport and my successor (1993–1995) also served under four ministers of transport and every minister had his own ideas."[17] Chidi claimed that this constant changeover in management led to many unsuccessful initiatives and wasted resources. He explained, "Each new appointee brought in different styles and ideas which never endured let alone yield the desired fruits."[18] Seamen blamed the politicization of the NNSL for its demise: "The NNSL failed because of the people that were managing the company. They do not know anything about the sea. Some of them have never been to the sea in their life. Some have not even seen a ship in their life, yet they were brought to manage the company and from there they started embezzling the money. They did not care about us and the nation that has the ships."[19]

The political intrusion into the running of the NNSL led to abuses by some politicians who redirected resources of the company to their own interests, but an equally damaging impact of the political establishment on the running of the national line was the inaction of the government. All decisions regarding capital investments and fleet expansion, the extension of activities, rates and charges for services rendered to the public, investment of surplus funds, borrowing money, or raising capital had to be decided by the government. Ultimately, it was the lack of action on the part of politicians that was most debilitating for the NNSL. Many critics have noted that there is a deep incongruence between the successful running of a company in a competitive and cutthroat market such as shipping, and the operation of a government bureaucracy. Rather than running the NNSL as a profit-driven venture in a highly competitive and complex industry, Iheduru argued that the state ran the shipping company as an extension of a government ministry.[20] This handicapped the NNSL. Bassey Ekong explained, "The company is a marginal firm in the oligopoly—the conference—which itself faces intern-conference rivalries as well as the competition from well-entrenched tramps. . . . This means that the National Line has got to monitor its market and act swiftly to catch up opportunities by judicious extensions and curtailments of its services if it must survive in the economic sense. How then can the National Shipping Line perform these tasks, calling for prompt reflex decision making when it is supposed to work within the iron-clad controls of such ministerial directives?"[21] Turning the NNSL into an economically viable enterprise would have required the government to make a long-term commitment to the venture and to take risks when necessary. But the government was overly cautious. Ekong wrote in 1974, "While security is being pursued, over-cautiousness had tended to slow down real progress capable of any able management personnel." Ekong charged that the government was too slow to invest capital, and resources were therefore not properly exploited: "Red-tapism of public service has been allowed to influence this business venture decision making process."[22] New ships had to be purchased, and old ships required large investments in maintenance to keep them running properly, but the government mainly deliberated without taking action. According to Ekong, throughout the 1970s, the federal government feared the instability that characterized the shipping industry and wanted to be convinced of the soundness of any expansion proposal before risking capital investments.[23]

This kind of conservatism and politicization in a dynamic business such as shipping was indefensible and devastating, and many capable staff members left in frustration or were pushed out, further weakening the potential for the NNSL to succeed.[24] Thus, the first Nigerian general manager, Nelson Oyesiku, who was appointed in 1964 to replace Donald Tod, left in 1968, claiming he was tired and disgusted by the politicization of the shipping line: "I am a professional and it got to the point where I could not bear the intrigues anymore. The nepotism, politics and what have you were unbecoming and I did not think it was good enough for a company like the NNSL so I quit."[25] In 1991, the *African Maritime Economist* described the organization as a Mafia, claiming, "If you belong to the reigning camp even if you do not qualify for a particular post, you will get it. Efficiency or inefficiency is irrelevant and if you try to correct the flaws therein, you get the boot for being a loud mouth."[26]

The NNSL ships bore the signs of the mismanagement and political gridlock that plagued the company. By 1972, 60 percent of the fleet was more than ten years old, and maintenance costs rose along with the age of the vessels. From the very start, the NNSL ships were smaller and slower than those of the other conference lines. Already in 1960, GM Donald Tod wrote, "Records show on average that our ships are much worse than others."[27] A former captain of the NNSL described the situation: "The NNSL was our pride, though it started with old ships. This was why most of our engineers became very proficient at their work, very knowledgeable and hardworking because the conditions were terrible. They did all the repairs themselves. And we were very proud of them. In ED and Palm Line, most of the ships were air-conditioned, unlike the ships of the NNSL. Some of the ships such as MV *Jaja*, the *Oduduwa*, et cetera, were very old."[28] A former engineer with the NNSL recalled his first journey in 1968: "I went on ship a month after school with a ship that was not too healthy to go to Liverpool. We were about six cadets from Lagos to Liverpool on the ship that was going for repair. And it took us about a month to Liverpool. And this was a trip that was supposed to take us nine days. And it was my first experience."[29] British seamen who worked on the Nigerian ships in the early years recalled the immense problems they faced in trying to properly operate and maintain the vessels:

> The *Dan Fodio* seemed to be jinxed, as whenever she was in port she gained fines for polluting—she ALWAYS had a plume of thick, black oily smoke from her funnel when the port authorities were

around. The *Cross River* was another exciting ship, always having engine problems! I remember she had an engine malfunction just at the wrong time (aren't they always!) putting the ship, with my mother and father on board, onto the rocks on the way up to Grangemouth. Took an Admiralty tug to pull her off, doing minor damage to the ship, but a huge amount of damage to my father's pride![30]

One British officer, who worked as an engineer with the NNSL from 1962 to 1965, had worked on various ships including the *Ahmadu Bello*, *King Jaja*, *Herbert Macauley*, and *Oranyan*, all of which had some ongoing mechanical problems. But it was particularly the *Dan Fodio*, which he referred to as "Dirty Dan," that was most ill-fated: "All we seemed to do was change banjo pipes, to stop water leaks, and cage fuel valves, to try and stop sparks coming out the lum. When I look back I must have been off my own trolley to keep going back."[31] He claimed that the *Oranyan* also had a very poor reputation among the British officers, and it was rumored that one engineer left that ship "in a straight jacket." Another British engineer who had worked for the NNSL from 1966 to 1968 wrote: "The trip in the *Oranyan* was a nightmare trip and my last trip to sea. I flew out to join her in Dakar, Senegal replacing the 3rd engineer. The company told me he had missed the ship at Dunkirk, he actually refused to sail in her and tried to stop her sailing as he thought she was unsafe. He was right."[32]

The management of the NNSL made the case for fleet expansion throughout the 1970s, claiming the national line was in dire need of new ships in order to increase the line's cargo share. At the time, the NNSL carried only 10 percent of the total volume of traffic in Nigerian ports.[33] Political circumstances made the situation worse, as Gerald Chidi explained: "It took the Federal Government almost five years to approve the tonnage expansion programme and modernisation of NNSL ships in the seventies. By the time the vessels were eventually built and introduced into the market, a measure of obsolescence had set into the original concept."[34] The nineteen ships ordered in 1977 at the cost of $180 million arrived within two years, but no sooner were these ships delivered to Nigeria than it was acknowledged that they were not optimally suited to changes in the industry brought on by containerization. At this point, Chidi claimed, "it took another five years to convince the government about the need to phase out the 19 combo vessels with a view to introducing appropriate vessels that were technologically up to-date as well as meeting market demands."[35] In 1984, the NNSL owned twenty-four vessels, but most of the ships were badly in need of repair. Even if the NNSL ships had functioned at full capacity, the fleet still remained minuscule in comparison to the 6,080 ships that called at Nigerian ports annually in the 1980s.[36] By 1991, the NNSL had only twelve aging and extremely uneconomical vessels, and management made plans to auction off several of these in order to finance the purchase of new ships.[37]

Historians of the international shipping industry have bemoaned the "traditional veil of secrecy" that has shrouded its operations over time. As British historian S. G. Sturmey wrote, "Shipping is not an industry which enjoys scrutiny," and much information about rates for services, income, and expenses is simply not available, as it has never been collected.[38] But even in an industry traditionally known for its lack of transparency, record keeping and preservation within the NNSL was particularly scanty. Very little information regarding the financial status of the NNSL was made public, and few sources of the financial records of the company have been preserved. In a 1974 doctoral thesis that studied the economic viability of the NNSL, Bassey Ekong wrote, "The published data in the company's annual report does not seem to offer sufficient information for serious study of the company's operations." Ekong continued, "The secrecy behind the data has been defended on reasons of protecting the company's interests."[39] Thus, a full and detailed reckoning of the company's finances is not possible to undertake, but a few studies conducted over the years by scholars, journalists, and members of the shipping industry in Nigeria provide important insights into the internal workings of the company. From the information available, it is clear that the inefficiency and waste that plagued the NNSL were largely glossed over by accounting practices that concealed losses over the long term. The minister of transportation and management of the NNSL took liberties in determining what information was included in annual reports and the balance sheet. According to Ekong, many costs were simply not included in the annual budget, including some very basic and highly significant expenses such as maintenance of the fleet and the interest paid on government loans. Ekong charged, "Apparently this was in a bid to reduce the level of operational expenses and to inflate the capital value of the company."[40] With much information missing from annual budgets, Ekong claimed that the financial problems facing the NNSL were not reflected in the published accounts and balance sheets. As maintenance fees were not part of annual budgets, the repairs needed were never made. He wrote, "During the first 13 years of the company's operations, profits before depreciations were positive throughout the entire period. When the long-term costs of maintaining and renewing ships was being delayed or avoided all together in the short run, it was possible to cover the variable short-term costs. But over the long term, the ships fell into disrepair and needed renewal and this was not budgeted.

And, the depreciation of the ships, when taken into account, meant that the company was running at a loss over its entire life."[41]

THE NNSL AND THE INTERNATIONAL
POLITICAL ECONOMY OF SHIPPING

Even if the Nigerian government had invested the necessary resources and commitment into the Nigerian National Shipping Line, the NNSL would have still have had to contend with the hegemonic structures of power that shaped the world shipping industry. As Iheduru has argued, developing nations have faced enormous challenges in their latecomer efforts to develop national fleets and to compete in an industry dominated by industrialized nations. West African states, Iheduru claimed, could not keep apace with the revolutionary changes taking place in the world shipping industry from the 1970s onward: technological innovations in the size and quality of ships, the development of new cargo-handling techniques, and fast-changing communication and information systems, to name just a few.[42] The organization of the industry into shipping conferences also came with challenges for late-industrializing nations. West African nations entered into these cartels as junior partners and, as such, had little power to influence decisions regarding freight rates or volume. Ekong wrote, "Where the market is characterized by pure oligopoly or cartelized oligopoly on the part of service suppliers while consumers of the services have no appreciable joint action form in the market, the most powerful decides unilaterally for the less powerful on the frequency, adequacy, and rates of the services supplied."[43] At the point in time when the NNSL was founded, shipping conferences decided on the frequency and quantum of services offered, as well as freight rates.[44]

Despite their junior status, the newly established Ghanaian and Nigerian shipping lines entered willingly into the conference system in order to ensure a share of the trade for their national ventures. Subsequently, a whole new set of challenges emerged when the power and influence of the conferences waned over the course of the 1980s. Iheduru wrote, "Just as West Africans were scrambling to join the conferences, the dominance of this form of organizing the shipping trade globally began to crumble under the weight of the technological revolution in the industry which in turn led to structural changes in the industry."[45] The breakdown in the influence and control of the conferences over the trade meant that West African states suffered a "drastic decline in the ability of their national governments to enforce cargo reservation and flag discrimination policies upon which they depended for their existence."[46] The Nigerian National Shipping Line thus entered into the shipping industry in an era of revolutionary changes with which the company could not keep pace. The result of this, Iheduri argued, was a "series of unethical behaviors adopted by shipping companies in order to break-even."[47]

NIGERIAN SEAMEN AND THE NNSL

The sordid history of the NNSL has provided fodder for critics of post-colonial governance in Nigeria, the failed development of the Nigerian maritime sector, and the inequalities of the international shipping industry. What has been largely left out of these studies is the impact that the ill-fated venture had on the lives and livelihood of Nigerian seamen. In turning our attention to the destiny of seamen employed by the Nigerian National Shipping Line during the years of the company's decline, we can gain a working-class perspective on this history that has been written largely from above. In what follows, it will be seen that the mismanagement of resources in the NNSL had dire consequences for the terms of employment and the working lives of seamen. As resources were increasingly mishandled and plundered, seamen experienced a worsening of conditions on board ships and deterioration in compensation and benefits under the Nigerian national line. According to Iheduru, the managerial instability and administrative vacuum led to a "leakage of authority" within the organization.[48] Archival material and interviews with seamen reveal the extent to which this leakage of authority came to bear on the work culture and work regimes on NNSL ships. The dynamic is reflected in the following testimony of a seaman who had worked for both Elder Dempster and the NNSL:

> When we were working under ED line, whenever we left Liverpool for Lagos, when we got there, we conducted general maintenance and repairs on the engine before we sail again. Maybe we had just two days to stay in Lagos, but we must conduct this general maintenance. From this general maintenance, we engine crew had a lot of experience about the ship engine. . . . Under national line, we, the engine room crew, were left alone to do the general maintenance and repairs unlike in ED Line, where both European officers and African crew members did the work together. Nigerian officers would abandon everything. Sometimes, when the ship broke down in the national line, we were left alone to repair the engine at night, and that was in the middle of the sea.[49]

As will be seen in what follows, in the absence of authority and dedicated leadership, the competition over a share of increasingly scarce resources led to a breakdown in discipline and a disregard for maintenance. The scarcity of resources, endemic uncertainty, and the lack of authority also drove employees of the NNSL—from ratings to officers and management—to maximize the opportunities available to them through their employment with the shipping company. This included widespread engagement with private trading of secondhand goods on Nigerian ships, but increasingly also led to a turn toward illegality on the part of crews, officers, captains, and management of the Nigerian line.

As the working class, seamen were the most vulnerable to the scarcity of resources that shaped the history of the NNSL. Their experiences as employees of the Nigerian line testified to their disempowerment and lack of recourse. Already in the early years of NNSL's existence, seamen complained that despite early promises, the terms of employment on NNSL ships were not an improvement on those of Elder Dempster vessels. Seamen's first major protest against the NNSL management came in 1966 because of a decision to retire seamen over the age of fifty-five without any compensation. In a *Daily Times* article regarding the protest, the seamen's union described the agreement "as most wicked and damaging" and represented a worsening of "the already deplorable condition of the Nigerian seamen since the inception of sea jobs in Nigeria."[50] Nigerian seamen were viewed as contracted labor by the management of the NNSL and were offered none of the same benefits enjoyed by the NNSL management and officers, such as pension plans and cash advances for buying cars.[51] By contrast, already in 1964 the management of Elder Dempster considered offering basic benefits to Nigerian seamen employed on their ships. Discussions were held around the option of offering employment benefits and pensions for at least a portion of Nigerian seamen, and some form of compensation for those who retired after working for the company for many years. Records from an Elder Dempster management meeting in Lagos revealed that while the management was not anxious to extend these benefits to the seamen, they recognized the inevitability of granting some basic rights, and acknowledged that seamen who had dedicated many years of service to Elder Dempster were entitled to them. As the meeting notes recorded: "Mr. Glasier said that he did not wish that this matter would be put forward or even suggested to the seamen or the Union at the present moment, but it would be a useful thing to clear one's thoughts on the matter in case at some time in the future we wanted to make the offer. He then went on to say, what he had in mind was some reward for a man who had completed 20, 25, 30 or even upwards years of service."[52] The management of the NNSL, on the other hand, showed no inclination to extend basic employment benefits to Nigerian seamen. On the contrary, seamen were seen as an unskilled and expendable workforce. In an interview with a former training and development officer of the NNSL, Isaac Bezi, seamen were described as migrant labor: "The ratings came in as migrant workers or laborers. You need no experience before you could become a rating. Ratings are like casual workers or auxiliary staff on board, not permanent staff. Ratings were not part of NNSL development."[53]

The characterization of seamen as "casual labor" rather than permanent employees of the NNSL meant that seamen received a salary only for those periods when they were signed on to ships. While waiting for employment back at home, they received no compensation. By contrast, British seamen received a weekly allocation for time ashore.[54] The arrangement caused great hardships for Nigerian seamen, particularly during the slowdowns and recessions that plagued the global shipping industry in the 1970s and 1980s. Over the first decade of operations, the number of seamen actively employed by the NNSL fell by half. According to archival records, there were 1,543 seamen employed between 1962 and 1963, while that number dropped to 863 in 1968.[55] In his notes from a visit to West Africa in 1969, Malcolm Glasier described the scene outside the seamen's union office in Lagos, where large numbers of unemployed seamen congregated, noting, "I was told that this is a permanent feature and was not specially arranged for my visit." Union president Benson Yogoi told the British officials that his chief worry was "the constant pressure of unemployed seamen."[56]

In an effort to alleviate the situation, the seamen's union negotiated for a rotational hiring system from the 1970s onward. According to this system, seamen on the register were given employment for six months at a time, and then dropped off to enable others to sign on. While the arrangement was initially deemed preferable to removing large numbers of seamen from the register, the system opened the way to abuses. Rather than providing security, the rotational system made seamen feel increasingly vulnerable, as one seaman explained:

> The rotational longshore was initially fair to all but later it became
> a punishment. . . . The Nigerian line wanted to lay us off because
> of redundancy. But the union insisted that rather than totally lay off
> all seamen like it was done in the railway sector, let us rotate the job
> among seamen. Every six month we will rotate seamen so that every-
> one would be fairly treated and will not go hungry. So those who
> have been in town for so long, we called them "longshore." When

the ship comes, those who have been longshore took over. . . . But the [NNSL] overstaffed the crew members so that the six-month longshore became one year, one year and a half, and longshore seamen in town never had their turn as was due. This made people to succumb to the whims and caprices of the company, and they became totally submissive. So, before seamen could get job, they must be ready to obey. Even the union complicated matters. They kept the arrival of the ship secret and they invited their folks and friends to come and work in the ship, so seamen were at the mercy of both the company and the union. Whenever we asked questions, the union told us that the call was an emergency and according to the shipping law, whenever there is an emergency call, you can invite any available person. So, the union connived with the captains to sideline seamen.[57]

As seen in this seaman's testimony, the increasing competition for work opened the way for conflicts and abuses. Against this backdrop, tensions were increasingly framed in ethnic terms, and Nigerian ships soon became another playing field for the ethnic politics that shaped the broader Nigerian political landscape. Seamen invoked ethnic identities in explaining the roots and causes of onboard conflicts, and often framed the discriminatory practices of the ships' officers in ethnic terms. This engagement with ethnic identities can be linked to what Bruce Berman has described as the instrumental use of ethnicity among working classes in postcolonial Africa to make demands for the redistribution of resources.[58] In Nigeria in particular, scholars have put forth a utilitarian view of ethnicity, arguing that ethnic identification has been an expedient reaction to the scarcity and competition for resources in the postindependence era.[59] As Dauda Abubakar has argued, ethnicity was "activated, mobilized and deployed as a resource for the pursuit of political and economic power."[60] Ships might therefore be identified as another arena in the Nigerian landscape where struggles for power and resources were contested along ethnic lines.[61] Early visions of Nigerian unity among crews of the NNSL gave way to ethnic divisions, and seamen began to associate the misconduct of officers with their ethnic background, as can be seen in the testimonies of two Ijaw seamen:

> The captain was an Igbo man, but I can't remember his name. This captain and the Calabar chief officer were in their rooms drinking. After everyone had finished eating and left, these two officers came

out and look at me and asked, "Are you annoyed?" because I waited
for them even when I was supposed to be resting. I did not answer.
These officers were like that, they abused us and underrated us.
Another Ijaw captain took over, he was very good to crew members.
When another Igbo captain came on board he had a very bad character. He abused my kinsmen indirectly. For example, he said Ijaw
people performed a rite by putting a newborn baby inside the water
for three to four days. He was fond of this statement. Then, one day
I replied to him, I said when an Igbo man eats pounded yam, he
will rub some pounded yam on his leg before he eats. I also told him
that when an Igbo man is not potent enough to impregnate his wife,
he gave her to his younger brother to impregnate the woman on his
behalf. With these responses, we became enemies.[62]

I was on board of a ship and there was this Calabar officer who told
me that the glass cup I washed was not clean and he gave it back to
me. As a pantryman, I had to wash the glass cup again. Imagine a
man like me washed a glass cup and it is not clean?[63]

The anti-Igbo sentiment expressed by Ijaw seamen was linked to resent-
ment over what they saw as the quick promotion of newly recruited Igbo
seamen to positions of authority, bypassing the Ijaw, who prided themselves
on their longer history of seafaring. As ethnic tensions rose, they contributed
to an overall sense that work for the NNSL led to the Nigerianization of
seafaring.

SECONDHAND TRADING ON NNSL SHIPS

As previously seen, the trade in secondhand goods provided African seamen
with a much-needed supplement to the meager wages they earned on colonial vessels. Nigerian seamen had hoped that the move to employment in
the NNSL would result in better terms of employment, but they soon discovered that the conditions of work were not substantially improved under the
Nigerian line. For many, the outcome was quite the opposite, and the move
to the NNSL resulted in an increased sense of uncertainty and vulnerability. In this context, Nigerian seamen needed to rely even more heavily
on their earnings from independent trade. As one seaman explained, the
secondhand trade alleviated the insecurity they experienced as employees
of the NNSL:

There were some exploitations in terms of wages. Probably because we were allowed to do some trading that is why the facts did not come out. . . . Because of the free trading, nobody cared and nobody bothered to find out. And that was what they used to exploit us and they exploited us successfully. . . . The NNSL suffered from a lot of mismanagement unfortunately, it wasn't given to those who have the company line at heart. So, they grab and grab and grab until they sank the company. . . . Seamen never bother much because we were benefiting from the free trade. We were doing our best to make sure that the vessels were moving from port to port and distributing cargo from place to place.[64]

In terms of the independent trade, some seamen felt that it was better to work for the NNSL than the European companies. Several reported that independent trade was easier to conduct on the ships of the Nigerian line, as some Nigerian captains did not impose the same kinds of restrictions as were seen on the British ships:

We had some level of freedom. In Nigeria shipping line, we had a Nigerian captain, chief officer, and probably a British chief engineer. . . . They were good because when we traveled on board we were not restricted on what to buy, we could buy a large quantity of goods, unlike in ED line, where we were restricted. There were some British captains who never allowed us and if anyone was caught, he would be paid off. Sometimes some of us did not make more than two trips, they were paid off because of these captains . . . but when we had the National Shipping Line, we had liberty and we did more trade than in British ships.[65]

Indeed, many of the British captains took a hard line with seamen caught with goods on board that were not declared on the crew manifest. As one British captain wrote with regard to a greaser found with lappa clothes on the *Ebani* in 1976, "Preboye was told by the master that he would take into consideration his previous good behavior but for his own good and that of the discipline of the ship he would be repatriated immediately."[66] Nigerian captains, on the other hand, demonstrated more compassion for the seamen's status and understood that the trade in secondhand goods was a legitimate way for the ratings to augment their earnings. As one captain interviewed said, "Yes, some crew and officers traded in [drugs]. This was why we allowed people who were doing secondhand legitimate trade to do so instead of carrying of drugs."[67]

While some Nigerian captains tolerated the independent trade, others actually took an active role in the trade themselves. Former seamen, captains, and management of the NNSL all testified that NNSL employees of every level took advantage of the opportunities opened up through the shipping line and participated in independent trade. Moreover, when officers and management got involved, the scope of the trade reached entirely new proportions. Unlike seamen who had meager resources, captains and management had money to invest and more freedom to develop a lucrative side business. In some instances, the independent trading interests of captains and management took priority over the official business of NNSL ships. As one former manager said, "Some people could buy up to one thousand television sets and there would not be room to carry cargo."[68] Those with abundant resources and an entrepreneurial spirit could develop very profitable ventures. Several seamen recalled the business success of one captain who began importing cow's feet into Nigeria, earning himself the nickname "Captain Cow Foot." His initiative tapped into a large market in Nigeria and later spread to England. As one seaman who conducted Captain Cow Foot's business for him recalled:

> In those days, I would go to slaughterhouses in Europe and booked for all the legs of the cattle slaughtered for that day. We eat them and trade with them. Sometimes, I will load about ten freezers on board with the cow legs. [We traded] to the Nigerians here in Lagos. In Europe they were thrown to the dogs, but we eat them here in Nigeria. From this, we enlightened the Europeans that the cow foot was edible. Very delicious, and at the end of the day, the European started to put them into cans. Today, it's now canned food in Europe. When the English discovered that this was good for Africans, they decided to can it.[69]

This particular seaman recognized that through his good relations with captains, he could gain access to trade on this larger scale. He explained that the blurring of lines between Nigerian officers and seamen created more opportunities for him than on British ships:

> The British officer would distinguish himself from the ratings. But in terms of being Nigerians, we traded together and bought

merchandize together to sell in Nigeria together and in terms of food, everybody was Nigerian, so we fed on the Nigerian diet. One thing we also enjoyed in the Nigerian vessels was a lot of free trading. We bought things to sell and everybody enjoyed it. Most Nigerian captains were businessmen too. We ratings do their business for them. I was close to three of our captains who wanted to sail with me all the time. In fact, they looked for me around when I was on leave to sail with them because I handled their businesses for them satisfactorily. So, that is a lot of evidence of free trade on the NNSL vessels. Most of us that traded have our personal houses and live good.[70]

This particular seaman reaped the benefits of an NNSL organizational culture that allowed those in positions of power to exploit every opportunity to improve their personal standing, and to reward those in their inner circle. But this seaman was clearly an exception, and the vast majority of those interviewed recounted a very different type of experience. Many claimed that Nigerian captains sought greater profits for themselves, and they attempted to maximize their own trading opportunities by limiting or eliminating the involvement of seamen in the independent trade.[71] Seamen blamed the failure of the NNSL on the selfishness and greed of the Nigerian captains:

When we had our own ship, initially, we were paid overtime and we added that to our little salary to buy different items abroad to sell. Later, ship officers planned and they stopped paying us overtime. They alleged that if we were paid overtime, we were going to buy more items abroad than them and when the ship officers bought their own items, we carried and loaded it in the ship for them. We were really used as slaves by these Nigerian chief officers. And they also threatened us that they would pay us off, in Lagos. There was nothing we could do. There are a lot of stories to tell.[72]

For seamen, what began as a symbol of freedom and opportunity ended in dysfunction and disappointment. In interviews, seamen voiced a broad range of complaints regarding employment on the NNSL: the arbitrary punishments employed by Nigerian ship officers, the lack of discipline among the entire crew of NNSL ships, and the absence of a maintenance culture on the ships. But the most virulent critique was aimed at the trading practices of the Nigerian officers of the NNSL, which grew at such a fast rate that soon entire ships were used for their private trading purposes. Not only were crew barred from importing their own goods, but they were compelled to carry, load, and unload the officers' cargo, without any compensation for this work:

> The European captains even understood us better than our own black Nigeria captains. European captains were very good. [Nigerian captains] treated us as slaves. The Nigerian captains often asked you to carry their goods they brought on board and this you can carry from morning till night outside your normal duty. The Nigerian captains punished us. All the captains collected their pension, but we were never paid. Captains did not help us during and after liquidation. Many of our fellow seamen have died because no money to take care of ourselves. We are suffering and dying. Some of us are sleeping under the bridge.[73]

In this testimony and many others, the exploitation of seamen as porters for the officers' trade was described again and again by seamen as the ultimate abuse, and in describing the treatment they received at the hands of Nigerian officers, they declared, "They treated us as slaves."[74] The historical and cultural significance of being compelled to carry someone else's load without being properly compensated was associated with the lowest rungs of society, those suffering the greatest exploitation and having no power to exercise their autonomy. The sense of powerlessness and anger was captured by one seaman: "When you cheat people, do not show it to them. But they are cheating us and they are showing it to us. So we must be angry."[75]

Carrying the officers' loads was insulting to seamen who did not see this as their responsibility, but more significant was the end of the seamen's ability to conduct their own trade once ships were monopolized by officers. As can be seen in the testimony above, seamen also suspected that captains stopped their overtime pay in order to make sure that the crew would not have the financial resources needed to engage in independent trade. Seamen claimed as well that captains would not provide them with cash advances due to them in ports of call, and would instead use the funds for their own business in secondhand goods. Adding insult to injury, they would then force seamen to carry and load this cargo:

> Things were moving fine when the white captains were in the NNSL until we trained our black captains. However, the black captains were the worst. . . . NNSL captains were selfish. They wanted everything in their own care. For instance, if they brought money

to the ship to share for all the crew, some of the captains used the money for their own interest. They used the money to buy second-hand goods and used the ratings to be carrying the goods for them. Sometime you can carry them from night till the following day morning. And in the morning, you will start the normal company work again. If you refuse, you will be the number one to be dropped from the ship when you get to Lagos.[76]

This seaman accused Nigerian captains of charging the seamen freight rates in order to deter seamen from trading, but they themselves did not pay for the cargo they loaded:

The Nigeria captain did not want us to trade because they did not want us to have more money like them. So they say no trading on board. If you buy goods, you would pay freight, but the British captain did not make us pay for it. The captains never pay for freight, but we the ratings were compelled to do so by the Nigeria captains. They thought that it was the only way to stop trading on board. Once you paid for freight, the trading is no longer profitable because how much would you have left, and you have wife and children back home in Nigeria. So, once the paying for freight was introduced, that means you are working for nothing.[77]

Several seamen interviewed claimed that captains of the NNSL earned additional cash through the manipulation of exchange rates. Seamen were given cash advances in ports of call, and many claimed that captains paid them at a lower rate than was due to them. The distrust ran so deep that several seamen claimed that they contacted the local embassy to verify the exchange rates rather than taking the captain's word.[78] In some cases, one seaman charged, the money that was wired for cash advances simply disappeared:

Sometimes our people changed the exchange rate and seamen protest to the embassy for conformation before we were paid; this exchange problem was a common thing. When crew members request for certain amount of money, telex is sent to the receiving company and the agent of the company brings the money to the ship, but after two days Nigerian captains denied the arrival of such money and crew members must protest before he pays. It is a regular routine with black people, but it was not so with the white man.[79]

Seamen expressed a sense of powerlessness in the face of these abuses. The small benefits they had came to expect under the British slowly disappeared as Nigerian captains and officers tried to maximize their own opportunities. For example, the same seaman recalled that when rice cargo was loaded onto ships, the company made provisions to distribute some of this to seamen, but only the British captains followed through. As he recounted: "The British captains would give us one or two bags of rice each, but Nigeria captains offloaded those bags of rice in the cargo first, they sold them and kept the money. That was outright exploitation; we really suffered." Seamen recognized the injustices and yet they lacked the resources necessary to combat them:

> In short, we were downtrodden. What I mean is that the NNSL itself used us the way they like. No one could raise any issue because we were contract staff. You are only paid when you sail with a ship. No permanent job. The majority of those working for the union were not literate. The majority of them do not even know their right from left. The only thing they knew was that they would say "I went to England," that's all. Even the payment system was characterized by fraud, as more often than before, you are paid less than what you signed for. And for a very long time, we never knew about this.[80]

Not all captains were engaged in the exploitation of seamen, and, indeed, many attempted to uphold the highest standards on board the ships they commanded. But these captains did not necessarily identify with the seamen's plight, and they expressed disdain for seamen's attempts to exploit opportunities in order to improve their standing. For example, Captain Niagwan boasted in an interview that seamen used to call him "Black Hitler" because he forbade independent trade on his ship. He was undeterred by their anger and claimed the trade was evidence of seamen's lack of dedication to the job. When I asked him about their lack of options, he replied, "Nobody put a gun to their heads." At the same time, he acknowledged that one seaman died in the course of loading tires purchased by an NNSL captain in Hamburg.[81]

The history of the independent trade in the NNSL reveals that most of the management and officers did not share in Captain Niagwan's conviction. On the contrary, the widespread engagement in independent trade among management and officers was a key factor in the breakdown of authority, regulation, and leadership in the NNSL. As Engineer Akinsoji claimed, seamen would have acted differently had the leadership of the NNSL set a different tone: "Corruption to me was not the issue for failure. Failure goes beyond corruption. If you have focus, and good leadership that maintains focus, people will line up behind him. In fact, this country will transform within six months if you have good leadership that maintains focus."[82] In a poignant testimony, Akinsoji argued that the engagement with the independent trade was both a symptom and a cause of the NNSL demise:

> I will tell you a story. When I was still a superintendent I went to Liverpool to inspect a ship, but there was this cabin that was locked and I insisted to see what was inside the cabin. And when it was opened, it was full of carpets owned by the crew, captains, officers, and cadets. I just lined them up and I asked who owned what? I later called a meeting on the ship and then wrote the names of everyone against his carpets. Although the captain of this particular ship did not have a carpet, I drew his attention to what his ship is being used for. His chief engineer had put his name there. So, unfortunately, some of those carpets were sent to be bought by those in management in the office through the crew on board. So, when I came back and wrote my report, it never had any headway because the management knew about it. I rounded all up by saying that we do not have the culture of what it takes to run shipping. Even the office did not have that culture. You would imagine a shipping company that condones that in a competitive world? It will certainly be out of business. That is why I say comparative cultural virtue is important in shipping. If you don't have it, you can't keep afloat because your counterparts, their crew are busy working while your crew are busy buying secondhand carpets. So, how did you compete? So, while you are still doing this, your counterpart would have completed a voyage while you are still on half voyage. So, it is a must. Until that culture is developed among those in the chain of shipping, we are not likely to have our quota in shipping.[83]

ILLEGALITY ON NNSL SHIPS

As work conditions deteriorated and authority and discipline waned on NNSL ships, growing numbers of seamen turned to illegality. Archival records and interviews with seamen reveal that rank-and-file ratings increasingly engaged in illicit activities, particularly theft and drug smuggling. Ship logs document many instances of theft on board ships, with the crew taking equipment and supplies from vessels, as well as cargo from the holds.

In some instances, these records reveal a strong correlation between the turn to illegality and seamen's discontent with working conditions, and the breakdown of authority and discipline on board ships. This could be seen in the logbook of the MV *Bareeb* in 1972. The journey began in Lagos, with the crew complaining that they were not being paid their salaries or given enough food. Over the course of the next week, seamen began deserting the ship in protest, and the captain reported there were no day or night watchmen on guard. Within a few days, the cargo was broken into, and the captain conducted searches in crew's accommodations, where he found many of the missing items.[84] Similarly, on the *River Benue* in 1981, the crew refused to secure the cargo on the deck unless they were paid an overtime bonus of twenty hours each. The captain refused, and the safety of the cargo was compromised.[85]

Seamen and captains interviewed reported that there were many hiding places on ships, and it was never easy to discover items that went missing. In several instances, stolen goods were found among the belongings of crew only after they were hospitalized or logged off for disciplinary action, and other crew members were sent to gather their personal items. This could be seen on the MV *Ileoluji* in 1979, when the captain reported finding corn-flakes, tea, ketchup, toilet paper, evaporated milk, and some electric cables from the supply rooms among the personal belongings of a greaser who was sent to the hospital.[86]

Captains determined what punishments were given to those caught stealing, and there was a wide range of responses. Thus, on the *River Benue* in 1970, the captain ordered a search of the ship when it was reported that one hundred bolts of cloth were missing from a cargo hold. In the course of the search, the cloth was found hidden under old mooring ropes. Four crew members came forward to confess one week later and begged for mercy, to which the captain responded, "No promises were made."[87] Some captains would dole out very harsh punishments for these infractions, and it was particularly the British captains who demonstrated no tolerance for perpetrators. This could be seen on the *Salamat Ambi*, when Captain Lancaster fined the cook three days' pay for stealing one frozen chicken and three pounds of beef.[88]

Nigerian captains often adopted a more lenient position toward these infractions, as seen in the logbook of the *River Benue* in 1980: "Mr. A. Nwanegbo, Greaser, was this day caught carrying a case of Guinness to his cabin. When questioned, he admitted having obtained it from among the ones landed on deck for the ship's stores. He claimed it was given to him by one of the riggers and pleads for leniency. He was ordered to return the case of Guinness and further more warned that severe measures will be taken against such behavior in future."[89] In another incident reported in the logbook from the *River Oji* in 1981, the captain discovered some ship supplies among the personal belongings of a radio officer taken ashore: "When he was removing his deep sea kit from the ship just before sailing, it was hinted that he had in the company's van that was to take him ashore some items belonging to the ship. On intercepting him, Mr. Aluge, in the van, I found one table fan belonging to the ship in the van, together with his luggage. He claimed that he took it in error. I then asked him to return it to the ship. This he did. [I] had to give him D.R. for conduct in his discharge as what it boils down to is stealing ship's property, which is not condonable as a ship's officer."[90]

In these instances and many like them, the crew, often buttressed by discontent over working conditions, took advantage of opportunities to boost their earnings and improve their circumstances. Living and working on the ships presented seamen with multiple prospects, and seamen exploited them to the fullest. Tools, foodstuff, and cargo could be taken for personal use or for resale. One captain reported that the crew had sold cement that had been swept up from the cargo hold to people ashore in Sapele rather than dumping it at sea.[91] Those who took alcohol from the cargo hold or from supply rooms sponsored parties in their rooms for other members of the crew.[92] Ships logs and interviews reveal that seamen, discontented with the terms of employment and work conditions on board ships, subsequently capitalized on the opportunities that presented themselves.

It is within this context that drug smuggling among seamen must be understood. From the establishment of the NNSL until its demise, there was a steady rise in the number of seamen engaged in drug smuggling. Thus, in 1973, the captain of the *Oduduwa* claimed that "the carriage of cannabis was rampant among the crew."[93] While none of the seamen interviewed claimed to have been personally involved, almost all of them talked about the practice as widespread. Ship logs reveal countless discoveries of drugs, and the ceaseless efforts of captains to conduct searches and put a stop to the practice. The captains' efforts were largely fruitless because, as many seamen and captains testified, there was little difficulty in bringing drugs on board and finding a hiding place for them during the journey:

> Because of the lower wages that they are paying people, most of the former seamen who are older than me when I started the work, they all carry drugs to Europe. I am not talking of cocaine, but I am talking about marijuana, which some seamen took to Europe from Nigeria so as to make more money. And not every time they

get away with it. Sometime they were caught by the customs and excise men who often bring detective dogs to the ships. They used different ways to carry the drugs. They sometime kept them in the waste bin and sometimes inside the empty can of beer. They made a lot of money just as many of them were caught.[94]

This seaman's testimony draws a distinction between cannabis on the one hand, and cocaine and heroin on the other. Incidents involving marijuana were not looked upon as severely by Nigerian captains, and many incidents were reported of crew members smoking marijuana on board. For example, the captain of the *King Jaja* in 1975 reported that M. Fowoshade was found walking around in the middle of the night covered in paint. The next morning, he was found in his cabin, which was filled with smoke and "smelled like Indian hemp." When asked, the greaser said that "he regularly smoked Indian hemp and that it helped him to perform his duties better."[95]

Nigerian captains beseeched their crews to throw goods overboard rather than risk being caught by local authorities in ports of call. Thus, the captain of the *River Ogun* reported that he "drew the attention of all crewmembers to the danger the involvement with cannabis or any contraband may have and warned all crews that if anyone has it, he should dump it overboard before the vessel arrives Tilbury Dock, London."[96] In another incident on the *King Jaja* in 1971, a bag of cannabis was discovered hidden in the engine room. The captain of the ship ordered the fourth engineer to dump "the ownerless bag" overboard "in order to avoid delays at Dakar."[97] He posted a sign warning the crew that it is a very serious offense to smuggle or smoke cannabis on the company's vessels. He recommended that the crew throw the drugs overboard: "In view of a recent accidental discovery of a bag of cannabis in this ship and signs of crew smoking cannabis, I am posting this notice warning all those concerned to dispose of whatever quantity they have in their possessions and hiding places before the ship gets to England." He asked the crew to come forward in confidence to report anyone smoking or smuggling cannabis and claimed in frustration that his search had turned up nothing: "My recent search was a legal obligation and was fruitless. The spies quickly passed the news round. But do not think that is the end, as more drastic action will follow. Be warned." The captain's warning apparently had fallen on deaf ears, because one week later, another bag of cannabis was discovered in the same hiding place. At this point, the suitcase was confiscated and the captain reported his plans to turn the bag over to the police in Middlesbrough.[98]

The frustrations of another captain can be seen in the logbook of the *King Jaja* in 1973. The captain delivered a stern warning to the entire crew to refrain from using or dealing in drugs. He reported conducting a thorough search before sailing, which turned up nothing. Despite these efforts, when the fourth engineer entered the pilot's cabin four days later, he perceived "a very strong, smoky odor." He immediately notified the captain, the chief officer, and the chief engineer, and together they agreed that the strong odor was that of cannabis and that someone must have been smoking in the room: "It therefore became established that after the thorough search for cannabis conducted and despite the chief officer's address to the crew and officers alike that the company does not permit any crew member to have onboard any quantity of cannabis either for personal use or for commercial purpose, a diehard or some diehards amongst the crew or officers still have onboard some quantity of cannabis."[99]

As the problem proliferated, captains and management took increasingly harsh measures to prevent and prosecute drug smugglers. The Nigerian Maritime Board imposed very strict punishments, and seamen caught smuggling drugs were permanently removed from the register. In light of this hard line, customs officers in Hull, England, did not prosecute the head greaser of the *Salamat Ambi* in 1977, who was caught with a small quantity of cannabis. As the captain's log reported, "No action was taken by the authorities in view of the severity of punishment imposed upon members by the rules of the Nigerian Maritime Board. They consider that dismissal is sufficient punishment in this case."[100] The increasingly hard line toward drug smuggling could be seen in the following announcement posted on the *River Benue*:

> Crew members are warned that should any member be misguided enough to indulge in the trafficking of cannabis or other drugs, he will not only suffer the full penalties of the law in the port of discovery, but also that information regarding the offence shall be conveyed to the military in Nigeria. . . . Any crew member convicted or suspected of being implicated in this trafficking will be blacklisted with either the Nigerian or British Federation. . . . Crew members are no doubt aware of the suffering of drug addicts and are morally implicated should he be the carrier. Heavy gaol sentences and fines will be imposed on any crew member being convicted in the above practice.[101]

Efforts to stop the trade became institutionalized practices on Nigerian ships. Ship logs from the 1970s and 1980s reported routine and extensive searches of all parts of the ship. Crew and officers had to submit to searches and were not allowed to carry any unauthorized parcels on board.[102] Some captains complained that drug searches were hampered by the presence of female visitors in crew's accommodations, and harsh punishments were instituted against those who brought unauthorized females on board.[103] In many ships, crew members were stationed on the gangway night and day, and every parcel or bag brought on board was subjected to inspection. In addition, crew members were put on night patrol on each end of the deck to make sure that no parcels were thrown on board from ashore.[104] But harsh punishments had little impact on the volume of the trade, and seamen continued to engage in drug trafficking throughout the history of the NNSL.

The flourishing drug trade among seamen on NNSL ships, despite enormous efforts to put a stop to it, cannot be divorced from the complex and troubled history of the Nigerian National Shipping Line and the place of seamen in this history. Seamen's turn to illegality must be understood against the backdrop of seamen's increasing disempowerment within the NNSL. Scholars have examined the roots and causes of the demise of the Nigerian line from the perspective of the political economy of international shipping and within the context of broader political and economic instability that plagued Nigeria in the postcolonial era. It has been argued that the history of the NNSL cannot be separated from deeper processes that contributed to a crisis of leadership and the growth of corruption. An investigation into seamen's efforts to maneuver this volatile landscape sheds new light on the ways in which the most disempowered and marginalized continually made efforts to reap benefits and exploit opportunities over the short term. Their experiences as employees of the Nigerian National Shipping Line are a poignant testimony to the ways in which the working class experiences, interprets, and navigates political and economic landscapes not of their choosing.

The history of seamen's experiences in the Nigerian line demonstrates how hierarchies of power originating at the international level in the world shipping industry ultimately filtered down through the national context and locked seamen into the lowest rungs of the industry. In this context, seamen could obtain their share of power only through creative maneuvering and steadfast commitment to grab at opportunities when they presented themselves. Seamen pulled from a diverse set of tools in navigating this world. Some benefited from patrimonialism, others embraced ethnic solidarity, and most sought to preserve their autonomy and combat their proletarianization through their independent trade. As circumstances worsened, illegality also became a viable means for maintaining some autonomy and wealth. But the increasing disempowerment led many to bitter disappointment and despair. This despair soon translated into a deep sense of disillusionment with the NNSL and, ultimately, with the national project of Nigeria itself. As Engineer Akinsoji said: "When I was on the ship, everyone was enthusiastic about the NNSL, and I was enthusiastic also. It was a pride to be a seaman then, but I don't know now. But I think a lot of people still have interest to be seaman. . . . Nigerians are very good people when they want to get things done, but the influence of the society sometime takes you away from your determination. And shipping is such a business that you can't allow anything to take you away from your determination."[105]

Conclusion

OVER THE LAST TWENTY YEARS, the Atlantic Ocean has increasingly provided historians with an alternative frame of reference to national borders for shaping research agendas. The focus on the Atlantic enables scholars to document the interconnectedness of histories, cultures, and experiences between Africa, Europe, and the Americas. Historians of the black diaspora have demonstrated that from the very first forced migrations of slaves across the Atlantic, Africans and their descendants throughout the Atlantic Basin have shared notions of identity, community, and culture as a result of ongoing flows and exchanges between black communities on all sides of the ocean. In taking the Atlantic Ocean as a single complex unit of analysis, or "an integrated whole," many have argued that the identities and ideologies of Africans and their descendants across the Atlantic remain demographically, economically, culturally, and intellectually linked.[1] These histories commonly invoke the terms "transnational," "cosmopolitan," and "intercultural" to describe the cultures and worldviews of communities and individuals living around the "Black Atlantic." The field of African history has also been greatly influenced by these trends. Even with regard to African communities and individuals who have never ventured beyond the continent, the flow of people, ideas, and commodities across the ocean has played a significant role in shaping local circumstances in the past and the present. As a result of these transatlantic connections, it has been argued that African experiences and worldviews are "shaded with inflections of a transnational black public sphere."[2]

From the start of the transatlantic trade, black seamen played a key role in the emergence of these diaspora connections. Through their travels, seamen conveyed news, commodities, and ideas between black communities across four continents, and thus fostered the emergence of shared consciousness, cultural trends, and political organizing. Seamen were not only instruments of change; rather, their own lives and experiences were fundamentally imprinted with the border crossings, hybridity, and cosmopolitanism that characterized the migratory flows across the ocean. Black seamen's transient lifestyle enabled them to push back against the racial and colonial hierarchies at the foundation of societies back home. Historians have argued that ships themselves represented a liminal space that enabled the emergence of transnational and interracial solidarities. Drawing heavily upon Foucault's notion of "heterotopias," historians of black seafaring argue that ships became vehicles that created circumstances for bypassing national and racial boundaries.[3] Particularly with regard to the Age of Sail, scholars such as Jeffrey Bolster, Markus Rediker, and Peter Linebaugh have claimed that the dangers and isolation of the sea fostered camaraderie between black and white sailors.[4] Working together in precarious conditions, solidarity emerged within multiracial crews that defied the hierarchies deeply embedded ashore.[5]

In approaching the history of Nigerian seamen, I had an eye to this burgeoning body of literature, and I anticipated finding evidence of these alternative spaces and experiences that defied borders and bordering processes. Some preliminary findings revealed that, indeed, many aspects of Nigerian seamen's lives conformed to this cosmopolitan vision. For Nigerians in the colonial era, the allure of seafaring was rooted in opportunities to travel beyond Nigeria and exploit new economic, social, and cultural possibilities. Their descriptions of life at sea and in foreign ports of call often reflected an empowered transience, a fluid and noncommittal lifestyle. Seamen established relations with foreign women that defied racial and national boundaries. They embraced new definitions for family, and they exploited opportunities for romantic connections that did not carry the commitments and obligations associated with family life in Nigeria. In addition, they were engaged in a vibrant independent trade that defied their categorization as a cheap and easily exploited source of labor for European shipping companies. Interviews confirmed that seamen saw themselves as what Pico Iyer characterized as "global souls"—the products of "blurred boundaries and global mobility."[6]

But while there were indeed dimensions of seamen's lives in which they enjoyed varying forms of economic and cultural autonomy, this study has ultimately shown that ships, and the seamen employed on them, did not exist in isolation of the forces of history. Seamen confronted international border regimes, racism on board ships and in ports of call, and economic exploitation as a cheap source of labor for colonial shipping companies. In the face of exclusion and discrimination, seamen drew upon the available ideologies of liberation. In the colonial era, the black diaspora provided material and ideological support for seamen in their struggles to improve their lot. But gradually, the historical processes of decolonization and the rise of nationalism overtook alternative forms of solidarity. Seamen were initially drawn to nationalist ideology as an answer to their exploitation, but their entanglement in the history of decolonization finally resulted in a loss of autonomy. As ships and the seamen who worked on them became national-ized, it was increasingly hard to find traces of the heterotopias of the Age of Sail. Stuart Hall's vision of the cosmopolitan, "the ability to stand outside of having one's life written and scripted by any one community,"[7] gradually gave way to the hegemonic influence of nationalization. In sharp contrast to the depictions of nineteenth-century seafaring as a vehicle for liberation and alterity, this history of Nigerian seafaring in the twentieth century traces a gradual but steady process of seamen's disempowerment.

The fate of Nigerian seamen in the transition from colonialism to in-dependence reaffirms that nation-building and nationalization were all-powerful forces that trampled alternative forms of alliance and identifica-tion. Seamen who had once seen themselves as "citizens of the world" faced a new set of hardships and obstacles when they became Nigerian sea-men. The potent force of nationalization extended its reach far beyond the borders of Nigeria. Far out at sea, or in foreign ports throughout the world, seamen confronted work regimes, ship hierarchies, and terms of employ-ment that increasingly bore the footprint of Nigerianization. It has been seen that in this transition from colonial ships to the Nigerian National Shipping Line (NNSL), seamen slowly experienced a loss of options for operating outside of their Nigerian identity. According to their testimo-nies, the conditions of work in the NNSL soon became an admonition of the opportunities they no longer had. As both local and transnational imaginaries lost ground to the nationalist perspectives, it was ultimately the nation-state that became the preeminent framework within which class struggles were negotiated and fought in the postcolonial era.[8] This border-ing process could be seen in the following testimony of one seaman, who claimed that the Nigerian government blocked seamen's efforts to gain international backing for their labor disputes, and prevented them from seeking recourse from international organizations such as the International Transport Workers' Federation (ITF):

> The government suppressed us, the crew, by that time. If anything new happened abroad and we told the government about an ITF decision, the government refused to listen to us. And when we invited ITF for anything here, to intervene, the ITF responded that the Nigerian government did not want them to intervene. . . . There was a strike and I went to Rotterdam, in Holland, to invite the ITF and I was told, boldly, by the Federation that the Nigerian government did not want external interference. . . . It was because the government knew that the ITF was going to take sides with us seamen.[9]

Nationalism emerged as an all-powerful force in seamen's lives, but this study also unpacks how we conceptualize and study nationalism. The power of nationalism and national borders has been evidenced in countless studies of Africa in the postcolonial era. But few of these studies have taught us what nationalism has signified in the lives of nonelites. This history of Nigerian seamen in the transition from colonialism to independence has argued that nationalism resonated in specific ways for the working class. The study has demonstrated the need to understand nationalism "from below." Seamen's experiences reveal how working classes embraced what Jon Fox and Cynthia Miller-Idriss have referred to as "everyday nationhood." This nationhood is expressed and performed in the routine contexts of everyday life. As they wrote, the nation is "the practical accomplishment of ordinary people talking about themselves and their surroundings in ways that implicate and reproduce a national view."[10] Thus, for seamen, "Nigeria" was found in ship menus and work routines. Seamen identified "Nigeria" in onboard relations between crews and officers, and in the slow deterioration of the terms of their employment. Their hopes for national liberation were tied up with their hopes for better working conditions, and their disillusionment with the reality of employment in the NNSL. This history instructs us that African working classes in the era of decolonization were not passive receptors of broader political changes, and they crafted their own notions for nationhood. The mundane associations seamen made between the Nigerianization of shipping and the broader political project of nation-building in Nigeria provide a rare look into how everyday Africans wrote themselves into history. Craig Calhoun wrote, "Nations are constituted largely by [these] claims themselves, by the way of talking and thinking and acting that relies on these sorts of claims to produce collective identity, to mobilize people for collective projects, and to evaluate peoples and practice."[11]

For seamen, the disillusionment with the Nigerianization of shipping became the basis for their disillusionment with Nigeria as a nation-state. Their experiences should therefore be considered against the backdrop of an immense body of scholarly literature that has emerged to explain the failures of nation-building in Nigeria. In focusing on the working class, this study sheds new light on this troubled history. Much of the literature regarding the devastating instability and ineffectiveness of the Nigerian state points to ethnicity and regionalism as the roots to ongoing political crises and lack of effective governance. It is beyond dispute that regional interests and ethnic chauvinism have been a destructive force in the history of postcolonial Nigeria. But ethnicity was not the central factor shaping the history of the NNSL and the fate of the individuals who played a role in the Nigerian National Shipping Line. Seamen's testimonies of their experiences with the NNSL continually downplayed ethnicity as the most significant determinant shaping their engagement with the national line. Instead, their experiences reveal that class was the most significant factor determining the ways in which each interest group involved in the NNSL anticipated the establishment of the line, and the ways in which they experienced it.

The history of the NNSL makes it clear that we need to bring class back to the forefront of the study of postcolonial Africa in general, and Nigeria in particular. It is doubtful whether the African indigenous shipping lines created as part of nationalist political platforms could have overcome the unequal structures of power shaping the world of international shipping. Former colonial giants maintained an advantage that perhaps no reasonable measure of investment and commitment by the Nigerian government could have overcome in order for the NNSL to succeed and thrive. But for those back in Nigeria, the consequences of this failure, whatever its causes were, were not experienced evenly across class lines. Politicians appointed their cronies as managers, and together they slowly bled the company of resources. Captains, officers, and middle management also positioned themselves to best exploit opportunities for personal gain on NNSL ships. By contrast, rank-and-file seamen, who had invested their hopes and aspirations in the NNSL as a homecoming, gradually experienced disempowerment and disillusionment. While officers, management, and politicians maneuvered to protect and maximize their opportunities, working-class seamen faced a loss of prospects and autonomy. The history of the NNSL brings into clear focus that the failures of nationalism were not experienced evenly by all Africans. This book has thus argued that for both working classes and ruling elites, class played a pivotal role in determining how nationalism and nationalization shaped their lives.

This is not just a matter of historical significance. The inequalities that characterized this history still deeply resonate in the lives of all those who played a part in the NNSL. These inequalities also surfaced in the process of researching this history, and they played a significant role in shaping whose stories were told and how they were told. We must remain aware of how historical hierarchies of power continue to find expression in the material circumstances of the present, and how the process of historicization can constitute another form of marginalization for those who have been marginalized by history. A few examples from the processes of interviewing can demonstrate this point. Former politicians and management who were involved with the NNSL came to interviews with a clear agenda of telling their version of events, and some had various forms of archives to validate their claims. Thus, I met Sen. Cosmos Niagwan in his air-conditioned office in Apapa, where he provided a long and detailed account of the NNSL liquidation process that he oversaw in 1994. Beginning his career as an NNSL captain, Niagwan eventually went into politics and was elected senator from the Plateau State. Niagwan was extremely well versed in the interview process, and he provided a wealth of information on his personal experiences both on board NNSL ships and as the liquidator of the company. He had a well-preserved personal archive regarding the liquidation, and he generously made this available for me to photocopy in his office. Key aides were present in interviews and offered their assistance in providing me with documents and other information.

Another member of management, Isaac Bezi, also provided a long and detailed interview. At first, Bezi was extremely reluctant to provide an interview at all. The meeting was arranged only after he itemized the subjects he would be willing to talk about and set rules for how the interview was to be conducted. We met at the exclusive Apapa Club in Lagos. This country club is well guarded and private, and I was severely warned by guards after innocently taking a picture of the entrance from the street. During the interview, Bezi directed the conversation, and I carefully avoided topics that were clearly off-limits. During the interview, it was clear to me that Bezi had agreed to meet in order to formally record his version of events, some of which was contradicted and refuted in interviews with other former managers.

I met with Capt. Tajudeen Alao in his home in a middle-class neighborhood in Lagos. Alao's house was full of guests — family and friends who either lived there or had stopped in to visit. The interview was conducted in his living room, with many onlookers. Alao was an extremely warm and forthcoming interviewee. He recounted many stories of life at sea and work for the NNSL. Like other captains and officers, he had studied many years in England and he had logged thousands of hours on foreign vessels before becoming a captain for the NNSL. Throughout the years, Alao had a camera and took many photos of his career at sea, and he had several photo albums and scrapbooks to show me. As we went through the pictures, he recalled incidents and people he encountered. His scrapbooks provided a rich basis for jogging his memory about his years with the NNSL. As we looked through these "scrapbook archives," he told me colorful stories about seamen's antics and showed me pictures of his friends abroad. In making and saving these photo albums, Alao had preserved a rare archive of knowledge, and this helped to make the interview with him extremely informative and insightful.

Thus, in the case of the elites—the politicians, management, and officers who had worked for the NNSL—interviews exposed the deep links between the construction of knowledge and the exercise of power. Former politicians and management were aware of how the collection and use of knowledge can be a political tool, and many came to the interview process with a clear agenda. They demonstrated a keen awareness of the potential for interviews to establish their own version of events and the ways in which this knowledge could later be used. Former management, officers, and captains had either a personal or an official archive that they drew upon in the interview process. Thus, the men who had held positions of power in the NNSL continued to wield this power in the process of historicizing the NNSL.

The process of interviewing those who had been rank-and-file seamen in the NNSL provides a stark contrast to interviews with former management and officers. Unlike the elites who left the NNSL with academic degrees, comfortable pensions, and necessary connections for finding alternative employment, seamen left the NNSL without any of these financial, political, or social resources. Most live in dire poverty; some are homeless and living under bridges in Lagos. This situation made it far more difficult to contact and establish interview times and meeting places. With both elites and the working class, the interview process was deeply influenced by the physical spaces in which interviews were conducted, and these physical spaces were in turn another form of evidence of the past. Whereas captains and management met me in exclusive country clubs or air-conditioned offices with an administrative staff and filing cabinets full of documents, seamen lived in the low-income neighborhoods of Lagos with poor infrastructure and access. In some cases, their homes lacked electricity or even a place that was convenient to sit for conducting an interview. They had fewer, if any, souvenirs or photos that could be presented as evidence. Seamen did not have the letters, documents, photo albums, or scrapbooks that officers had in their homes and offices. This had significant implications for the interview process and the ways in which seamen's memories could be recovered and preserved. This case study teaches us that history is not just a matter of the past, but remains embedded in the material lives of both ruling elites and working classes in the African present.

But interviews with seamen revealed a deeper divide between the ways in which the relationship between knowledge and power had shaped their lives. Unlike former officers and management, seamen did not approach the interview process as a tool for crafting a narrative that would potentially serve or empower them in the broader political landscape. Rather, they provided interviews with a more personal material agenda. Some welcomed the opportunity to tell their stories to someone who would listen. Many sought a tangible, material benefit in the form of a small gift at the end of the interview. Others hoped that I might be able to help them get a job with a foreign shipping company. Unlike elites, rank-and-file seamen saw little utility in the process of historicization itself. Having been so marginalized from history, seamen's lives did not reflect any benefits that "history" could provide. Thus, as the research grew and developed, I became increasingly aware of the ways in which the history itself was imprinted in the process of historicization. The underclass of history were also the underclass in the process of recovering this history.

Yet, seamen continue to look for ways to maneuver around this status. In seeking out the immediate material potential the interviews provided, seamen were in fact continuing to identify and exploit opportunities as they presented themselves, much in the same way they had as a colonial working class, and as the working class of the NNSL. Both in the past and the present, seamen were continually drawing from whatever toolboxes were available to meet their immediate, material needs. In their lives as seamen, they had found emotional consolation in their connections with foreign wives, and financial opportunities in their independent trade. When these opportunities slowly disappeared, some turned to the clandestine and lucrative drug trade. Thus, time and again, seamen exploited whatever opportunities made themselves available to overcome the hierarchies of power that rested upon their exploitation.

It has been seen that despite these efforts, the move to the NNSL represented a gradual narrowing of possibilities and opportunities for Nigerian seamen. The ultimate price was paid when the NNSL folded and seamen had to forfeit seafaring entirely. Whereas officers and management found employment in various branches of government or private shipping enterprises, seamen no longer had any alternatives to exploit. The dissolution of the NNSL left them without any horizons. Occasionally, Nigerian seamen still manage to sign on to foreign vessels as they pass through Lagos, but this is fairly rare. Some of the seamen interviewed nevertheless maintained a hope that seafaring can still provide a springboard for improving their economic, social, and political options. One seafarer said, "Just as you know, it is not easy to get a visa, and some of these people use this shipping work to sail abroad and then abscond. This is still going on."[12]

Nigerian seamen experienced, and subsequently evaluated, nationalism through the prism of their work as seafarers. When the move to the national lines proved ruinous, for many seamen this became a metaphor for their own plight as Nigerian nationals. As one seafarer said of the officials who managed the NNSL, "They just tarnished Nigeria's image."[13] The rise and development of nationalist consciousness in Africa is too often studied as a process engendered by political elites within the borders of nation-states. This history of Nigerian seafaring in the transition from colonialism to independence has argued that nationalism was experienced as a process that both created and eliminated solidarities and opportunities. The history of seamen deepens our understanding of the promise that nationalism held for some Africans, and the extent to which they experienced disillusionment with its ultimate outcomes.

Notes

INTRODUCTION

1. Diane Frost, ed., *Ethnic Labour and British Imperial Trade: A History of Ethnic Seafarers in the UK* (London: Cass, 1995); Frost, *Work and Community among West African Migrant Workers since the Nineteenth Century* (Liverpool: Liverpool University Press, 1999).

2. British shipping agents and colonial officials referred to all colonial seamen as "coloured," thus including all seamen of African and Asian origins in this category.

3. Robin D. G. Kelley, *Freedom Dreams: The Black Radical Imagination* (Boston, MA: Beacon Press, 2003).

4. Bill Freund, *The African Worker* (Cambridge: Cambridge University Press, 1988), 2.

5. Frederick Cooper, *Decolonization and African Society: The Labor Question in French and British Africa* (Cambridge: Cambridge University Press, 1996).

6. Ibid., 369–73; Monica M. van Beusekom, "From Underpopulation to Over-population: French Perceptions of Population, Environment, and Agricultural Development in French Soudan (Mali), 1900–1960," *Environmental History* 4, no. 2 (1999): 198–221; Lynn Schler, "Historicizing the Undisclosed: Questions of Authority and Authenticity in Writing the History of Birth in Colonial Cameroon," *Lagos Notes and Records* 13 (2008): 1–34.

7. Cooper, *Decolonization and African Society*, 54.

8. Elliot J. Berg, "Urban Real Wages and the Nigerian Trade Union Movement, 1939–60: A Comment," *Economic Development and Cultural Change* 17, no. 4 (1969): 604–17; Paul M. Lubeck, "Unions, Workers and Consciousness in Kano, Nigeria: A View from Below," in *The Development of an African Working Class: Studies in Class Formation and Action*, ed. Richard Sandbrook and Robin Cohen (London: Longman, 1975), 139–60; Jon Kraus, "African Trade Unions: Progress or Poverty?" *African*

Studies Review 19, no. 3 (1976): 95–108; Richard Sandbrook, *Proletarians and African Capitalism: The Kenyan Case, 1960–1972* (Cambridge: Cambridge University Press, 1975).

9. Tijani M. Yesufu, *An Introduction to Industrial Relations in Nigeria* (Oxford: Oxford University Press, 1962), 178.

10. Elliot J. Berg and Jeffrey Butler, "Trade Unions," in *Political Parties and National Integration in Tropical Africa*, ed. James S. Coleman and Carl G. Rosberg Jr. (Berkeley: University of California Press, 1964), 340–81.

11. W. M. Warren, "Urban Real Wages and the Nigerian Trade Union Movement, 1939–60," *Economic Development and Cultural Change* 15, no. 1 (1966): 21–36; Peter Kilby, "Industrial Relations and Wage Determination: Failure of the Anglo-Saxon Model," *Journal of Developing Areas* 1, no. 4 (1967): 489–520; John F. Weeks, "A Comment on Peter Kilby: Industrial Relations and Wage Determination," *Journal of Developing Areas* 3, no. 1 (1968): 7–18; Weeks, "Further Comment on the Kilby/Weeks Debate: An Empirical Rejoinder," *Journal of Developing Areas* 5, no. 2 (1971): 165–74.

12. Adrian J. Peace, *Choice, Class and Conflict: A Study of Southern Nigerian Factory Workers* (Brighton: Harvester Press, 1979).

13. Peter Waterman, *Division and Unity amongst Nigerian Workers: Lagos Port Unionism, 1940s–60s* (The Hague: Institute of Social Studies, 1982).

14. Robin Cohen, *Labor and Politics in Nigeria, 1945–71* (London: Heinemann, 1974).

15. Adrian J. Peace, "The Lagos Proletariat": Labour Aristocrats or Populist Militants?" in *The Development of an African Working Class: Studies in Class Formation and Action*, ed. Richard Sandbrook and Robin Cohen (London: Longman, 1975), 281.

16. William H. Sewell Jr., "Toward a Post-Materialist Rhetoric for Labor History," in *Rethinking Labor History: Essays on Discourse and Class Analysis*, ed. Lenard R. Belanstein (Urbana: University of Illinois Press, 1993), 15, quoted in Beverly J. Silver, *Forces of Labor: Workers' Movements and Globalization since 1870* (Cambridge: Cambridge University Press, 2003), 1.

17. Robin Cohen, "Resistance and Hidden Forms of Consciousness amongst African Workers," *Review of African Political Economy* 7, no. 19 (1980): 8–22.

18. See, for example, Keletso E. Atkins, *The Moon Is Dead! Give Us Our Money!: The Cultural Origins of an African Work Ethic, Natal, South Africa, 1843–1900* (Porstmouth, NH: Heinemann, 1993).

19. Paul M. Lubeck, *Islam and Urban Labor in Northern Nigeria: The Making of a Muslim Working Class* (Cambridge: Cambridge University Press, 1987); and Lubeck, "Islamic Protest under Semi-Industrial Capitalism: 'Yan Tatsine Explained," *Africa* 55, no. 4 (1985): 369–89.

20. Carolyn A. Brown, *"We Were All Slaves": African Miners, Culture, and Resistance at the Enugu Government Colliery* (London: Heinemann, 2003), 327.

21. Lisa A. Lindsay, *Working with Gender: Wage Labor and Social Change in Southwestern Nigeria* (Portsmouth, NH: Heinemann, 2003).

22. Philip Bonner, Jonathan Hyslop, and Lucien Van Der Walt, "Rethinking Worlds of Labour: Southern African Labour History in International Context," *African Studies* 66, nos. 2–3 (2007): 137–67.

23. Ibid., 144.

24. For a broader discussion of the disempowerment of rank-and-file labor in post-colonial Nigeria, see Waterman, *Division and Unity amongst Nigerian Workers*; Lubeck, "Unions, Workers and Consciousness"; and Peace, "Lagos Proletariat," 281–302.

25. Richard Roberts, "History and Memory: The Power of Statist Narratives," *International Journal of African Historical Studies* 33, no. 3 (2000): 513–22.

26. David Newman, "On Borders and Power: A Theoretical Framework," *Journal of Borderlands Studies* 18, no. 1 (Spring 2003): 13–25.

27. Susan Geiger, "Tanganyikan Nationalism as 'Women's Work': Life Histories, Collective Biography and Changing Historiography," *Journal of African History* 37, no. 3 (1996): 466.

28. Jean M. Allman, *The Quills of the Porcupine: Asante Nationalism in an Emergent Ghana* (Madison: University of Wisconsin Press, 1993).

29. Geiger, "Tanganyikan Nationalism,'" 466. Meredith Terretta makes a similar argument about women's petition writing in Cameroon. See Terretta, *Petitioning for Our Rights, Fighting for Our Nation: The History of the Democratic Union of Cameroonian Women, 1949–1960* (Mankon: Langaa, 2013).

30. Tefetso H. Mothibe, "Zimbabwe: African Working Class Nationalism, 1957–1963," *Zambezia* 23, no. 2 (1996): 157–80.

31. Frederick Cooper, *The Dialectics of Decolonization: Nationalism and Labor Movements in Postwar Africa* (Ann Arbor: University of Michigan, 1992).

32. Cooper, *Decolonization and African Society*, 6.

33. Gregory Mann, *Native Sons: West African Veterans and France in the Twentieth Century* (Durham, NC: Duke University Press, 2006), 7–8. See also Ruth Ginio, "African Colonial Soldiers between Memory and Forgetfulness: The Case of Post-Colonial Senegal," *Outre-Mers* 93, no. 350 (2006): 141–55.

34. Frederick Cooper, *Africa since 1940: The Past of the Present*, vol. 1 (Cambridge: Cambridge University Press, 2002).

35. Mahmood Mamdani, *Citizen and Subject: Contemporary Africa and the Legacy of Late Colonialism* (Princeton, NJ: Princeton University Press, 1996).

36. Timothy Burke, "Eyes Wide Shut: Africanists and the Moral Problematics of Postcolonial Societies," *African Studies Quarterly* 7, nos. 2–3 (2003): 205–9.

37. Patrick Chabal and Jean-Pascal Daloz, *Africa Works: Disorder as Political Instrument* (Bloomington: Indiana University Press, 1999), 44.

38. Jean-François Bayart, *The State in Africa: The Politics of the Belly* (New York: Longman, 1993), 233.

39. J. P. Olivier de Sardan, "A Moral Economy of Corruption in Africa?" *Journal of Modern African Studies* 37, no. 1 (1999): 44.

40. Daniel J. Smith, *A Culture of Corruption: Everyday Deception and Popular Discontent in Nigeria* (Princeton, NJ: Princeton University Press, 2007), 6.

41. For logistical reasons, in Nigeria I conducted interviews only in the area of Lagos. Many former seamen settled in Lagos after retirement, and it was therefore possible to locate a large and diverse group of informants. Although the study was limited to the greater Lagos area, the seamen interviewed represented a diverse group of ethnicities with large concentrations of Yoruba, Ijaw, and Igbo, but also included men who originated in the Middle Belt and Northern Region of Nigeria.

CHAPTER 1: THE WORKING LIVES
OF NIGERIAN SEAMEN IN THE COLONIAL ERA

1. W. Jeffrey Bolster, "'Every Inch a Man': Gender in the Lives of African American Seamen, 1800–1860," in *Iron Men, Wooden Women: Gender and Seafaring in the Atlantic World, 1700–1920,* ed. Margaret S. Creighton and Lisa Norling (Baltimore, MD: Johns Hopkins University Press, 1996), 138.

2. Walter Hawthorne, "Gorge: An African Seaman and His Flights from 'Freedom' Back to 'Slavery' in the Early Nineteenth Century," *Slavery and Abolition* 31, no. 3 (2010): 416.

3. Peter Linebaugh and Marcus Rediker, *The Many-Headed Hydra: The Hidden History of the Revolutionary Atlantic* (Boston, MA: Beacon Press, 2001).

4. Laura Tabili, "'A Maritime Race': Masculinity and the Racial Division of Labor in British Merchant Ships, 1900–1939," in Creighton and Norling, *Iron Men, Wooden Women,* 178.

5. Laura Tabili, "The Construction of Racial Difference in Twentieth-Century Britain: The Special Restriction (Coloured Alien Seamen) Order, 1925," *Journal of British Studies* 33, no. 1 (January 1994): 63.

6. Tabili, "Maritime Race," 180.

7. Tabili, "Construction of Racial Difference," 63.

8. Tabili, "Maritime Race," 171.

9. W. Jeffrey Bolster, *Black Jacks: African American Seamen in the Age of Sail* (Cambridge, MA: Harvard University Press, 1997), 48.

10. Diane Frost, *Work and Community among West African Migrant Workers since the Nineteenth Century* (Liverpool: Liverpool University Press, 1999), 8.

11. Ibid., 25.

12. Ibid., 27.

13. Ibid., 45, 102.

14. Frederick Cooper, *Decolonization and African Society: The Labor Question in French and British Africa* (Cambridge: Cambridge University Press, 1996), 58–60.

15. Marika Sherwood, "Elder Dempster and West Africa, 1891–c. 1940: The Genesis of Underdevelopment?" *International Journal of African Historical Studies* 30, no. 2 (1997): 266.

16. Frost, *Work and Community,* 16–17.

17. Sherwood, "Elder Dempster and West Africa," 255.

18. Paul Wood, "The History of Elder Dempster," http://www.rakaia.co.uk/elder-dempster-history.html.

19. Sherwood, "Elder Dempster and West Africa."

20. Peter N. Davies, *The Trade Makers: Elder Dempster in West Africa, 1852–1972, 1973–1989,* Research in Maritime History 19 (St. John's, Newfoundland: IMEHA, 2000), 256–59.

21. Janet J. Ewald, "Crossers of the Sea: Slaves, Freedmen, and Other Migrants in the Northwestern Indian Ocean, c. 1750–1914," *American Historical Review* 105, no. 1 (2000): 69–91.

22. Frost, *Work and Community,* 47.

23. Marika Sherwood, "Strikes! African Seamen, Elder Dempster and the Government 1940–42," in *Ethnic Labour and British Imperial Trade: A History of*

Ethnic Seafarers in the UK, ed. Diane Frost (London: Cass, 1995), 130. See also PRO-British National Archives, CO 859/40/2, National Union of Seamen, 13 February 1941.

24. Interview with Festus Adekunle Akintade, 24 December 2007.

25. PRO-British National Archives CO 859/76/14, J. L. Keith, 1 December 1942.

26. PRO-British National Archives CO 876/45, Jewell, 12 March 1942.

27. PRO-British National Archives CO 859/76/14, Labour Officer's Memorandum, 24 May 1941.

28. PRO-British National Archives CO 859/76/14, J. L. Keith, 26 January 1942.

29. Quoted in Frost, *Work and Community*, 101.

30. Tabili, "Maritime Race," 178.

31. Clement A. Griscom, "How Steamship Operations Are Organized—Job Descriptions and Departments," Gjenvick-Gjonvik Archives, http://www.gjenvick.com/SteamshipArticles/SteamshipCrew/1904-02-HowSteamshipOperationsAreOrganized.html#ixzz2LzRfFAiv.

32. Interview with Peter Obeze, 24 January 2011.

33. Quoted in Frost, *Work and Community*, 52.

34. Frost, *Work and Community*, 48–49.

35. Winthrop Packard, "Stewards of an Ocean Liner Above and Below Decks," Gjenvick-Gjonvik Archives, http://www.gjenvick.com/SteamshipArticles/SteamshipCrew/1904-05-StewardsOfAnOceanLiner.html#ixzz2M1B30Wnh.

36. David Simpson et al., "Firemen, Trimmers and Stokers," Barry Merchant Seamen, http://www.barrymerchantseamen.org.uk/articles/BMSfiretrim.html.

37. Tabili, "Maritime Race," 179.

38. John C. Hoyt, "Ship Facts," in *Old Ocean's Ferry: The Log of the Modern Mariner, the Trans-Atlantic Traveler, and Quaint Facts of Neptune's Realm*, ed. John C. Hoyt (New York: Bonnell, Silver, 1900), 121.

39. Simpson et al., "Firemen, Trimmers and Stokers."

40. Ibid.

41. Ibid.

42. Frost, *Work and Community*, 53.

43. Ibid., 54.

44. Ibid., 57.

45. Ibid., 56.

46. Interview with Joseph Kehinde Adigun, 17 December 2007.

47. Frost, *Work and Community*, 62.

48. Ibid., 55.

49. Interview with Festus Adekunle Akintade, 24 December 2007.

50. Interview with Muritala Olayinka alli-Balogun, 15 December 2007.

51. Interview with Rita Anomorisa, 20 January 2011.

52. Interview with Bolaji Akintade, 24 December 2007.

53. Interview with Victoria Emonaye, 15 September 2011.

54. Interview with Margaret Bessan, 3 July 2011.

55. Interview with Catherine Akpan, 20 September 2011.

56. Interview with Rita Anomorisa, 20 January 2011.

57. Interview with Catherine Akpan, 20 September 2011; interview with Essien Ben-Efang, 20 January 2011.

58. Frost, *Work and Community*, 59.

59. Quoted in Frost, *Work and Community*, 59.

60. Interview with Abiola Falola, 20 September 2011.

61. Interview with Stella Mojisola Ogundare, 20 September 2011.

62. Merseyside Maritime Museum, 4C 1908 Nigerian Union 1959–1962, Memorandum presented by the Nigerian Union of Seamen to Elder Dempster Shipping Lines, 10 January 1959.

63. Ibid.

64. Interview with Chief Charles Oloma Kose Kroseide, 17 January 2008.

65. Merseyside Maritime Museum, 4C 1908 Nigerian Union 1959–1962, Memorandum presented by the Nigerian Union of Seamen to Elder Dempster Shipping Lines, 1 October 1959.

66. Merseyside Maritime Museum, 4C 1908 Nigerian Union 1959–1962, General Secretary Monday to Elder Dempster Shipping Lines, 15 October 1958.

67. Frost, *Work and Community*, 65.

68. Interview with Adebowale Adeleye, 16 December 2007.

69. Merseyside Maritime Museum, 4C 1908 Nigerian Union 1959–1962, Letter of Ekore to M. B. Glasier at Elder Dempster Shipping Lines, 11 October 1958.

70. Merseyside Maritime Museum, 4C 1908 Nigerian Union 1959–1962, Letter of Accra Crew to Elder Dempster Shipping Lines, 21 January 1959.

71. PRO-British National Archives, CO 876/45, Trade Unions Registered in Nigeria, February 1942.

72. *Report of the Board of Enquiry into the Trade Dispute between the Elder Dempster Lines Limited and the Nigerian Union of Seamen* (Lagos: Federal Government Printer, 1959).

73. Hakeem I. Tijani, *Union Education in Nigeria: Labor, Empire, and Decolonization since 1945* (London: Palgrave Macmillan, 2012).

74. Merseyside Maritime Museum, Nigerian Union of Seamen and the Apapa Strike 1959, Precis on the view of Elder Dempster Lines, 1954.

75. Cooper, *Decolonization and African Society*, 3.

76. Merseyside Maritime Museum, Nigerian Union of Seamen and the Apapa Strike, Agent's Department, Lagos, Elder Dempster Lines, 7 October 1952.

77. Merseyside Maritime Museum, Nigerian Union of Seamen and the Apapa Strike, letter from Franco Olugbake to Elder Dempster Lines, 22 October 1956.

78. Merseyside Maritime Museum, 4C 1908 Nigerian Union of Seamen 1959–1962, letter from the Shipping Federation to M. B. Glasier, 25 June 1959.

79. Merseyside Maritime Museum, 4C 1908 Nigerian Union of Seamen 1959–1962, Nigerian Union of Seamen: Rules, 1959.

80. Merseyside Maritime Museum, 4C 1908 Nigerian Union of Seamen 1959–1962, meeting notes from R. H. Chalcroft, 13 January 1959.

81. Merseyside Maritime Museum, 4C 1908 Nigerian Union of Seamen 1959–1962, Nigerian Union of Seamen: Rules, 1959.

82. Interview with Adeola Lawal, 20 January 2011.

83. Merseyside Maritime Museum, 4C 1908 Nigerian Union of Seamen 1959–1962, letter from Akpan Monday to M. B. Glasier, 15 October 1958.

84. Merseyside Maritime Museum, 4C 1908 Nigerian Union of Seamen 1959–1962, letter from Sidi Khayam to M. B. Glasier, 1 October 1959.

85. Merseyside Maritime Museum, 4C 1908 Nigerian Union of Seamen 1959–1962, meeting notes, 1 November 1959.

86. Merseyside Maritime Museum, 4C 1908 Nigerian Union of Seamen 1959–1962, meeting notes, 1 November 1959.

87. Merseyside Maritime Museum, 4C 1908 Nigerian Union of Seamen 1959–1962, meeting notes, 3 November 1959.

88. Tijani, *Union Education in Nigeria*, 88.

89. *Report of the Board of Enquiry*, 4–5.

90. Merseyside Maritime Museum, 4C 1908 Nigerian Union of Seamen 1959–1962, Mr. Dyson to Mr. Glasier, 23 December 1958.

91. Merseyside Maritime Museum, 4C 1908 Nigerian Union of Seamen 1959–1962, Presidential Address by S. M. Ekore, 15 May 1959.

92. Ibid.

93. Merseyside Maritime Museum, 4C 1908 Nigerian Union of Seamen 1959–1962, letter of Chief Steward of the m.v. *Aureol* to Mr. Boswell, 28 May 1959.

CHAPTER 2: SEAMEN AND THE
COSMOPOLITAN IMAGINARY

Epigraph: Charles Taylor, "Modern Social Imaginaries," *Public Culture* 14, no. 1 (2002): 91.

1. Interview with Capt. Cosmos Niagwan, 27 January 2011.

2. Taylor, "Modern Social Imaginaries," 106.

3. Alberta Arthurs, "Social Imaginaries and Global Realities," *Public Culture* 15, no. 3 (2003): 580.

4. Elisa Pieri, "Contested Cosmopolitanism," *Collegium* 15 (2014): 14.

5. Stuart Hall, "Political Belonging in a World of Multiple Identities," in *Conceiving Cosmopolitanism: Theory, Context and Practice*, ed. Steven Vertovec and Robin Cohen (Oxford: Oxford University Press, 2002), 26.

6. Steven Vertovec and Robin Cohen, "Introduction: Conceiving Cosmopolitanism," in Vertovec and Cohen, *Conceiving Cosmopolitanism*, 2.

7. Jacqueline N. Brown, *Dropping Anchor, Setting Sail: Geographies of Race in Black Liverpool* (Princeton, NJ: Princeton University Press, 2005), 20–21. See also Roy May and Robin Cohen, "The Interaction between Race and Colonialism: A Case Study of the Liverpool Race Riots of 1919," *Race and Class* 16, no. 2 (1974): 111–26; Laura Tabili, *We Ask for British Justice: Workers and Racial Difference in Late Imperial Britain* (Ithaca, NY: Cornell University Press, 1994).

8. Romain Garbaye, "British Cities and Ethnic Minorities in the Post-War Era: From Xenophobic Agitation to Multi-Ethnic Government," *Immigrants and Minorities* 22, nos. 2–3 (2003): 298–315.

9. Laura Tabili, "The Construction of Racial Difference in Twentieth Century Britain: The Special Restriction of (Coloured Alien Seamen) Order, 1925," *Journal of British Studies* 33, no. 1 (1994): 84.

10. Carina E. Ray, "The White Wife Problem: Sex, Race and the Contested Politics of Repatriation to Interwar British West Africa," *Gender and History* 21, no. 3 (2009): 628–46.

11. Ibid., 633–34.

12. Ibid., 630, 639.

13. Muriel Fletcher, "Report on an Investigation into the Colour Problem in Liverpool and Other Ports," pp. 14, 19, quoted in Brown, *Dropping Anchor*, 28.

14. Mark Christian, "The Fletcher Report 1930: A Historical Case Study of Contested Black Mixed Heritage Britishness," *Journal of Historical Sociology* 21, nos. 2–3 (2008): 238.

15. Brown, *Dropping Anchor*, 28.

16. Christian, "Fletcher Report 1930," 238.

17. Randall Hansen, *Citizenship and Immigration in Post-War Britain: The Institutional Origins of a Multicultural Nation* (Oxford: Oxford University Press, 2000), 55.

18. Roxanne L. Doty, "Immigration and National Identity: Constructing the Nation," *Review of International Studies* 22, no. 3 (1996): 243–45.

19. Brown, *Dropping Anchor*, 61.

20. Many of the Nigerian seamen's complaints concerning discrimination on board Elder Dempster ships can be found in the archives of the Merseyside Maritime Museum in Liverpool. See, for example, *Report of the Board of Enquiry into the Trade Dispute between the Elder Dempster Lines Limited and the Nigerian Union of Seamen* (Merseyside Maritime Museum 1959a).

21. Interview with Adeola Lawal, 21 December 2007.

22. Interview with Reuben Lazarus, 16 December 2007.

23. Interview with Niyi Adeyemo, 24 January 2011.

24. Interview with Festus Adekunle Akintade, 24 December 2007.

25. Interview with Anthony Davies Eros, December 15, 2007.

26. Interview with Lawrence Miekumo, 27 December 2007.

27. Interview with Joseph Kehinde Adigun, 21 January 2011.

28. Interview with Daniel Ofudje, 14 January 2008.

29. For an explanation of the term "Liverpoool-born blacks," see Brown, *Dropping Anchor*, 94.

30. Of course, narrower ethnic and national ties were significant, as identification as a Yoruban or Nigerian, for example, often formed the basis of ties to other communities and individuals outside of Nigeria. But seamen insisted that ethnic and national affiliations were less prominent than race as a signifier of community and loyalty. Particularly with regard to the prenationalist era, seamen described themselves as African or black seamen, and characterized relations with others of African descent in familial terms.

31. Barbara Bush, *Imperialism, Race and Resistance: Africa and Britain, 1919–1945* (London: Routledge, 2002), 14.

32. Lissoni and Suriano have invoked the term "lived pan-Africanism" in describing relationships between South African ANC exiles and Tanzanian women. See Arianna Lissoni and Maria Suriano, "Married to the ANC: Tanzanian Women's Entanglement in South Africa's Liberation Struggle," *Journal of Southern African Studies* 40, no. 1 (2014): 129–50.

33. Interview with John Larry, 17 January 2008.

34. Ibid.

35. Brown, *Dropping Anchor*, 221.

36. Interview with Anthony Davies Eros, 15 December 2007.

37. Interview with Adeola Lawal, 21 December 2007; interview with Joseph Kehinde Adigun, 17 December 2007.

38. Sarah J. Zimmerman noted a similar dynamic among *tirailleurs sénégalais* of the colonial and postcolonial eras. These Senegalese soldiers recruited to the French

military sought out romantic and social companionship with foreign women while on duty in Europe and Asia. See Zimmerman, *Living beyond Boundaries: West African Servicemen in French Colonial Conflicts, 1908–1962* (PhD diss., University of California, Berkeley, 2011).

39. Interview with Adeola Lawal Andrew, 20 January 2011.

40. Interview with Pa Agbaosi, 15 December 2007.

41. Interview with Ganui Agoro, 15 December 2007.

42. Interview with Capt. S. A. Omoteso, 20 January 2011.

43. Interview with Lawrence Miekumo, 27 December 2007.

44. Interview with John Larry, 17 January 2008; interview with Anthony Davies Eros, 15 December 2007. On the relationships between black seamen and Irish women in Liverpool, see Brown, *Dropping Anchor*.

45. Interview with Anthony Davies Eros, 15 December 2007; interview with Reuben Lazarus, 16 December 2007.

46. Interview with Joseph Kehinde Adigun, 17 December 2007.

47. Interview with Anthony Ademola, 15 December 2007.

48. Interview with Ganui Agoro, 15 December 2007.

49. Interview with Lawrence Miekumo, 27 December 2007.

50. Interview with Alhadja Bisi Moore, 20 September 2011.

51. Interview with Adeola Lawal Andrew, 20 January 2011.

52. Interview with Modupe Lazarus, 17 January 2011.

53. Interview with Kojo George, 27 December 2007.

54. Interview with Muritala Olayinka alli-Balogun, 15 December 2007; interview with Ari Festus, December 2007.

55. Interview with Adebowale Adeleye, 16 December 2007.

56. Interview with Adeola Lawal, 21 December 2007.

57. Interview with Ari Festus, 24 December 2007.

58. Interview with Anthony Davies Eros, 15 December 2007.

59. Interview with Ganui Agoro, 15 December 2007.

60. Interview with Anthony Ademola, 15 December 2007.

61. Interview with Alex Dediara, 20 January 2011.

62. Racial segregation in Liverpool has been well documented by several historians and sociologists. See, for example, Ferdinand Dennis, *Behind the Frontlines: Journey into Afro-Britain* (London: Gollancz, 1988); and Brown, *Dropping Anchor*.

63. Interview with Pa Agbaosi, 15 December 2007.

64. Interview with Muritala Olayinka alli-Balogun, 15 December 2007.

65. Interview with Anthony Davies Eros, 15 December 2007.

66. Interview with Reuben Lazarus, 16 December 2007; interview with Muritala Olayinka alli-Balogun, 15 December 2007.

67. Interview with Joseph Kehinde Adigun, 21 January 2011.

68. Interview with Adeola Lawal Andrew, 20 January 2011.

69. Merseyside Maritime Museum, 4C 1908 Nigerian Union 1959–1962, letter from A. Monday to M. B. Glasier, 10 October 1958.

70. Interview with Anthony Davies Eros, 15 December 2007.

71. Ibid.

72. Interview with Joseph Kehinde Adigun, 17 December 2007.

73. Interview with Festus Adekunle Akintade, 24 December 2007.

74. Interview with Ari Festus, 24 December 2007.

75. Interview with Bolaji Akintade, 24 December 2007; interview with Evelyn Miekumo, 27 December 2007.

76. Interview with Bolaji Akintade, 24 December 2007.

77. Interview with Evelyn Miekumo, 27 December 2007; interview with Theresa Obezi, 28 July 2011.

78. Interview with Theresa Obezi, 28 July 2011.

79. Interview with Ganui Agoro, 15 December 2007; interview with Adebowale Adeleye, 16 December 2007; interview with Pa Agbaosi, 15 December 2007.

80. Interview with Margaret Bessan, 3 July 2011.

81. Interview with Ari Festus, 24 December 2007; interview with Anthony Davies Eros, 15 December 2007.

82. Interview with Anthony Davies Eros, 15 December 2007.

83. Interview with Kojo George, 27 December 2007.

84. Interview with Festus Adekunle Akintade, 24 December 2007.

85. As one informant explained, "You cannot use two fridges if you already have one." Interview with Ganui Agoro, 15 December 2007.

86. Interview with Margaret Bessan, 3 July 2011.

87. Interview with Anthony Davies Eros, 15 December 2007.

88. Interview with Daniel Ofudje, 14 January 2008.

89. Interview with Pa Agbaosi, 15 December 2007.

90. Peter N. Davies, *The Trade Makers: Elder Dempster in West Africa, 1852–1972, 1973–1989*, Research in Maritime History 19 (St. John's, Newfoundland: IMEHA, 2000), 306, 346.

91. Interview with Kojo George, 27 December 2007.

92. Interview with Festus Adekunle Akintade, 24 December 2007.

93. Interview with Daniel Ofudje, 14 January 2008.

94. Interview with Festus Adekunle Akintade, 24 December 2007.

95. Interview with Muritala Olayinka alli-Balogun, 17 January 2011.

96. Interview with Alex Dediara, 20 January 2011.

97. Interview with Festus Adekunle Akintade, 24 December 2007.

98. Interview with Chief Charles Oloma Kose Kroseide, 14 January 2008; interview with John Larry, 17 January 2008; interview with T. T. Mensah, 25 January 2007.

99. Interview with Pa Agbaosi, 15 December 2007; interview with John Larry, 17 January 2008.

100. Interview with Pa Agbaosi, 15 December 2007.

101. Interview with Adeola Lawal, 21 December 2007.

102. Ibid.

103. Interview with Anthony Davies Eros, 15 December 2007.

104. Ibid.

105. Paul Gilroy, *The Black Atlantic: Modernity and Double Consciousness* (Cambridge, MA: Harvard University Press, 1993).

106. Interview with Ari Festus, 24 December 2007.

107. See, for example, Deborah A. Thomas and Kamari M. Clarke, "Introduction: Globalization and the Transformations of Race," in *Globalization and Race: Transformations in the Cultural Production of Blackness*, ed. Kamari M. Clarke and Deborah A. Thomas (Durham, NC: Duke University Press, 2006), 1–34.

CHAPTER 3: FROM CITIZENS OF THE WORLD
TO CITIZENS OF NIGERIA

1. Frederick Cooper, "Possibility and Constraint: African Independence in Historical Perspective," *Journal of African History* 49, no. 2 (2008): 167–96.

2. Philip S. Zachernuk, *Colonial Subjects: An African Intelligentsia and Atlantic Ideas* (Charlottesville: University Press of Virginia, 2000), 141.

3. Ibid., 163.

4. Frantz Fanon, *The Wretched of the Earth*, trans. Constance Ferrington (London: Penguin, 1990), 126.

5. Michael Neocosmos, *The Contradictory Position of "Tradition" in African Nationalist Discourse: Some Analytical and Political Reflections* (Durban: Centre for Civil Society, 2004), 6.

6. Hakim Adi, "Pan-Africanism and West African Nationalism in Britain," *African Studies Review* 43, no. 1 (April 2000): 69–82.

7. Paul Gilroy, *The Black Atlantic: Modernity and Double Consciousness* (Cambridge, MA: Harvard University Press, 1991).

8. W. Jeffrey Bolster, "'Every Inch a Man': Gender in the Lives of African American Seamen, 1800–1860," in *Iron Men, Wooden Women: Gender and Seafaring in the Atlantic World, 1700–1920*, ed. Margaret S. Creighton and Lisa Norling (Baltimore, MD: Johns Hopkins University Press, 1996), 39.

9. Michael A. Gomez, *Reversing Sail: A History of the African Diaspora* (Cambridge: Cambridge University Press, 2004), 194.

10. Merseyside Maritime Museum, 4C 1908 Nigerian Union of Seamen 1959–1962, letter Ekore to M. B. Glasier, 11 October 1958.

11. Merseyside Maritime Museum, 4C 1908 Nigerian Union of Seamen 1959–1962, letter A. Monday to M. B. Glasier, 10 October 1958.

12. Ibid.

13. Merseyside Maritime Museum, 4C 1908 Nigerian Union of Seamen 1959–1962, letter A. Monday to M. B. Glasier, 11 October 1958.

14. Merseyside Maritime Museum, 4C 1908 Nigerian Union of Seamen 1959–1962, Chief Steward of the m.v. *Aureol* to Mr. Boswell, 5 May 1959 (written from Las Palmas).

15. Jacqueline N. Brown, *Dropping Anchor, Setting Sail: Geographies of Race in Black Liverpool* (Princeton, NJ: Princeton University Press, 2005), 91.

16. Marika Sherwood, *Pastor Daniels Ekarte and the African Churches Mission, Liverpool, 1931–64* (London: Savannah Press, 1994).

17. Diane Frost, *Work and Community among West African Migrant Workers since the Nineteenth Century* (Liverpool: Liverpool University Press, 1999), 198.

18. See Merseyside Maritime Museum, 4C 1908 Nigerian Union of Seamen 1959–1962, letter from John Holt at ED to M. B. Glasier, 6 May 1959.

19. Modern Records Centre, University of Warwick, mss/292/966.3/3, letter from G. D. Gibbins to M. Nicholson, 3 April 1958.

20. Merseyside Maritime Museum, 4C 1908 Nigerian Union of Seamen 1959–1962, letter from the seamen's union to Elder Dempster Lines in Lagos, 12 June 1959.

21. Modern Records Centre, University of Warwick, mss/292/966.3/3, Public Notice, Nigerian Union of Seamen, April 1958.

22. Merseyside Maritime Museum, Nigerian Union of Seamen Apapa Strike 1959, letter from ED officer in Lagos to M. Glasier, 21 June 1959.

23. Merseyside Maritime Museum, 4C 1908 Nigerian Union of Seamen 1959–1962, letter from the seamen's union to Elder Dempster Lines in Lagos, 22 January 1959.

24. Merseyside Maritime Museum, 4C 1908 Nigerian Union of Seamen 1959–1962, notes from Mr. Glasier's interview with Captain Perkins of the s.s. *Winneba*.

25. Ibid.

26. Merseyside Maritime Museum, 4C 1908 Nigerian Union of Seamen 1959–1962, P. A. R. Lindsay to G. Foggon (Labour Advisor to the Secretary of State for the Colonies, Colonial Office), 6 February 1959.

27. Merseyside Maritime Museum, 4C 1908 Nigerian Union of Seamen 1959–1962, Mr. Dyson to Mr. Glasier, 23 December 1958.

28. Modern Records Centre, University of Warwick, mss/292/966.3/3, letter from Tom Yates to Sir Vincent Tewson, 26 June 1958.

29. Merseyside Maritime Museum, Nigerian Union of Seamen Apapa Strike 1959, letter from ED officer in Lagos to M. Glasier, 21 June 1959.

30. Merseyside Maritime Museum, 4C 1908 Nigerian Union of Seamen 1959–1962, P. A. R. Lindsay to G. Foggon (Labour Advisor to the Secretary of State for the Colonies, Colonial Office), 6 February 1959.

31. Merseyside Maritime Museum, 4C 1908 Nigerian Union of Seamen 1959–1962, letter from G. H. Neville in Nigeria to M. B. Glasier, 24 January 1959.

32. Merseyside Maritime Museum, 4C 1908 Nigerian Union of Seamen 1959–1962, R. H. Chalcroft to M. Glasier, 10 February 1959.

33. Ibid.

34. This conversation was reported in a letter from R. H. Chalcroft to M. Glasier on 10 February 1959, Merseyside Maritime Museum, 4C 1908 Nigerian Union of Seamen 1959–1962.

35. Merseyside Maritime Museum, 4C 1908 Nigerian Union of Seamen 1959–1962, letter from the Secretariat and Education Bureau to the general membership, 10 January 1959.

36. *Report of the Board of Enquiry into the Trade Dispute*, appendix C.

37. *Daily Telegraph* (Lagos), 27 May 1959.

38. Merseyside Maritime Museum, 4C 1908 Nigerian Union of Seamen 1959–1962, letter from M. B. Glasier to R. N. Chalcroft, 6 July 1959.

39. Merseyside Maritime Museum, 4C 1908 Nigerian Union of Seamen 1959–1962, letter from M. B. Glasier to R. N. Chalcroft, 24 June 1959.

40. Merseyside Maritime Museum, 4C 1908 Nigerian Union of Seamen 1959–1962, African Defense Association (and signing the letter from Sojourner Truth) to Mr. Glasier, 30 June 1959.

41. Merseyside Maritime Museum, Nigerian Union of Seamen Apapa Strike 1959, report from *Apapa* voyage, June 1959.

42. Merseyside Maritime Museum, Nigerian Union of Seamen Apapa Strike 1959, report from R. R. Worthington, June 1959.

43. Merseyside Maritime Museum, 4C 1908 Nigerian Union of Seamen 1959–1962, Charles Elston to Mr. Glasier, 30 June 1959.

44. Merseyside Maritime Museum, 4C 1908 Nigerian Union of Seamen 1959–1962, Elder Dempster representative in Lagos to Mr. Glasier, 1 July 1959.

45. Frederick Cooper, *Decolonization and African Society: The Labor Question in French and British Africa* (Cambridge: Cambridge University Press, 1996), 16.

46. Merseyside Maritime Museum, 2047 Mr. Glasier 1951–1961, Glasier to the University of Liverpool, 29 October 1959.

47. Merseyside Maritime Museum, 4C 1908 Nigerian Seamen's Union, Sidi Khayam address to the First Delegates Conference (no date, but must be in 1960 at the earliest because of reference to Salubi inquiry).

48. Ibid.

49. Modern Records Centre, University of Warwick, mss/292/966.3/1, report on the m.v. *Dan Fodio* crisis, 12 August 1960.

50. Cooper, *Decolonization and African Society*, 416.

51. Modern Records Centre, University of Warwick, mss/292/966.3/1, report on the m.v. *Dan Fodio* crisis, 12 August 1960..

52. Merseyside Maritime Museum, 4C 1908 Nigerian Seamen's Union, Nigeria Shipping Federation to M. B. Glasier, 9 January 1960.

53. Elder Dempster, Lagos, Robertson, to Steamship Nautical Dept Liverpool, 26 April 1960.

54. Merseyside Maritime Museum, 4C 1908 Nigerian Seamen's Union, Sidi Khayam address to the First Delegates Conference (no date, but must be in 1960 at the earliest because of reference to Salubi inquiry).

55. Modern Records Centre, University of Warwick, mss/292/966.3/1, report on the m.v. *Dan Fodio* crisis, 12 August 1960.

56. Ibid.

57. Ibid.

58. Zachernuk, *Colonial Subjects*, 141.

59. Merseyside Maritime Museum, 2047 Mr. Glasier 1951–1961, Glasier to Tod, 13 November 1959.

60. Merseyside Maritime Museum, 1908 Nigerian Seamen's Union, Paxton to Holt, 10 August 1962.

61. Merseyside Maritime Museum, 1908 Nigerian Seamen's Union, extract from a letter from Mr. Gale, 12 January 1960.

62. Merseyside Maritime Museum, 1908 Nigerian Seamen's Union, Nigerian Shipping Federation to M. B. Glasier, 4 February 1960.

63. Modern Records Centre, University of Warwick, mss/292/966.3/11, Paxton to Yates, 16 February 1960.

64. Modern Records Centre, University of Warwick, mss/292/966.3/11, Paxton to Yates, 25 August 1960.

65. Merseyside Maritime Museum, 1908 Nigerian Seamen's Union, letter to Gale, 6 October 1959.

66. Merseyside Maritime Museum, 1908 Nigerian Seamen's Union, B. Koffe to Elder Dempster, 24 September 1959.

67. Björn Beckman, Sakhela Buhlungu, and Lloyd Sachikonye, eds., *Trade Unions and Party Politics: Labour Movements in Africa* (Cape Town: HSRC Press, 2010), 13.

68. Peter Waterman, *Division and Unity amongst Nigerian Workers: Lagos Port Unionism, 1940s–60s*, vol. 11 (The Hague: Institute of Social Studies, 1982), 23.

69. For a broader discussion of the disempowerment of rank-and-file labor in postcolonial Nigeria, see ibid.; also Paul M. Lubeck, "Unions, Workers and Consciousness in Kano, Nigeria: A View from Below," in *The Development of an African Working Class: Studies in Class Formation and Action*, ed. Richard Sandbrook and Robin Cohen

(London: Longman, 1975), 139–60; Adrian J. Peace, "The Lagos Proletariat: Labour Aristocrats or Populist Militants?" in *The Development of an African Working Class: Studies in Class Formation and Action,* ed. Richard Sandbrook and Robin Cohen (London: Longman, 1975), 281–302; and Bill Freund, *The African Worker* (Cambridge: Cambridge University Press, 1988), 103–4.

70. Abubakar Momoh, "Popular Struggles in Nigeria, 1960–1982," *African Journal of Political Science* 1, no. 2 (1996): 164.

71. Björn Beckman and Salihu Lukman, "The Failure of Nigeria's Labour Party," in Beckman, Buhlungu, and Sachikonye, *Trade Unions and Party Politics,* 60.

72. Interview with Sunday Nwachukwu, 24 December 2007.

73. Merseyside Maritime Museum, 1909 Commander Shelbourne, Palm Line to Glasier, 7 June 1963.

74. Interview with Adebowale Adeleye, 16 December 2007.

75. Interview with Muritala Olayinka alli-Balogun, 15 December 2007.

76. Merseyside Maritime Museum, 4C 1908 Nigerian Seamen's Union, crew letter from the m.v. *Apapa* in Liverpool to Gen. Sec. Sidi Khayam, 18 July 1961.

CHAPTER 4: THE BIRTH OF THE NIGERIAN
NATIONAL SHIPPING LINE

1. Okechukwu C. Iheduru, *The Political Economy of International Shipping in Developing Countries* (Newark: University of Delaware Press, 1996), 21.

2. Ibid.

3. Ibid., 233.

4. Ebere Nwaubani, "Constitution-Making and the Nigerian Identity, 1914–1960," in *The Transformation of Nigeria: Essays in Honor of Toyin Falola,* ed. Adebayo Oyebade (Trenton, NJ: Africa World Press, 2002), 88–89.

5. Toyin Falola and Matthew M. Heaton, *A History of Nigeria* (Cambridge: Cambridge University Press, 2008), 149.

6. Rotimi T. Suberu, *Federalism and Ethnic Conflict in Nigeria* (Washington: US Institute of Peace Press, 2001), 24.

7. Akanmu G. Adebayo, "The Collapse of Nigeria's Federal System of Government," in Oyebade, *Transformation of Nigeria,* 120.

8. Peter P. Ekeh, "The Structure and Meaning of Federal Character in the Nigerian Political System," in *Federal Character and Federalism in Nigeria,* ed. Peter P. Ekeh and Eghosa E. Osaghae (Ibadan: Heinemann, 1989), 21.

9. Suberu, *Federalism and Ethnic Conflict in Nigeria,* 24–25.

10. Okwudiba Nnoli, *Ethnicity and Development in Nigeria* (Aldershot: Avebury, 1995), 83.

11. Ismaila Mohammed, "The Nigerian Enterprises Promotion Decrees (1972 and 1977) and Indigenisation in Nigeria" (PhD diss., University of Warwick, 1985), 38.

12. Falola and Heaton, *History of Nigeria,* 159.

13. Axel Harneit-Sievers, "African Business, 'Economic Nationalism,' and British Colonial Policy: Southern Nigeria, 1935–1954," *African Economic History* 24 (1996): 87.

14. Ibid.

15. Quoted in Robert L. Tignor, *Capitalism and Nationalism at the End of Empire: State and Business in Decolonizing Egypt, Nigeria, and Kenya, 1945–1963* (Princeton, NJ: Princeton University Press, 1998), 239–40.

16. Tignor, *Capitalism and Nationalism at the End of Empire*.

17. Ibid., 261.

18. Olakunle A. Lawal, "British Commercial Interests and the Decolonization Process in Nigeria, 1950–60," *African Economic History* 22 (1994): 93–110; Tignor, *Capitalism and Nationalism at the End of Empire*, 274.

19. Harneit-Sievers, "African Business," 115.

20. E. O. Akeredolu-Ale, "Private Foreign Investment and Underdevelopment of Indigenous Entrepreneurship in Nigeria," in *Nigeria: Economy and Society*, ed. Gavin Williams (London: Rex Collins, 1976), 67–82; Larry J. Diamond, *Class, Ethnicity and Democracy in Nigeria: The Failure of the First Republic* (Syracuse, NY: Syracuse University Press, 1988), 30.

21. Björn Beckman, "Whose State? State and Capitalist Development in Nigeria," *Review of African Political Economy* 9, no. 23 (1982): 39.

22. Olasupo Ojedokun, "The Changing Pattern of Nigeria's International Economic Relations: The Decline of the Colonial Nexus, 1960–1966," *Journal of Developing Areas* 6, no. 4 (1972): 535–36.

23. Chibuzo N. Nwoke, "Towards Authentic Economic Nationalism in Nigeria," *Africa Today* 33, no. 4 (1986): 56.

24. Ibid., 62.

25. Michael Adejugbe, "The Myths and Realities of Nigeria's Business Indigenization," *Development and Change* 15, no. 4 (1984): 578.

26. Nwoke, "Towards Authentic Economic Nationalism in Nigeria," 60.

27. Adejugbe, "Myths and Realities of Nigeria's Business Indigenization," 578.

28. Adeoye A. Akinsanya, "The Power Structure in Nigeria and the Indigenization of the Economy," *Pakistan Horizon* 47, no. 2 (1994): 66.

29. Ibid., 67.

30. Ibid.

31. Charlotte Leubuscher, *West African Shipping Trade, 1909–1959* (Leiden: Sythoff, 1963).

32. Ibid.

33. Iheduru, *Political Economy of International Shipping*, 53.

34. Ayodeji Olukoju, "A 'Truly Nigerian Project'? The Politics of the Establishment of the Nigerian National Shipping Line (NNSL), 1957–1959," *International Journal of Maritime History* 15, no. 1 (2003): 69–90.

35. PRO-British National Archives, CO 554/1683, notes from NEC meeting, January 1957.

36. Ibid.

37. PRO-British National Archives, CO 554/1683, extract from fifth meeting of the NEC, 8 October 1957.

38. PRO-British National Archives, COM 201/11/01 Shipping Service West Africa, M. Terry, 12 August 1958.

39. Ibid.

40. PRO-British National Archives, CO 554/1683, extract from seventh NEC meeting, 6 September 1958.

41. Ibid.

42. Merseyside Maritime Museum, 2247 J. Joyce 1959–1961, Joyce to Lindenberg, 20 January 1958.

43. Ibid.

44. PRO-British National Archives, CO 554/1683, press release of Njoku's speech, 25 November 1958.

45. Ibid.; emphasis in the original.

46. Ibid.

47. Ibid.; emphasis in the original.

48. Bassey U. Ekong, "Survival Opportunities and Strategies of a Marginal Firm in a Cartelized Oligopoly: Case Study of the Nigerian National Shipping Line" (PhD diss., Michigan State University, 1974), 179.

49. PRO-British National Archives, COM 201/11/01 Shipping Service West Africa, Ministry of Transport to Saker, 27 July 1959.

50. PRO-British National Archives, COM 201/11/01 Shipping Service West Africa, Cheeseman to Innes, 27 January 1959.

51. PRO-British National Archives, CO 554/1683, Stapleton to Robertson, 4 February 1959.

52. PRO-British National Archives, COM 201/11/01, Shipping Service West Africa, Ministry of Transport to Saker, 27 July 1959.

53. Ibid.

54. PRO-British National Archives, CO 554/1683, Remarks of Minister Amanze Njoku in House of Representatives, 19 February 1959; emphasis in the original.

55. "The Shipping Muddle," *Daily Times*, 23 February 1959.

56. *Daily Service*, 24 April 1959.

57. *Daily Service*, 25 April 1959.

58. "Nationalists in Office," *West African Pilot*, 4 April 1959.

59. Merseyside Maritime Museum, 2247 J. Joyce 1959–1961, Minister of Transport Njoku, House of Representatives Debates, 17 August 1959.

60. Ibid.

61. Merseyside Maritime Museum, 2247 J. Joyce 1959–1961, Leif Hoegh to Joyce, 28 January 1958.

62. Ironically, it was the Black Star Line that initially opposed the membership of the Nigerian National Shipping Line, hoping to negotiate a better cargo share for themselves before voting in the Nigerians. This effort was abandoned after pressure from Elder Dempster. See Merseyside Maritime Museum, 2247 J. Joyce 1959–1961, Joyce to Traub, 12 May 1959.

63. Leubuscher, *West African Shipping Trade*, 77.

64. Ibid., 86–88.

65. Ibid., 9–12.

66. Merseyside Maritime Museum, 2247 J. Joyce 1959–1961, notes on a visit to West Africa, Stapleton, 25 May 1959.

67. Leubuscher, *West African Shipping Trade*, 88.

68. Merseyside Maritime Museum, 2247 J. Joyce 1959–1961, Joyce to Evans, 10 April 1959.

69. Ibid.

70. Leubuscher, *West African Shipping Trade*, 92.

71. Diamond, *Class, Ethnicity, and Democracy in Nigeria*, 30.

72. PRO-British National Archives, CO 554/1683, Remarks of Minister Amanze Njoku, 8 June 1959.

73. Quoted in Tignor, *Capitalism and Nationalism at the End of Empire*, 257.

74. PRO-British National Archives, COM 201/11/01, Shipping Service West Africa, extract from West Africa press survey, 30 December 1959.

75. Ekong, "Survival Opportunities and Strategies," 182.

76. Leubuscher, *West African Shipping Trade*, 68.

77. Quoted in Tignor, *Capitalism and Nationalism at the End of Empire*, 259.

78. Merseyside Maritime Museum, 2247 J. Joyce 1959–1961, Joyce to Hoffman, 5 June 1959.

79. Merseyside Maritime Museum, 2247 J. Joyce 1959–1961, NNSL to Muirhead, 23 July 1959.

80. Merseyside Maritime Museum, 2247 J. Joyce 1959–1961, Joyce to Ojukwu, 17 February 1961.

81. Gerald Chidi, "Nigerian National Shipping Lines, the Beginning and the End," Vanguard, 1 November 2011, http://www.vanguardngr.com/2011/11/nigerian-national-shipping-lines-the-beginning-and-the-end.

82. Merseyside Maritime Museum, 2247 J. Joyce 1959–1961, Ojukwu to Joyce, 16 May 1959.

83. Merseyside Maritime Museum, 2247 J. Joyce 1959–1961, "Establishment of Branch Offices in West Africa," 10 July 1961.

84. Merseyside Maritime Museum, 2247 J. Joyce 1959–1961, Press release, 28 September 1960.

85. Leubuscher, *West African Shipping Trade*, 68.

86. Merseyside Maritime Museum, 2247 J. Joyce 1959–1961, board meeting notes, 31 May 1960.

87. Merseyside Maritime Museum, 2247 J. Joyce 1959–1961, Ojukwu to Minister of Transport, 19 May 1960.

88. Merseyside Maritime Museum, 2247 J. Joyce 1959–1961, board meeting notes, 31 May 1960.

89. Ibid.

90. Merseyside Maritime Museum, 2247 J. Joyce 1959–1961, Minister of Transport and Aviation to Chairman of NNSL, 31 December 1960.

91. Merseyside Maritime Museum, 2247 J. Joyce 1959–1961, meeting notes on new ships for NNSL, 27 January 1961.

92. Merseyside Maritime Museum, 2247 J. Joyce 1959–1961, Chairman NNSL to Minister of Transport, 1961.

93. Merseyside Maritime Museum, 2247 J. Joyce 1959–1961, Accounts and Control, 30 January 1961.

94. Merseyside Maritime Museum, 2247 J. Joyce 1959–1961, Hoffman to Muirhead, 18 January 1961.

95. Chidi, "Nigerian National Shipping Lines."

96. Bolaji Akinola, *Arrested Development: A Journalist's Account of How the Growth of Nigeria's Shipping Sector Is Impaired by Politics and Inconsistent Policies* (Bloomington, IN: AuthorHouse, 2012).

97. Dele Aderibigbe, "How Bureaucracy Led to the NNSL Demise—Chidi," *Nigerian Tribune*, 25 July 2012.

98. Merseyside Maritime Museum, 2247 J. Joyce 1959–1961, Passage to Joyce, 8 April 1960.

99. Merseyside Maritime Museum, 2247 J. Joyce 1959–1961, Passage to Joyce, 7 April 1960.

1. Ships Nostalgia, http://www.shipsnostalgia.com/newreply.php?do=newreply&p= 26643.

2. Ibid.

3. Merseyside Maritime Museum, 2247 J. Joyce 1959–1961, Minister of Transport Njoku, House of Representatives Debates, 17 August 1959.

4. See, for example, Leslie L. Rood, "Nationalisation and Indigenisation in Africa," *Journal of Modern African Studies* 14, no. 3 (1976): 427–47; Stephanie Decker, "Building Up Goodwill: British Business, Development and Economic Nationalism in Ghana and Nigeria, 1945–1977," *Enterprise and Society* 9, no. 4 (2008): 602–13; Ernest J. Wilson III, "Strategies of State Control of the Economy: Nationalization and Indigenization in Africa," *Comparative Politics* 22, no. 4 (1990): 401–19; Adeoye A. Akinsanya, *The Expropriation of Multinational Property in the Third World* (New York: Praeger, 1980).

5. See, for example, Chibuzo S. A. Ogbuagu, "The Nigerian Indigenization Policy: Nationalism or Pragmatism?" *African Affairs* 82, no. 327 (1983): 241–66; Paul Collins, "Public Policy and the Development of Indigenous Capitalism: The Nigerian Experience," *Journal of Commonwealth and Comparative Politics* 15, no. 2 (1977): 127–50; Adeoye A. Akinsanya, "The Power Structure in Nigeria and the Indigenization of the Economy," *Pakistan Horizon* 47, no. 2 (1994): 63–79; Fiona C. Beveridge, "Taking Control of Foreign Investment: A Case Study of Indigenisation in Nigeria," *International and Comparative Law Quarterly* 40, no. 2 (1991): 302–33; Michael Adejugbe, "The Myths and Realities of Nigeria's Business Indigenization," *Development and Change* 15, no. 4 (1984): 577–92.

6. Modern Records Centre, University of Warwick, mss/292/9663/1, Conditions of Service for West African Seamen, 1960.

7. For example, see interview with Lawrence Miekumo, 27 December 2007; interview with Festus Adekunle Akintade, 24 December 2007; interview with Daniel Ofudje, 14 January 2008.

8. Interview with Muritala Olayinka alli-Balogun, 15 December 2007.

9. Interview with Festus Adekunle Akintade, 24 December 2007.

10. Interview with Anomorisa Johnson, 22 January 2011.

11. Interview with Jimmy Bessan, 3 July 2011.

12. Interview with Pa Agbaosi, 15 December 2007.

13. Craig J. Calhoun, "'Belonging' in the Cosmopolitan Imaginary," *Ethnicities* 3, no. 4 (2003): 543.

14. Interview with Kojo George, 27 December 2007.

15. Interview with Daniel Ofudje, 14 January 2008.

16. Interview with Patric Pereira, 24 January 2011.

17. Interview with Muritala Olayinka all-Balogun, 15 December 2007.

18. Interview with Muritala Olayinka all-Balogun, 16 December 2007.

19. Interview with Anthony Eros, 15 December 2007.

20. Interview with Gold Agbodobiri, 24 January 2011.

21. Interview with Anomorisa Johnson, 22 January 2011.

22. Interview with John Larry, 20 January 2008.

23. Interview with Adebowale Adeleye, 16 December 2007.

24. Merseyside Maritime Museum, 2247 J. Joyce 1959–1961, notes of meeting on Nigerian crew matters, 4 September 1959.

25. Ibid.

26. Modern Records Centre, University of Warwick, mss/292/966.3/1, report on the m.v. *Dan Fodio* crisis, 12 August 1960.

27. Modern Records Centre, University of Warwick, mss/292D/966.3/1, Comprehensive Report—m.v. *Dan Fodio* crisis, 1960.

28. Modern Records Centre, University of Warwick, mss/292/966.3/1, report on the m.v. *Dan Fodio* crisis, 12 August 1960.

29. Merseyside Maritime Museum, 2273 Muirhead inward 1962–1964/5, Operational Agent's Report, December quarter, 1959.

30. Merseyside Maritime Museum, 2247 J. Joyce 1959–1961, Minister of Transport Njoku, House of Representatives Debates, 17 August 1959.

31. Merseyside Maritime Museum, 2247 J. Joyce 1959–1961, NNSL board meeting notes, 27 October 1959.

32. Bassey U. Ekong, "Survival Opportunities and Strategies of a Marginal Firm in a Cartelized Oligopoly: Case Study of the Nigerian National Shipping Line" (PhD diss., Michigan State University), 328.

33. Ibid., 329.

34. Merseyside Maritime Museum, 2273 Muirhead inward 1962–1964/5, NNSL Board of Directors Meeting, 28 September 1960.

35. Merseyside Maritime Museum, 2273 Muirhead inward 1962–1964/5, NNSL Board of Directors Meeting, 26 February 1960.

36. Merseyside Maritime Museum, 1908, Khayam to Crews Manager, 27 October 1959.

37. Modern Records Centre, University of Warwick, mss/292D/966.3/1, Comprehensive Report—m.v. *Dan Fodio* crisis, 1960.

38. Ibid.

39. Ibid.

40. Ibid.

41. Ibid.

42. Interview with Adebowale Adeleye, 16 December 2007.

43. Interview with Capt. Alao Tajudeen, 23 January 2011.

44. Interview with Jimmy Bessan, 3 July 2011.

45. Ship's logbook: *River Ogun*, 25.9.80, entry: 4.4.81 at sea: 5.4.81.

46. Ship's logbook: *King Jaja*, 31.10.73, entry: 26.3.74 Liverpool.

47. Ship's logbook: *Oduduwa*, 20.8.73, entry: 16.9.73 N.A.: 17.9.73.

48. Ship's logbook: *River Majidum*, 30.9.82, entry: 5.4.83.

49. Ship's logbook: *River Benue*, 25.5.74, entry: 31.7.74 at sea: 1.8.74.

50. Ship's logbook: *River Adada*, 24.7.82, entry: 14.12.82 Singapore.

51. Ship's logbook: *River Ogun*, n.d. entry: 21.1.78.

52. Bailey, http://www.shipsnostalgia.com/showthread.php?t=3654.

53. Ships Nostalgia, http://www.shipsnostalgia.com/showthread.php?t=3154&highlight=biafra.

54. Ship's logbook: *Yinka Folawiyo*, 24.5.76, entry: date and place n/a.

55. Ship's logbook: *River Ogun*, 2.4.70, entry: 17.7.70 Calabar.

56. Ship's logbook: *Oranyan*, 4.4.74, entry: 27.12.74 Lagos Bar.

57. Ship's logbook: *King Jaja*, 1.4.75, entry: 6.6.75 Lagos.

58. Ship's logbook: *King Jaja*, N/A, entry: 3.1.69 Avonmouth.

59. Ship's logbook: *Ahmadu Tijani* 14.2.78, entry: 31.5.78 Antwerp.

60. Ibid.

61. Ibid.

62. Ship's logbook: *Ahmadu Tijani* 14.2.78, entry: 21.6.78 at sea.

63. Ship's logbook: *Ahmadu Tijani*, 14.2.78, entry: 28.7.78 Lagos Bar.

64. Ship's logbook: *River Ogun*, n.d. entry: 1.4.78.

65. Ship's logbook: *River Benue*; 21.7.76, entry: 22.12.76.

66. Ship's logbook: *King Jaja*, 31.10.73, entry: 10.5.74 N/A.

67. Ship's logbook: *River Ngada*, 5.11.80.

68. Ship's logbook: *River Ethiope*, 19.8.1980, entry: 4.10.80.

69. Ship's logbook: *River Oshun*, 12.12.80, entry: 14.4.81 Hamburg.

70. Ship's logbook: *River Benue*, 25.5.74, entry: 25.7.74 Lagos: 26.7.73.

71. Ship's logbook: *Oduduwa*, 20.8.73, entry: 23.9.73 Sapele: 24.9.73.

72. Ship's logbook: *River Oji*, 11.12.80, entry: 20.4.81 Port of Abidjan.

73. Ship's logbook: *River Niger*, 13.6.71, entry: 7.7.71 Hamburg.

74. Eghosa E. Osaghae, *Crippled Giant: Nigeria since Independence* (Bloomington: Indiana University Press, 1998), 19.

75. Isaac O. Albert, "Problems of Democratic Governance in Nigeria: The Past in the Present" (paper prepared for presentation at the Triennial History Workshop on Democracy, "Popular Precedents, Popular Practice and Popular Culture," University of the Witwatersrand, Johannesburg, 13–16 July, 1994).

76. Augustine Ikelegbe, "The Perverse Manifestation of Civil Society: Evidence from Nigeria," *Journal of Modern African Studies* 39, no. 1 (2001): 7.

77. Osaghae, *Crippled Giant*, 313.

78. Interview with Reuben Lazarus, 17 January 2011.

79. Modern Records Centre, University of Warwick, mss/292D/966.3/1, Conditions of Service for West African Seamen, 1960.

80. Interview with Pa Agbaosi, 15 December 2007.

81. Interview with John Rafaal, 24 January 2011.

82. Interview with Ari Festus, 24 January 2011.

83. Ibid.

84. Interview with Ari Festus, 24 December 2007.

85. Ship's logbook: *King Jaja*, N/A, entry: 10.6.72 Rotterdam.

86. Interview with Lawrence Miekumo, 27 December 2007.

87. Interview with Joseph Kehinde Adigun, 21 January 2011.

88. Interview with Adebowale Adeleye, 16 December 2007.

89. Interview with Ari Festus, 24 December 2007.

CHAPTER 6: SEAMEN IN THE SHADOW
OF THE NNSL DECLINE AND DEMISE

1. Interview with Kenneth Birch, Liverpool, England, 8 June 2009.

2. Interview with Olukayode Akinsoji, 25 January 2011.

3. Mahmood Mamdani, *Citizen and Subject: Contemporary Africa and the Legacy of Late Colonialism* (Princeton, NJ: Princeton University Press, 1996).

4. Alois S. Mlambo, "Western Social Sciences and Africa: The Domination and Marginalisation of a Continent," *African Sociological Review* 10, no. 1 (2006): 170.

5. Eghosa E. Osaghae, *Crippled Giant: Nigeria since Independence* (Bloomington: Indiana University Press, 1998), 12.

6. Abonyi N. Nnaemeka, "Towards an Alternative Development Paradigm for Africa," *Journal of Social Science* 21, no. 1 (2009): 39–48.

7. Patrick Chabal and Jean-Pascal Daloz, *Africa Works: Disorder as Political Instrument* (Bloomington: Indiana University Press, 1999).

8. Richard A. Joseph, *Democracy and Prebendal Politics in Nigeria: The Rise and Fall of the Second Republic*, African Studies Series 56 (Cambridge: Cambridge University Press, 2014), 67. See also Olufemi Vaughan, *Nigerian Chiefs: Traditional Power in Modern Politics, 1890s–1990s*, Rochester Studies in African History and the Diaspora 7 (Rochester, NY: University of Rochester Press, 2006), 156.

9. Chudi Uwazurike, "Ethnicity, Power and Prebendalism: The Persistent Triad as the Unsolvable Crisis of Nigerian Politics," *Dialectical Anthropology* 21, no. 1 (1996): 1–20.

10. Isaac O. Albert, "Explaining 'Godfatherism' in Nigerian Politics," *African Sociological Review* 9, no. 2 (2005): 79–105; Albert, "Problems of Democratic Governance in Nigeria: The Past in the Present" (paper prepared for presentation at the Triennial History Workshop on Democracy, "Popular Precedents, Popular Practice and Popular Culture," University of the Witwatersrand, Johannesburg, 13–16 July 1994).

11. Daniel J. Smith, *A Culture of Corruption: Everyday Deception and Popular Discontent in Nigeria* (Princeton, NJ: Princeton University Press, 2007), 5.

12. Gerald Chidi, "Nigerian National Shipping Lines, the Beginning and the End," *Vanguard*, 1 November 2011, http://www.vanguardngr.com/2011/11/nigerian-national-shipping-lines-the-beginning-and-the-end.

13. Merseyside Maritime Museum, 2247 J. Joyce 1959–1961, Nigeria ED Manager, 3 October 1962.

14. *Lloyd's*, 3 October 1962.

15. Bassey U. Ekong, "Survival Opportunities and Strategies of a Marginal Firm in a Cartelized Oligopoly: Case Study of the Nigerian National Shipping Line" (PhD diss., Michigan State University, 1974), 194.

16. Okechukwu C. Iheduru, *The Political Economy of International Shipping in Developing Countries* (Newark: University of Delaware Press, 1996), 214.

17. "How Bureaucracy Led to NNSL Demise," *Nigerian Tribune*, 27 July 2012.

18. Ibid.

19. Interview with Joseph Kehinde Adigun, 21 January 2011.

20. Iheduru, *Political Economy of International Shipping*, 237.

21. Ekong, "Survival Opportunities and Strategies," 196.

22. Ibid., 193.

23. Ibid., 197.

24. Ibid., 195.

25. Bolaji Akinola, *Arrested Development: A Journalist's Account of How the Growth of Nigeria's Shipping Sector Is Impaired by Politics and Inconsistent Policies* (Bloomington, IN: AuthorHouse, 2012); see also Merseyside Maritime Museum, 2273 Muirhead inward 1962–1964/5, Muirhead to Oyesiku, 2 October 1964.

26. Quoted in Iheduru, *Political Economy of International Shipping*, 212.

27. Merseyside Maritime Museum, 2247 J. Joyce 1959–1961, Joyce to Tod, 2 July 1960.

28. Interview with Capt. Niyi Adeyemo, 25 January 2011.

29. Interview with Olukayode Akinsoji, 25 January 2011.

30. Ships Nostalgia, http://www.shipsnostalgia.com/archive/index.php?t-3154.html.

31. Ibid.

32. Ibid.

33. Ismaila Mohammed, "The Nigerian Enterprises Promotion Decrees (1972 and 1977) and Indigenisation in Nigeria" (PhD diss., University of Warwick, 1985), 269.

34. "How Bureaucracy Led to NNSL Demise."

35. Ibid.

36. Mohammed, "Nigerian Enterprises Promotion Decrees," 269.

37. Iheduru, *Political Economy of International Shipping*, 165.

38. S. G. Sturmey, *British Shipping and World Competition* (London: Athlone, 1962), 3.

39. Ekong, "Survival Opportunities and Strategies," 234.

40. Ibid., 238.

41. Ibid., 242.

42. Iheduru, *Political Economy of International Shipping*, 230–32.

43. Ekong, "Survival Opportunities and Strategies," 121.

44. Ibid., 160.

45. Iheduru, *Political Economy of International Shipping*, 234.

46. Ibid., 231.

47. Ibid., 134.

48. Ibid., 214.

49. Interview with Pa Agbaosi, 15 December 2007.

50. "Seamen Protest over Sack Move," *Daily Times*, 19 May 1966.

51. Merseyside Maritime Museum, 2273 Muirhead inward 1962–1964/5, NNSL Board of Directors Meeting, 28 September 1960.

52. Merseyside Maritime Museum, 1909 Nigerian Shipping Federation, Commander Shelbourn, Williams to Duncan, 25 June 1964.

53. Interview with Isaac T. A. Bezi, 26 January 2011.

54. *Daily Times*, 19 May 1966.

55. Merseyside Maritime Museum, 2047, M. Glasier 1951–1961, "Notes on a visit to West Africa 1969."

56. Ibid.

57. Interview with Ari Festus, 24 December 2007.

58. Bruce J. Berman, "Ethnicity, Patronage and the African State: The Politics of Uncivil Nationalism," *African Affairs* 97, no. 388 (1998): 331.

59. Julius O. Ihonvbere, "The 'Irrelevant' State, Ethnicity, and the Quest for Nationhood in Africa," *Ethnic and Racial Studies* 17, no. 1 (1994): 42–60; Jeffrey Herbst, *States and Power in Africa: Comparative Lessons in Authority and Control* (Princeton, NJ: Princeton University Press, 2000), 130–31.

60. Dauda Abubakar, "Ethnic Identity, Democratization, and the Future of the African State: Lessons from Nigeria," *African Issues* 29, nos. 1–2 (2001): 32.

61. Abu Bakarr Bah, *Breakdown and Reconstitution: Democracy, the Nation-State, and Ethnicity in Nigeria* (Lanham, MD: Lexington Books, 2005), 5.

62. Interview with Lawrence Miekumo, 27 December 2007.

63. Interview with Daniel Ofudje, 14 January 2008.

64. Interview with Adeola Lawal, 20 January 2011.

65. Interview with Anthony Davies Eros, 15 December 2007.

66. Ship's logbook: *Ebani*, 22.1.76 entry: 1.6.76 Tema.

67. Interview with Capt. Alao Tajudeen, 23 January 2011.

68. Interview with Benneth Achilefu, 7 February 2011.

69. Interview with Adeola Lawal, 20 January 2011.

70. Ibid.

71. See Ayodeji Olukojo, "A 'Truly Nigerian Project'?: The Politics of the Establishment of the Nigerian National Shipping Line (NNSL), 1957–1959," *International Journal of Maritime History* 15, no. 1 (June 2003): 69–90. Also, interview with Joseph Kehinde Adigun, 17 December 2007; interview with John Larry, 17 January 2008.

72. Interview with Daniel Ofudje, 14 January 2008.

73. Interview with France Zeinebro, 1 January 2011.

74. Interview with Ari Festus, 24 December 2007; interview with Joseph Kehinde Adigun, 17 December 2007; interview with Sunday Nwahukwu, 17 December 2007; interview with Daniel Ofudje, 14 January 2008; interview with Adeola Lawal, 21 December 2007.

75. Interview with Joseph Kehinde Adigun, 21 January 2011.

76. Ibid.

77. Ibid.

78. Interview with Ari Festus, 24 January 2011.

79. Interview with Ari Festus, 24 December 2007.

80. Interview with Alex Dediara, 18 January 2011.

81. Interview with Capt. Cosmos Niagwan, 27 January 2011.

82. Interview with Olukayode Akinsoji, 25 January 2011.

83. Ibid.

84. Ship's logbook: *Bareeb*, 12.3.72, posted message, no date.

85. Ship's logbook: *River Benue*, 30.3.80, entry: 31.5.81 Freetown.

86. Ship's logbook: *Ileoluji*, 28.9.79, entry: 22.11.76 Santos.

87. Ship's logbook: *River Benue*, 8.11.70, entry: 30.12.70.

88. Ship's logbook: *Salamat Ambi*, 29.10.76, entry: 9.2.77 Hull.

89. Ship's logbook: *River Benue*, 7.11.80, entry: 4.2.81 Middlesbrough.

90. Ship's logbook: *River Oji*, 22.6.81 entry: 4.6.81 Apapa.

91. Ship's logbook: *River Niger*, 22.11.73, entry: 9.12.73 Sapele.

92. Ship's logbook: *Oduduwa*, 31.8.68, entry: 8.11.68 Tilbury: 14.11.68.

93. Ship's logbook: *Oduduwa*, 20.8.73, entry: 26.9.73 at sea.

94. Interview with Joseph Kehinde Adigun, 21 January 2011.

95. Ship's logbook: *King Jaja*, 1.4.75, entry: 11.6.75 Lagos.

96. Ship's logbook: *River Ogun*, 30.4.81 entry: 18.5.81 at sea.

97. Ship's logbook: *King Jaja*, 18.8.71, entry: 8.12.71 at sea.

98. Ibid.

99. Ship's logbook: *King Jaja*, 31.10.73, entry: 30.11.73 at sea.

100. Ship's logbook: *Salamat Ambi*, 29.10.76, entry: 3.3.77 Hull.

101. Ship's logbook, *River Benue*, 26.7.72, posted message, no date.

102. Ship's logbook: *el Kanemi*, 29.7.72, posted message.

103. Ship's logbook: *River Benue*, 26.7.72, posted message, no date.

104. Ship's logbook: *King Jaja*, 31.10.73, entry: 8.3.74 at sea.

105. Interview with Olukayode Akinsoji, 25 January 2011.

CONCLUSION

1. See Bernard Bailyn, *Atlantic History: Concept and Contours* (Cambridge, MA: Harvard University Press, 2005); Kristin Mann, "Shifting Paradigms in the Study of the African Diaspora and of Atlantic History and Culture," in *Rethinking the African Diaspora: The Making of a Black Atlantic World in the Bight of Benin and Brazil*, ed. Kristin Mann and Edna G. Bay (New York: Routledge, 2013), 3–21.

2. Bayo Holsey, "Black Atlantic Visions: History, Race, and Transnationalism in Ghana," *Cultural Anthropology* 28, no. 3 (2013): 513.

3. Jo Stanley, "And after the Cross-Dressed Cabin Boys and Whaling Wives? Possible Futures for Women's Maritime Historiography," *Journal of Transport History* 23, no. 1 (2002): 9–22.

4. W. Jeffrey Bolster, *Black Jacks: African American Seamen in the Age of Sail* (Cambridge, MA: Harvard University Press, 1997); Peter Linebaugh and Marcus Rediker, *The Many-Headed Hydra: The Hidden History of the Revolutionary Atlantic* (Boston, MA: Beacon Press, 2001).

5. Lois E. Horton, "From Class to Race in Early America: Northern Post-Emancipation Racial Reconstruction," *Journal of the Early Republic* 19, no. 4 (1999): 629–49.

6. Pico Iyer, *The Global Soul: Jet Lag, Shopping Malls, and the Search for Home* (New York: Random House, 2011), 24.

7. Stuart Hall, "Political Belonging in a World of Multiple Identities," in *Conceiving Cosmopolitanism: Theory, Context and Practice*, ed. Steven Vertovec and Robin Cohen (Oxford: Oxford University Press, 2002), 26.

8. Richard Roberts, "History and Memory: The Power of Statist Narratives," *International Journal of African Historical Studies* 33, no. 3 (2000): 513–22.

9. Interview with Pa Agbaosi, 15 December 2007.

10. Jon E. Fox and Cynthia Miller-Idriss, "Everyday Nationhood," *Ethnicities* 8, no. 4 (2008): 542.

11. Craig J. Calhoun, *Nationalism* (Minneapolis: University of Minnesota Press, 1997), 5.

12. Interview with Ari Festus, 24 December 2007.

13. Interview with Muritala Olayinka alli-Balogun, 15 December 2007.

Bibliography

ARCHIVES CONSULTED

International Institute of Social History in Amsterdam (Peter Waterman Papers)
Merseyside Maritime Museum
Modern Records Centre, University of Warwick
Nigerian Institute of International Relations
Nigerian National Archives, Ibadan
Nigerian National Shipping Federation (Ship Logbooks)
Nigerian Shipping Federation
PRO-British National Archives

BOOKS AND ARTICLES

Abubakar, Dauda. "Ethnic Identity, Democratization, and the Future of the African State: Lessons from Nigeria." *African Issues* 29, nos. 1–2 (2001): 31–36.

Adebayo, Akanmu G. "The Collapse of Nigeria's Federal System of Government." In Oyebade, *Transformation of Nigeria*, 113–36.

Adejugbe, Michael. "The Myths and Realities of Nigeria's Business Indigenization." *Development and Change* 15, no. 4 (1984): 577–92.

Aderibigbe, Dele. "How Bureaucracy Led to the NNSL Demise—Chidi." *Nigerian Tribune*, 25 July 2012.

Adi, Hakim. "Pan-Africanism and West African Nationalism in Britain." *African Studies Review* 43, no. 1 (April 2000): 69–82.

Akeredolu-Ale, E. O. "Private Foreign Investment and Underdevelopment of Indigenous Entrepreneurship in Nigeria." In *Nigeria: Economy and Society*, edited by Gavin Williams, 67–82. London: Rex Collins, 1976.

Akinola, Bolaji. *Arrested Development: A Journalist's Account of How the Growth of Nigeria's Shipping Sector Is Impaired by Politics and Inconsistent Policies.* Bloomington, IN: AuthorHouse, 2012.

Akinsanya, Adeoye A. *The Expropriation of Multinational Property in the Third World.* New York: Praeger, 1980.

———. "The Power Structure in Nigeria and the Indigenization of the Economy." *Pakistan Horizon* 47, no. 2 (1994): 63–79.

Albert, Isaac O. "Explaining 'Godfatherism' in Nigerian Politics." *African Sociological Review* 9, no. 2 (2005): 79–105.

———. "Problems of Democratic Governance in Nigeria: The Past in the Present." Paper prepared for presentation at the Triennial History Workshop on Democracy, "Popular Precedents, Popular Practice and Popular Culture," University of the Witwatersrand, Johannesburg, 13–16 July 1994.

Allman, Jean M. *The Quills of the Porcupine: Asante Nationalism in an Emergent Ghana.* Madison: University of Wisconsin Press, 1993.

Arthurs, Alberta. "Social Imaginaries and Global Realities." *Public Culture* 15, no. 3 (2003): 579–86.

Atkins, Keletso E. *The Moon Is Dead! Give Us Our Money! The Cultural Origins of an African Work Ethic, Natal, South Africa, 1843–1900.* Portsmouth, NH: Heinemann, 1993.

Bah, Abu Bakarr. *Breakdown and Reconstitution: Democracy, the Nation-State, and Ethnicity in Nigeria.* Lanham, MD: Lexington Books, 2005.

Bailyn, Bernard. *Atlantic History: Concept and Contours.* Cambridge, MA: Harvard University Press, 2005.

Bayart, Jean-François. *The State in Africa: The Politics of the Belly.* New York: Longman, 1993.

Beckman, Björn. "Whose State? State and Capitalist Development in Nigeria." *Review of African Political Economy* 9, no. 23 (1982): 37–51.

Beckman, Björn, Sakhela Buhlungu, and Lloyd Sachikonye, eds. *Trade Unions and Party Politics: Labour Movements in Africa.* Cape Town: HSRC Press, 2010.

Beckman, Björn, and Salihu Lukman. "The Failure of Nigeria's Labour Party." In Beckman, Buhlungu, and Sachikonye, *Trade Unions and Party Politics,* 59–83.

Berg, Elliot J. "Urban Real Wages and the Nigerian Trade Union Movement, 1939–60: A Comment." *Economic Development and Cultural Change* 17, no. 4 (1969): 604–17.

Berg, Elliot J., and Jeffrey Butler. "Trade Unions." In *Political Parties and National Integration in Tropical Africa,* edited by James S. Coleman and Carl G. Rosberg Jr., 340–81. Berkeley: University of California Press, 1964.

Berman, Bruce J. "Ethnicity, Patronage and the African State: The Politics of Uncivil Nationalism." *African Affairs* 97, no. 388 (1998): 305–41.

Beveridge, Fiona C. "Taking Control of Foreign Investment: A Case Study of Indigenisation in Nigeria." *International and Comparative Law Quarterly* 40, no. 2 (1991): 302–33.

Bolster, W. Jeffrey. *Black Jacks: African American Seamen in the Age of Sail.* Cambridge, MA: Harvard University Press, 1997.

———. "'Every Inch a Man': Gender in the Lives of African American Seamen, 1800–1860." In Creighton and Norling, *Iron Men, Wooden Women,* 138–68.

Bonner, Philip, Jonathan Hyslop, and Lucien Van Der Walt. "Rethinking Worlds of Labour: Southern African Labour History in International Context." *African Studies* 66, nos. 2–3 (2007): 137–67.

Brown, Carolyn A. *"We Were All Slaves": African Miners, Culture, and Resistance at the Enugu Government Colliery*. London: Heinemann, 2003.

Brown, Jacqueline N. *Dropping Anchor, Setting Sail: Geographies of Race in Black Liverpool*. Princeton, NJ: Princeton University Press, 2005.

Burke, Timothy. "Eyes Wide Shut: Africanists and the Moral Problematics of Postcolonial Societies." *African Studies Quarterly* 7, nos. 2–3 (2003): 205–9.

Bush, Barbara. *Imperialism, Race and Resistance: Africa and Britain, 1919–1945*. London: Routledge, 2002.

Calhoun, Craig J. "'Belonging' in the Cosmopolitan Imaginary." *Ethnicities* 3, no. 4 (2003): 531–68.

——. *Nationalism*. Minneapolis: University of Minnesota Press, 1997.

Chabal, Patrick, and Jean-Pascal Daloz. *Africa Works: Disorder as Political Instrument*. Bloomington: Indiana University Press, 1999.

Chidi, Gerald. "Nigerian National Shipping Lines, the Beginning and the End." *Vanguard*, 1 November 2011. http://www.vanguardngr.com/2011/11/nigerian-national -shipping-lines-the-beginning-and-the-end.

Christian, Mark. "The Fletcher Report 1930: A Historical Case Study of Contested Black Mixed Heritage Britishness." *Journal of Historical Sociology* 21, nos. 2–3 (2008): 213–41.

Cohen, Robin. *Labor and Politics in Nigeria, 1945–71*. London: Heinemann, 1974.

——. "Resistance and Hidden Forms of Consciousness Amongst African Workers." *Review of African Political Economy* 7, no. 19 (1980): 8–22.

Collins, Paul. "Public Policy and the Development of Indigenous Capitalism: The Nigerian Experience." *Journal of Commonwealth and Comparative Politics* 15, no. 2 (1977): 127–50.

Cooper, Frederick. *Africa since 1940: The Past of the Present*. Vol. 1. Cambridge: Cambridge University Press, 2002.

——. *Decolonization and African Society: The Labor Question in French and British Africa*. Cambridge: Cambridge University Press, 1996.

——. *The Dialectics of Decolonization: Nationalism and Labor Movements in Postwar Africa*. Ann Arbor: University of Michigan, 1992.

——. "Possibility and Constraint: African Independence in Historical Perspective." *Journal of African History* 49, no. 2 (2008): 167–96.

Creighton, Margaret S., and Lisa Norling, eds. *Iron Men, Wooden Women: Gender and Seafaring in the Atlantic World, 1700–1920*. Baltimore, MD: Johns Hopkins University Press, 1996.

Davies, Peter N. *The Trade Makers: Elder Dempster in West Africa, 1852–1972, 1973–1989*. Research in Maritime History 19. St. John's, Newfoundland: IMEHA, 2000.

Decker, Stephanie. "Building Up Goodwill: British Business, Development and Economic Nationalism in Ghana and Nigeria, 1945–1977." *Enterprise and Society* 9, no. 4 (2008): 602–13.

Dennis, Ferdinand. *Behind the Frontlines: Journey into Afro-Britain*. London: Gollancz, 1988.

De Sardan, J. P. Olivier. "A Moral Economy of Corruption in Africa?" *Journal of Modern African Studies* 37, no. 1 (1999): 25–52.

Diamond, Larry J. *Class, Ethnicity and Democracy in Nigeria: The Failure of the First Republic*. Syracuse, NY: Syracuse University Press, 1988.

Doty, Roxanne L. "Immigration and National Identity: Constructing the Nation." *Review of International Studies* 22, no. 3 (1996): 235–55.

Ekeh, Peter P. "The Structure and Meaning of Federal Character in the Nigerian Political System." In *Federal Character and Federalism in Nigeria*, edited by Peter P. Ekeh and Eghosa E. Osaghae, 19–44. Ibadan: Heinemann, 1989.

Ekong, Bassey U. "Survival Opportunities and Strategies of a Marginal Firm in a Cartelized Oligopoly: Case Study of the Nigerian National Shipping Line." PhD diss., Michigan State University, 1974.

Ewald, Janet J. "Crossers of the Sea: Slaves, Freedmen, and Other Migrants in the Northwestern Indian Ocean, c. 1750–1914." *American Historical Review* 105, no. 1 (2000): 69–91.

Falola, Toyin, and Matthew M. Heaton. *A History of Nigeria*. Cambridge: Cambridge University Press, 2008.

Fanon, Frantz. *The Wretched of the Earth*. Translated by Constance Farrington. London: Penguin, 1990.

Fox, Jon E., and Cynthia Miller-Idriss. "Everyday Nationhood." *Ethnicities* 8, no. 4 (2008): 536–63.

Freund, Bill. *The African Worker*. Cambridge: Cambridge University Press, 1988.

Frost, Diane, ed. *Ethnic Labour and British Imperial Trade: A History of Ethnic Seafarers in the UK*. London: Cass, 1995.

——. *Work and Community among West African Migrant Workers since the Nineteenth Century*. Liverpool: Liverpool University Press, 1999.

Garbaye, Romain. "British Cities and Ethnic Minorities in the Post-War Era: From Xenophobic Agitation to Multi-Ethnic Government." *Immigrants and Minorities* 22, nos. 2–3 (2003): 298–315.

Geiger, Susan. "Tanganyikan Nationalism as 'Women's Work': Life Histories, Collective Biography and Changing Historiography." *Journal of African History* 37, no. 3 (1996): 465–78.

Gilroy, Paul. *The Black Atlantic: Modernity and Double Consciousness*. Cambridge, MA: Harvard University Press, 1993.

Ginio, Ruth. "African Colonial Soldiers between Memory and Forgetfulness: The Case of Post-Colonial Senegal." *Outre-Mers* 93, no. 350 (2006): 141–55.

Gomez, Michael A. *Reversing Sail: A History of the African Diaspora*. Cambridge: Cambridge University Press, 2004.

Griscom, Clement A. "How Steamship Operations Are Organized—Job Descriptions and Departments." Gjenvick-Gjonvik Archives. http://www.gjenvick.com/Steam shipArticles/SteamshipCrew/1904-02-HowSteamshipOperationsAreOrganized. html#ixzz2LzRfFAiv.

Hall, Stuart. "Political Belonging in a World of Multiple Identities." In Vertovec and Cohen, *Conceiving Cosmopolitanism*, 25–31.

Hansen, Randall. *Citizenship and Immigration in Post-War Britain: The Institutional Origins of a Multicultural Nation*. Oxford: Oxford University Press, 2000.

Harneit-Sievers, Axel. "African Business, 'Economic Nationalism,' and British Colonial Policy: Southern Nigeria, 1935–1954." *African Economic History* 24 (1996): 79–128.

Hawthorne, Walter. "Gorge: An African Seaman and His Flights from 'Freedom' Back to 'Slavery' in the Early Nineteenth Century." *Slavery and Abolition* 31, no. 3 (2010): 411–28.

Herbst, Jeffrey. *States and Power in Africa: Comparative Lessons in Authority and Control.* Princeton, NJ: Princeton University Press, 2000.

Holsey, Bayo. "Black Atlantic Visions: History, Race, and Transnationalism in Ghana." *Cultural Anthropology* 28, no. 3 (2013): 504–18.

Horton, Lois E. "From Class to Race in Early America: Northern Post-Emancipation Racial Reconstruction." *Journal of the Early Republic* 19, no. 4 (1999): 629–49.

Hoyt, John C. "Ship Facts." In *Old Ocean's Ferry: The Log of the Modern Mariner, the Trans-Atlantic Traveler, and Quaint Facts of Neptune's Realm,* edited by John C. Hoyt, 111–29. New York: Bonnell, Silver, 1900.

Iheduru, Okechukwu C. *The Political Economy of International Shipping in Developing Countries.* Newark: University of Delaware Press, 1996.

Ihonvbere, Julius O. "The 'Irrelevant' State, Ethnicity, and the Quest for Nationhood in Africa." *Ethnic and Racial Studies* 17, no. 1 (1994): 42–60.

Ikelegbe, Augustine. "The Perverse Manifestation of Civil Society: Evidence from Nigeria." *Journal of Modern African Studies* 39, no. 1 (2001): 1–24.

Iyer, Pico. *The Global Soul: Jet Lag, Shopping Malls, and the Search for Home.* New York: Random House, 2011.

Joseph, Richard A. *Democracy and Prebendal Politics in Nigeria: The Rise and Fall of the Second Republic.* African Studies Series 56. Cambridge: Cambridge University Press, 2014.

Kelley, Robin D. G. *Freedom Dreams: The Black Radical Imagination.* Boston, MA: Beacon Press, 2003.

Kilby, Peter. "Industrial Relations and Wage Determination: Failure of the Anglo-Saxon Model." *Journal of Developing Areas* 1, no. 4 (1967): 489–520.

Kraus, Jon. "African Trade Unions: Progress or Poverty?" *African Studies Review* 19, no. 3 (1976): 95–108.

Lawal, Olakunle A. "British Commercial Interests and the Decolonization Process in Nigeria, 1950–60." *African Economic History* 22 (1994): 93–110.

Leubuscher, Charlotte. *West African Shipping Trade, 1909–1959.* Leiden: Sythoff, 1963.

Lindsay, Lisa A. *Working with Gender: Wage Labor and Social Change in Southwestern Nigeria.* Portsmouth, NH: Heinemann, 2003.

Linebaugh, Peter, and Marcus Rediker. *The Many-Headed Hydra: The Hidden History of the Revolutionary Atlantic.* Boston, MA: Beacon Press, 2001.

Lissoni, Arianna, and Maria Suriano. "Married to the ANC: Tanzanian Women's Entanglement in South Africa's Liberation Struggle." *Journal of Southern African Studies* 40, no. 1 (2014): 129–50.

Lubeck, Paul M. *Islam and Urban Labor in Northern Nigeria: The Making of a Muslim Working Class.* Cambridge: Cambridge University Press, 1987.

——. "Islamic Protest under Semi-Industrial Capitalism: 'Yan Tatsine Explained." *Africa* 55, no. 4 (1985): 369–89.

——. "Unions, Workers and Consciousness in Kano, Nigeria: A View from Below." In Sandbrook and Cohen, *Development of an African Working Class,* 139–60.

Mamdani, Mahmood. *Citizen and Subject: Contemporary Africa and the Legacy of Late Colonialism.* Princeton, NJ: Princeton University Press, 1996.

Mann, Gregory. *Native Sons: West African Veterans and France in the Twentieth Century*. Durham, NC: Duke University Press, 2006.

Mann, Kristin. "Shifting Paradigms in the Study of the African Diaspora and of Atlantic History and Culture." In *Rethinking the African Diaspora: The Making of a Black Atlantic World in the Bight of Benin and Brazil*, edited by Kristin Mann and Edna G. Bay, 3–21. New York: Routledge, 2013.

May, Roy, and Robin Cohen. "The Interaction between Race and Colonialism: A Case Study of the Liverpool Race Riots of 1919." *Race and Class* 16, no. 2 (1974): 111–26.

Mlambo, Alois S. "Western Social Sciences and Africa: The Domination and Marginalisation of a Continent." *African Sociological Review* 10, no. 1 (2006): 161–79.

Mohammed, Ismaila. "The Nigerian Enterprises Promotion Decrees (1972 and 1977) and Indigenisation in Nigeria." PhD diss., University of Warwick, 1985.

Momoh, Abubakar. "Popular Struggles in Nigeria, 1960–1982." *African Journal of Political Science* 1, no. 2 (1996): 154–75.

Mothibe, Tefetso H. "Zimbabwe: African Working Class Nationalism, 1957–1963." *Zambezia* 23, no. 2 (1996): 157–80.

Neocosmos, Michael. *The Contradictory Position of "Tradition" in African Nationalist Discourse: Some Analytical and Political Reflections*. Durban: Centre for Civil Society, 2004.

Newman, David. "On Borders and Power: A Theoretical Framework." *Journal of Borderlands Studies* 18, no. 1 (Spring 2003): 13–25.

Nnaemeka, Abonyi N. "Towards an Alternative Development Paradigm for Africa." *Journal of Social Science* 21, no. 1 (2009): 39–48.

Nnoli, Okwudiba. *Ethnicity and Development in Nigeria*. Aldershot: Avebury, 1995.

Nwaubani, Ebere. "Constitution-Making and the Nigerian Identity, 1914–1960." In Oyebade, *Transformation of Nigeria*, 73–112.

Nwoke, Chibuzo N. "Towards Authentic Economic Nationalism in Nigeria." *Africa Today* 33, no. 4 (1986): 51–69.

Ogbuagu, Chibuzo S. A. "The Nigerian Indigenization Policy: Nationalism or Pragmatism?" *African Affairs* 82, no. 327 (1983): 241–66.

Ojedokun, Olasupo. "The Changing Pattern of Nigeria's International Economic Relations: The Decline of the Colonial Nexus, 1960–1966." *Journal of Developing Areas* 6, no. 4 (1972): 535–54.

Olukoju, Ayodeji. "A 'Truly Nigerian Project'? The Politics of the Establishment of the Nigerian National Shipping Line (NNSL), 1957–1959." *International Journal of Maritime History* 15, no. 1 (2003): 69–90.

Osaghae, Eghosa E. *Crippled Giant: Nigeria since Independence*. Bloomington: Indiana University Press, 1998.

Oyebade, Adebayo, ed. *The Transformation of Nigeria: Essays in Honor of Toyin Falola*. Trenton, NJ: Africa World Press, 2002.

Packard, Winthrop. "Stewards of an Ocean Liner Above and Below Decks." Gjenvick-Gjonvik Archives. http://www.gjenvick.com/SteamshipArticles/SteamshipCrew/1904-05-StewardsOfAnOceanLiner.html#ixzz2M1B3oWnh.

Peace, Adrian J. *Choice, Class and Conflict: A Study of Southern Nigerian Factory Workers*. Brighton: Harvester Press, 1979.

———. "The Lagos Proletariat: Labour Aristocrats or Populist Militants?" In Sandbrook and Cohen, *Development of an African Working Class*, 281–302.

Pieri, Elisa. "Contested Cosmopolitanism." *Collegium* 15 (2014): 14–38.

Ray, Carina E. "'The White Wife Problem': Sex, Race and the Contested Politics of Repatriation to Interwar British West Africa." *Gender and History* 21, no. 3 (2009): 628–46.

Report of the Board of Enquiry into the Trade Dispute between the Elder Dempster Lines Limited and the Nigerian Union of Seamen. Lagos: Federal Government Printer, 1959.

Roberts, Richard. "History and Memory: The Power of Statist Narratives." *International Journal of African Historical Studies* 33, no. 3 (2000): 513–22.

Rood, Leslie L. "Nationalisation and Indigenisation in Africa." *Journal of Modern African Studies* 14, no. 3 (1976): 427–47.

Sandbrook, Richard. *Proletarians and African Capitalism: The Kenyan Case, 1960–1972.* Cambridge: Cambridge University Press, 1975.

Sandbrook, Richard, and Robin Cohen, eds. *The Development of an African Working Class: Studies in Class Formation and Action.* London: Longman, 1975.

Schler, Lynn. "Historicizing the Undisclosed: Questions of Authority and Authenticity in Writing the History of Birth in Colonial Cameroon." *Lagos Notes and Records* 13 (2008): 1–34.

Sewell, William H., Jr. "Toward a Post-Materialist Rhetoric for Labor History." In *Rethinking Labor History: Essays on Discourse and Class Analysis,* edited by Lenard R. Belanstein, 15–38. Urbana: University of Illinois Press, 1993.

Sherwood, Marika. "Elder Dempster and West Africa, 1891–c. 1940: The Genesis of Underdevelopment?" *International Journal of African Historical Studies* 30, no. 2 (1997): 253–76.

———. *Pastor Daniels Ekarte and the African Churches Mission, Liverpool, 1931–64.* London: Savannah Press, 1994.

———. "Strikes! African Seamen, Elder Dempster and the Government 1940–42." In Frost, *Ethnic Labour and British Imperial Trade,* 130–45.

Silver, Beverly J. *Forces of Labor: Workers' Movements and Globalization since 1870.* Cambridge: Cambridge University Press, 2003.

Simpson, David, et al. "Firemen, Trimmers and Stokers." Barry Merchant Seamen. http://www.barrymerchantseamen.org.uk/articles/BMSfiretrim.html.

Smith, Daniel J. *A Culture of Corruption: Everyday Deception and Popular Discontent in Nigeria.* Princeton, NJ: Princeton University Press, 2007.

Stanley, Jo. "And after the Cross-Dressed Cabin Boys and Whaling Wives? Possible Futures for Women's Maritime Historiography." *Journal of Transport History* 23, no. 1 (2002): 9–22.

Sturmey, S. G. *British Shipping and World Competition.* London: Athlone, 1962.

Suberu, Rotimi. T. *Federalism and Ethnic Conflict in Nigeria.* Washington: US Institute of Peace Press, 2001.

Tabili, Laura. "The Construction of Racial Difference in Twentieth-Century Britain: The Special Restriction (Coloured Alien Seamen) Order, 1925." *Journal of British Studies* 33, no. 1 (January 1994): 54–98.

———. "'A Maritime Race': Masculinity and the Racial Division of Labor in British Merchant Ships, 1900–1939." In Creighton and Norling, *Iron Men, Wooden Women,* 169–88.

———. *We Ask for British Justice: Workers and Racial Difference in Late Imperial Britain.* Ithaca, NY: Cornell University Press, 1994.

Taylor, Charles. "Modern Social Imaginaries." *Public Culture* 14, no. 1 (2002): 91–124.

Terretta, Meredith. *Petitioning for Our Rights, Fighting for Our Nation: The History of the Democratic Union of Cameroonian Women, 1949–1960*. Mankon: Langaa, 2013.

Thomas, Deborah A., and Kamari M. Clarke. "Introduction: Globalization and the Transformations of Race." In *Globalization and Race: Transformations in the Cultural Production of Blackness*, edited by Kamari M. Clarke and Deborah A. Thomas, 1–34. Durham, NC: Duke University Press, 2006.

Tignor, Robert L. *Capitalism and Nationalism at the End of Empire: State and Business in Decolonizing Egypt, Nigeria, and Kenya, 1945–1963*. Princeton, NJ: Princeton University Press, 1998.

Tijani, Hakeem I. *Union Education in Nigeria: Labor, Empire, and Decolonization since 1945*. London: Palgrave Macmillan, 2012.

Uwazurike, Chudi. "Ethnicity, Power and Prebendalism: The Persistent Triad as the Unsolvable Crisis of Nigerian Politics." *Dialectical Anthropology* 21, no. 1 (1996): 1–20.

Van Beusekom, Monica M. "From Underpopulation to Overpopulation: French Perceptions of Population, Environment, and Agricultural Development in French Soudan (Mali), 1900–1960." *Environmental History* 4, no. 2 (1999): 198–221.

Vaughan, Olufemi. *Nigerian Chiefs: Traditional Power in Modern Politics, 1890s–1990s*. Rochester Studies in African History and the Diaspora 7. Rochester, NY: University of Rochester Press, 2006.

Vertovec, Steven, and Robin Cohen. "Introduction: Conceiving Cosmopolitanism." In *Conceiving Cosmopolitanism: Theory, Context, and Practice*, edited by Steven Vertovec and Robin Cohen, 1–22. Oxford: Oxford University Press, 2002.

Warren, W. M. "Urban Real Wages and the Nigerian Trade Union Movement, 1939–60." *Economic Development and Cultural Change* 15, no. 1 (1966): 21–36.

Waterman, Peter. *Division and Unity amongst Nigerian Workers: Lagos Port Unionism, 1940s–60s*. The Hague: Institute of Social Studies, 1982.

Weeks, John F. "A Comment on Peter Kilby: Industrial Relations and Wage Determination." *Journal of Developing Areas* 3 no. 1 (1968): 7–18.

———. "Further Comment on the Kilby/Weeks Debate: An Empirical Rejoinder." *Journal of Developing Areas* 5, no. 2 (1971): 165–74.

Wilson, Ernest J., III. "Strategies of State Control of the Economy: Nationalization and Indigenization in Africa." *Comparative Politics* 22, no. 4 (1990): 401–19.

Wood, Paul. "The History of Elder Dempster." http://www.rakaia.co.uk/elder-dempster-history.html.

Yesufu, Tijani M. *An Introduction to Industrial Relations in Nigeria*. Oxford: Oxford University Press, 1962.

Zachernuk, Philip S. *Colonial Subjects: An African Intelligentsia and Atlantic Ideas*. Charlottesville: University Press of Virginia, 2000.

Zimmerman, Sarah J. "Living beyond Boundaries: West African Servicemen in French Colonial Conflicts, 1908–1962." PhD diss., University of California, Berkeley, 2011.

NEWSPAPERS

Daily Telegraph
Daily Times
Daily Service
Lloyd's
West African Pilot

INTERVIEWS BY AUTHOR

(All interviews took place in Lagos, Nigeria, unless noted otherwise.)
Achilefu, Benneth: 7 February 2011
Adeleye, Adebowale: 16 December 2007
Ademola, Anthony: 15 December 2007
Adeyemo, Capt. Niyi: 24 and 25 January 2011
Adigun, Joseph Kehinde: 17 December 2007 and 21 January 2011
Agbaosi, Pa: 15 December 2007
Agbodobiri, Gold: 24 January 2011
Agoro, Ganui: 15 December 2007
Akinsoji, Olukayode: 25 January 2011
Akintade, Bolaji: 24 December 2007
Akintade, Festus Adekunle: 24 December 2007
Akpan, Catherine: 20 September 2011
alli-Balogun, Muritala Olayinka: 15 and 16 December 2007; 17 January 2011
Anomorisa, Rita: 20 January 2011
Ben-Efang, Essien: 20 January 2011
Bessan, Jimmy: 3 July 2011
Bezi, Isaac T. A.: 26 January 2011
Birch, Kenneth: Liverpool, England, 8 June 2009; and e-mail correspondence, 7 June
    2013
Dediara, Alex: 18 and 20 January 2011
Emonaye, Victoria: 15 September 2011
Eros, Anthony Davies: 15 December 2007
Falola, Abiola: 20 September 2011
Festus, Ari: 24 December 2007 and 24 January 2011
George, Kojo: 27 December 2007
Johnson, Anomorisa: 22 January 2011
Kroseide, Chief Charles Oloma Kose: 17 January 2008
Larry, John: 17 and 20 January 2008
Lawal, Adeola: 21 December 2007, and 20 January 2011
Lazarus, Modupe: 17 January 2011
Lazarus, Reuben: 16 December 2007; 17 January 2011
Mensah, T. T.: 25 January 2007
Miekumo, Evelyn: 27 December 2007
Miekumo, Lawrence: 27 December 2007
Moore, Alhadja Bisi: 20 September 2011
Niagwan, Cosmos: 27 January 2011
Nwachukwu, Sunday: 17 and 24 December 2007
Obeze, Peter: 24 January 2011
Ofudje, Daniel: 14 January 2008
Ogundare, Stella Mojisola: 20 September 2011
Omoteso, Capt. S. A.: 20 January 2011
Pereira, Patric: 24 January 2011
Rafaal, John: 24 January 2011
Tajudeen, Capt. Alao: 23 January 2011
Zeinebro, France: 1 January 2011

Index

British National Archives, 17
Brown, Carolyn, 9
Brown, Jacqueline, 52
Buhlungu, Sakhela, 97
Burke, Timothy, 15
Burns, Alan, 28, 39
Bush, Barbara, 55
Butler, Jeffrey, 7

Calhoun, Craig, 136, 196–97
cargo share, 121–22, 169, 172, 218n62
cargo ships, 19, 27, 29–30, 32, 33, 66, 71, 74, 167, 174
catering crews, 24, 30, 32, 133, 138–39
Chabal, Patrick, 15, 164
Chidi, Gerald, 126–27, 129–30, 166, 169, 172
citizenship, 13, 53
Cohen, Robin, 8
colonialism: economic and political interests, 108–9, 163; exploitation of resources, 163–64; idealization of, 2; inequality of, 15; labor movements and, 6; racism of, 52–53. *See also* decolonization; postcolonialism
Coloured Alien Seamen Order (1925), 51
Commonwealth borders, 53
Commonwealth Immigrants Act (1962), 53
Communist Party, 90
containerization, 29, 66, 172
Cooper, Fred, 12, 13–14, 26–27, 39, 77, 92, 93
cosmopolitanism, 5, 10; defined, 49, 195; imaginaries, 49–50, 135, 194; vs. nationalism, 134, 136; role of, 49, 50, 55

Daily Service (newspaper), 118, 119
Daily Times (newspaper), 118, 176
Daloz, Jean-Pascal, 15, 164
deckhands, 26, 29–30, 74
decolonization, 3, 10–11, 13, 77, 78, 109, 195. *See also* postcolonialism
Department of Commerce and Industries (Nigeria), 109
Diamond, Larry, 124
diaspora. *See* black diaspora
discipline: actions against seamen, 18, 45, 88, 145–47, 150, 152, 182, 186–87, 190–91; decline of, 150, 153, 159–60, 161, 176, 182, 186; due to race, 35–36, 82
Dosunnui, 150–51
drug trafficking, 16, 68–69, 165, 180–81, 186–87, 188–90

Eastern Region, 46, 106, 113, 114, 127
Ebani, 180
Ekarte, Daniels, 83

Ekeh, Peter, 107
Ekong, Bassey, 169, 173
Ekore, S. M., 44, 45, 84, 86
Elder Dempster Lines, 4, 16, 27–29, 37, 158; cargo regulation, 66; on Khayam, 95–96; as NNSL partner, 113–17, 118–19, 122, 123, 128–30; on unions, 39–41; in WALCON, 122. *See also* MV *Apapa* strike (1959); specific ships
Electricity Corporation, 130
ethnic chauvinism, 77, 78, 107
ethnicity, study of, 9–10
European crews, 42–43, 91, 133; officers and captains, 26, 36–38, 84–85, 133, 135–36, 139–41, 143, 144–45, 147–48, 152, 158, 175, 183; Nigerian officers and captains' relationship to, 36–37, 133, 143, 144–45, 175; Nigerian seamen's relationship to, 2, 3–4, 25–26, 28, 30, 32–33, 35–36, 38, 88–89, 137–41, 143–44, 147, 148–49, 151–52, 158, 175, 183
Ewald, Janet, 27
exclusion, 48, 50–54

Falola, Toyin, 106, 107–8
Fanon, Frantz, 78
Federal Ministry of Transport, 169
firemen, 24, 26, 29, 30–31, 32–33, 133
First Republic, demise of, 156
Fletcher, Muriel, 52
foreign investment, 110
Foucault, Michel, 194
Fox, Jon, 196
freedom, 1–2, 5, 48, 50, 180, 182
Freund, Bill, 6
Frost, Diane, 28, 29, 30, 32–33

Geiger, Susan, 11–12
General Strike (Nigeria, 1964), 7, 98
Ghanaian-Israeli shipping partnership, 113
Gilroy, Paul, 10, 70
Glasier, Malcolm, 43–44, 89–90, 176–77
globalization, 70
Gomez, Michael, 80–81
Goodluck, Wahab, 98
Guinea Gulf Line, 122

Hall, Stuart, 49, 195
Hansen, Randall, 53
Harneit-Sievers, Axel, 108, 109
Hawthorne, Walter, 24
Heaton, Matthew, 106, 107–8
Herbert Macauley, 172
heterotopias, use of term, 194
Hoegh Line, 122